Praise for *Speaking of Rape*

This book is a courageous and extremely insightful analysis of narrative agency in the aftermath of sexual violation. It is written with the author's whole self, bringing to the vexed subject of rape the lived experience of a survivor, the political consciousness of a feminist, and the profound compassion of a practical theologian.

—Susan J. Brison, author of *Aftermath: Violence and the Remaking of a Self*

Piercingly analytical and honest, *Speaking of Rape* situates the author's own experiences in the context of a sustained scholarly commentary on how we do things with words about sexual violations. Danielle Tumminio Hansen lays bare the complexity of naming rape and proposes pathways to reconstructing the self in the aftermath. The book is interdisciplinary, insisting that feminist philosophy and pastoral theology both be part of the conversation about sexual harm. Anyone from any background who reads this book will receive a rare gift: an invitation to remember and speak their own bodily truth. There is no prevention for rape. But after rape there is: Voice. Voice. Voice.

—Margaret D. Kamitsuka, Francis W. and Lydia L. Davis Professor Emeritus of Religion, Oberlin College

In this powerfully argued and beautifully written book, Danielle Tumminio Hansen highlights a conundrum that all survivors of sexual misconduct face—how to find the words to speak the unspeakable, to come up with the exact, right phrasing to convince others to believe something that is already in doubt, and within a society that is constantly changing the relevant terms and definitions. Through the lens of linguistics, story, narrative, and even notions of plot, Hansen does what her book title so boldly claims—she speaks of rape in order to point us to the ongoing paradoxes in which victim-survivors continually find themselves as they try to process what they've lived, and find the right words to tell their stories. Tumminio Hansen emerges as an important new voice on this subject and

her argument, an essential contribution to scholarly conversation about sexual misconduct and, yes, rape—one we must all be willing to hear.
—Donna Freitas, author of *Consent: A Memoir of Unwanted Attention* and *Sex and the Soul: Juggling Sexuality, Spirituality, Romance, and Religion on America's College Campuses*

In this authentic, unflinching, and beautifully written book, Danielle Tumminio Hansen tells us something deeply important about sexual harm. The words we use to describe it often cause more harm, fail to capture its depth, and obfuscate rather than empower; that law, religion, popular culture, and the media are all too often complicit. But this book is not just critique. Tumminio Hansen offers a path forward that includes storytelling and active, deep listening; she envisions a restorative justice approach that provides both accountability and healing for individuals and communities.
—David R. Karp, director, Center for Restorative Justice, University of San Diego

SPEAKING OF RAPE

SPEAKING OF RAPE

THE LIMITS OF LANGUAGE IN SEXUAL VIOLATIONS

DANIELLE TUMMINIO HANSEN

FORTRESS PRESS
Minneapolis

SPEAKING OF RAPE
The Limits of Language in Sexual Violations

Copyright © 2024 by Fortress Press, an imprint of 1517 Media. All rights reserved. Except for brief quotations in critical articles or reviews, no part of this book may be reproduced in any manner without prior written permission from the publisher. Email copyright@1517.media or write to Permissions, Fortress Press, PO Box 1209, Minneapolis, MN 55440-1209.

Parts of this text are derived from the article "Absent a Word: How the Language of Sexual Trauma Keeps Survivors Silent" by Danielle Tumminio Hansen (2020), published in *Journal of Pastoral Theology*. Copyright © Society for Pastoral Theology, reprinted by permission of Taylor & Francis Ltd, http://www.tandfonline.com on behalf of Society for Pastoral Theology.

Library of Congress Control Number: 2023943496 (print)

Cover image: Digital collage with Organic lines etched on wood using Lithography by mzajac/Getty Images
Cover design: Kristin Miller

Print ISBN: 979-8-8898-3132-7
eBook ISBN: 979-8-8898-3133-4

To Marilyn, Susan, Kristen, and Shannon,
who all found ways to speak.

CONTENTS

	Preface	ix
	Introduction	xiii
1.	Limiting Language	1
2.	Reclaiming Rape	45
3.	Speaking as a Narrative Self	81
4.	On Dominant Stories	101
5.	On Setting and Story	135
6.	On Listening Well	159
7.	On Restorative Justice	181
	Conclusion	209
	Acknowledgments	217
	Notes	221
	Bibliography	269
	Index	283

PREFACE

What follows is a story spoken through words, as many stories are. It is a story of hurt and hope, a story constructed through different ways of knowing and being in the world. It is a story about the wisdom of the body and the wisdom of logic and reason, scientific studies, transcendent spirituality, and community.

I believe it is a true story, though I would not be so bold as to say it is the only truth.

Whenever someone is writing about sexual violations, the question of trustworthiness comes up: What makes the writer a reliable narrator? How can the reader be sure that the survivors quoted aren't brainwashed or opportunistic, willing to lie for their own personal gain? These questions emerge from a number of other stories that the United States likes to tell about victims, stories you have probably heard before. They are the stories that cable news commentators tell about victim credibility, stories told to children in which women are by nature passive and histrionic, stories told over dinner tables in some Christian households where the plot is that men are made in the image of God and women are sinful descendants of Eve. These stories have an insidious place in the dominant culture of the United States, and, told in conjunction with the story that survivors of sexual violations aren't credible narrators of their own experiences, they lead to the convenient conclusion that victims lie.

This story suggests a different narrative, one in which the setting is a society that primes victims to distrust the experiences of their selves—their bodies, agency, and desires—and that primes individuals to undertake sexually harmful acts for the same reason. This setting is made up of misogyny, white supremacy, homophobia, transphobia, and classism, all made even more toxic when paired with the Descartes-inspired dualism that encourages us to distrust and denigrate experiences in which the body is front and center. Because setting impacts character, all of these ways of enacting systemic oppression get reflected in the ways that individuals think and speak about sexual violations. The plot, the conflict in which one person sexually violates another, emerges as a byproduct of the setting. In other words, sexual violations are birthed by destructive, insidious ways of knowing in which we all marinate and participate.

They are also not our singular stories, as each element of plot, character, and setting that we weave into a narrative is also intertwined with the narratives of others. I've done my best when possible to respect that intertwine, to obtain permission to share those stories that are part of my narrative and simultaneously not mine alone. Identifying information has been changed or withheld in cases where permission could not be obtained.

Some of what you read in this book may make you uncomfortable or trigger memories of violations that you've experienced. I encourage you to listen to your body and the needs that emerge from it as you read. If you feel distress while reading, then it may be time to put the book down for a while and do something that makes you feel safe and secure. Then pick it up again when you're ready. It will be here for you. In this way, your act of reading this book becomes an act in which you can practice claiming your own agency in a community made up of other readers and me, the author.

My hope, regardless of the speed at which you read the book, is that you will find yourself thinking, speaking, and acting differently. Speech, thought, and action exist in an intimate dance in which one leads and the other follows, depending on the moment. Our thoughts and the words we use to express them, therefore, influence every part of how we live and move and have our being in the world. They affect the choices we make and the communities we create, just as the choices we make and the communities we create affect our speech and thought. My hope, therefore, is that this book will change not only how you think and speak but also how you act in the world, so that you will become one more person who lives, holistically, in a way that helps end the practices of thinking, speaking, and acting that make sexual harm part of our individual and collective story.

INTRODUCTION

The Inciting Event

Here is what I remember.

My hands clenched an iron railing on the back of a bed, the rest of my body frozen, as unable to move as the icicles outside my dorm room window. I could not speak and I could not leave, and I sensed that I did not exist anymore, a sensation magnified by feeling that my self was floating above my body, watching the scene as if I were watching a film.

Only in movies, the women scream.

I did not scream.

I cried, and I repeatedly said, "No," but still, the whole event was so hauntingly quiet that if someone was reading a book in the room next door—as my roommate was—she could have finished the chapter uninterrupted. Absence complemented that silence—the absence of desire, the absence of agency, the absence of trust, the absence of consent. Mine was the textbook example of a sexual violation that never would have gone to trial, never mind received a conviction, and any movie director would have thrown the scripted version of this scene into the trash, remarking that the plot was eerie but unsensational.[1]

At the time, unremarkability was part of the shock. Now, I think the unremarkability was in and of itself remarkable because it leads to this question: What does it take to keep a person from naming her own sexual violation for what it is?

I knew the other person in the room that night, but that too is unremarkable because 80% of those who experience sexual violations are like me, known to those who harm them.[2] Still, the fact that I am telling you this, as if this person's prior relationship to me matters, shows the power of the rape script to skew who is believed and who is not. It places people like me on the defensive, because we lack the power to define harm through reference to our experiences—we have to conform our narratives to pre-made definitions of words like "rape" and "sexual assault." These are concepts we didn't create. They've been inherited, absorbed from birth, as pervasive and invisible as the air we breathe.

We know to conform to them. The words do not conform to us.

Statistically, you would be more likely to believe me—less likely to construct me as an unreliable narrator of my own story—if I said this person was someone I'd never met, if I told you that this stranger grabbed me from behind in the dead of night, pulled me into an alley, forced intercourse, and left me bruised and battered.[3] But what happened was nothing like that. We'd known each other for quite some time, been friends first and romantically involved. We studied together, went to parties together, took walks together, shared friends and beliefs, and some—though not all—of the other memories I have of this person involve cookies and movies and kindness.

Although the kindness, with the hindsight of time, I am not so confident about, because sometimes what appears to be kindness is really thickly cloaked manipulation.

On the night in question, the night in which this particular violation occurred, this individual took me out to dinner, walked me back to where I lived, and likely exchanged a few words with my roommate, who would have been doing problem sets in the room next door. At some point, the door to my room would have closed—who closed it, I don't recall—and some clothes came off, and I felt safe through all of this until this person tried to physically press me to do more than I was willing, and then I objected, but my words went unacknowledged. This person left no mark and drew no blood, which is different from saying there was no coercion, because there was. Instead of taking my tears and words seriously, this other human being picked up my body as if it were a doll, and then initiated a sexual act I did not desire. When the act was complete, the person

Introduction   xv

left, again walking past my roommate who was still solving problems by the light at her desk.

And then that chapter of my story ended.

*   *   *

Or did it?

Raised to believe stereotypes, scripts, and myths of what constituted "real rape"—namely a physically violent attack on a woman by a male stranger who forced her to engage in intercourse—I did not have a word to express what had happened to me. Indeed, it did not even occur to me to try to find one because the event seemed to defy categorization, and so, absent a word to express wrongdoing, I packaged the memory in a box and hid it in a dusty, cobwebbed corner. Here too, my response to this unremarkable event was also unremarkable. I didn't make a fuss, and I didn't complain, much like the other 71.9% of women—including my physics major roommate—who are sexually victimized during their college years but do not acknowledge it in so many words.[4]

I believed there was nothing more to say about it, and so I said nothing at all.[5]

If we think of life as a story that we construct over time and in community, then the story stopped for me after that night. Instead of being an embodied story, I became an embodied question mark: Why did I not leave if I was not tied down and forced to stay? Why was I in this relationship to begin with? How much agency had I ever had? Can I use the word "rape" when it connotes the myth of a stranger who grabs a woman from behind and assaults her in a dark alley, or does using that word make me look like a liar? These questions led to another one, the one that planted the seed for much of the material in this book: How does one talk about this kind of a violation with others when the English words and ideas available to encapsulate it are laden with associations that do not resonate with experience?[6] This question is not just theoretically interesting but practically pressing: Communication is imperative for survivors of any kind of trauma to recover, but if the words that survivors have do not assist in the process of being heard, then they face additional barriers in their own healing. This linguistic stalemate, in turn, ensures the perpetuation of harm, as well as the inability to personally identify and hold others accountable for the enactment of it.

The limits of language to describe sexual violations also implicates language more generally: Philosophers, linguists, and theologians have long asserted that language is more than just a system of symbols.[7] Language sets the limits of our world, as Wittgenstein famously writes, because what is beyond language is also, to some extent, beyond knowing.[8] But language is also a system of power, and that power performs so that some individuals are emboldened to speak while others are rendered silent.[9] This system of linguistic power affects all of us in our daily lives. It means that what we say, how we think, and even how we act are impacted by what we can conceptualize, and what we can conceptualize is delineated by the words we receive from culture. If those words are limited in scope, then some individuals are left without a vocabulary to express their experiences, often at the times they most need to speak. In other words, the way we construct language as a culturally dominant embedded belief that privileges the powerful and disempowers the vulnerable impacts us as English speakers in ways that extend beyond theoretical discussions.[10] I am interested in how this power struggle plays out in relation to the words and narratives that English speakers commonly invoke to describe sexual violations, how they are performed, and the effect that this performance has upon our collective ability to communicate to others what sexual harm is as well as what it does in the life of a person who has experienced it.

What I discovered from my own life is that my body found ways of speaking when words failed me.[11] It refused to forget and insisted on speaking in a different language—through flashbacks and fear, through hypervigilance and constant startling, through emotional numbness alternating with sudden and irrational outbursts of anger, through dissociation, anxiety, a dislike of being touched, crushing nightmares that inaugurated insomnia, and the relapse of a prior eating disorder. At times, I was so reactive that I felt that I might as well have been attached to an IV drip that released cortisol directly into my bloodstream. Most days, I felt like I had become the icicles outside my bedroom window on the night of the violation—jagged, frozen, and sharp. I began to wear red lipstick because I thought it would remind me that I was actually alive, that my lips had the color of life and not the blue of death. There were also practical signs of suffering: My grades sagged, I couldn't drive without startling when a car passed me, I had a petrifying fear of dying in my sleep, and my ability to concentrate was so compromised that I questioned whether I could finish my degree.

I couldn't find a way to tell the story, and so the story was telling me.[12]

Three years after that night, I began to name for myself that something terribly wrong had happened and that this terribly wrong thing had led to the psychological and physical distress that was dominating my life. Yet while these realizations were unnerving, it was the crisis of knowing—the epistemological crisis—that felt most torturous. Once I named what had happened in the privacy of my own heart, I had to reckon with the assumptions I held about myself and my safety in the world. Because this person was someone I had known for quite some time, what happened felt like a reflection on my ability to judge a human being's character. Mindful that I had made a mistake once, it seemed probable that I would trust the wrong person again, which turned the world into a more frightening place than it was before, a place where there were harmful people everywhere that I couldn't identify. I began to ruminate, my mind circling through the same questions over and over again: Who can I trust? Is there a litmus test for trust? If there isn't, how am I supposed to keep this from happening again? Will it happen again? What will I do if it does?

Curiously, I did not find myself experiencing one of the most common questions that suffering individuals ask—the question of "Why me?" or "Why did God allow this to happen?" These concerns broadly relate to what theologians call "theodicy," or the study of why a good, powerful, and loving God allows bad things to happen to people (see the biblical Book of Job for a paradigmatic example). Though I am a theologian, I did not engage theodicy much in my own journey because questions of this nature seemed to have an obvious answer to me: In a world where sexual harm—largely, but not exclusively harm inflicted upon women—is an assumed reality of the fallen world in which we live, there was no reason why I should be immune. This was sobering and says something about the extent to which sexual violations frame women's identity on the whole.[13]

I navigated this jagged terrain largely during my years in graduate school, where I found myself clinging to my closest friends as I became acutely aware that there were unpredictable limits to my own safety. Only with them, sitting on futons and watching episodes of *Survivor*, did I feel flashes of belonging and protection and hope, and so slowly, carefully, I told some of them about this part of my life—in the privacy of my apartment, on a long car ride, over homemade lentil soup and beer bread. Most of the time, they received what I said with belief, compassion, and rage on my behalf. Sometimes, my words elicited their own disclosures, which they'd held in the privacy of their own hearts up until that moment. Occasionally, they said thoughtless but well-intentioned things in response, and a few times, what I said caused us to drift apart. This distance sometimes blossomed from the hurt of disbelief, but more hauntingly, it occurred when my friends' own experiences of sexual violations made it too difficult to navigate the consequences that arose from living in a world in which our bodies and the bodies of the people we loved were vulnerable to such tremendous harm. The loss of those friendships feels like the greatest loss of all.

The response I had fits fairly closely into the narrative that the mental health community offers about the aftermath of undesired sexual contact—posttraumatic stress and anxiety, the brain trying to make sense of the trauma while simultaneously trying to avoid it. But what confounded me was that I seemed to be having this reaction for no reason because, for several years, I didn't think any inappropriate sexual contact had happened. Unwanted, yes, but inappropriate—no. What I was experiencing was an epistemic clash—a clash in ways of knowing—between the dominant narrative of psychology and the dominant narrative embedded in rape scripts, and, initially at least, the rape script played a far more influential role in the story I was telling myself about my relationships, my life, and myself. Perhaps this is why, when the therapist I started seeing asked whether I'd ever experienced any kind of rape or sexual assault, I told her that I hadn't, because I thought those words did not apply to me.[14] It wasn't that I'd forgotten what had happened. This wasn't a case of recovered memories.[15] I hadn't deleted any of the relevant details from my consciousness, but I wouldn't have called it "rape" or "sexual assault" or "sexualized violence" or any of the other words we commonly use, because they were too laden with stereotypes that did not apply to me. I would have told you at the time that I was not a "victim" of rape nor was I a "survivor." I still do not think of myself in these terms. I am a human. Humans are vulnerable to other humans, and it was my humanity—both in my physicality and in the way that physicality has been culturally constructed—that created the setting for the violation to occur. That violation then turned me into a person who possessed a memory that lacked a label, and without such a label, my logical conclusion was that harm had not taken place.

So although I was experiencing fairly debilitating psychological distress, I didn't attribute it to that night until I began to question the assumption that the way we talk about sexual violations doesn't always help us communicate what we want to say. In linguistic terms, it doesn't do the conversational work that's needed to express what sexual harm really looks like. You see, the gift of words is that they create boundaries, limits, categories, but when an experience defies these, then dissonance arises because a person must question what is more valid—her personal experience or the words in which her society collectively invests itself to explain reality. If the latter is true, then the person must question her own sanity. If the former, then the person is forced to recognize that the language subscribed to by the collective fails to represent her, and the narratives that derive from the language fail as well. Both, in effect, perform in a way that continues the violation. When such a person tries to speak, then, it becomes even more important for words to do this conversational work well because communication is essential for the alleviation of epistemic symptoms, by which I mean the symptoms that emerge from questions about how we construct knowledge about our world.¹⁶ As Susan Brison writes, "*Saying* something about the memory *does* something to it."¹⁷

But what happens when there's nothing to be said?

From my experience, I know that saying something can feel daunting. I didn't believe anyone could receive what I was trying to say because I didn't think the words represented me, and so I was afraid of being judged. I worried that listeners would think I was making a big deal out of nothing, which, in turn, made me worried that I *was* making a big deal out of nothing, that I was a histrionic woman making an unnecessary fuss. I became anxious, my mind going in loops as it tried to figure out whether what I experienced was bad enough to count as "rape," as if there were some kind of measure—like a joule or a centimeter—that could objectively quantify harm that someone hadn't told me about.

The absence of words also seemed to signal that, as a society, we had collectively agreed on the boundaries of what constituted sexual harm, and that what I had experienced—this event that had landed me with years of distress and therapy bills—didn't exist. Surely it would have a name if it did. This is how I came to realize that even though any given sexual violation takes place in private, it is the culmination of many public violations, of widely held philosophies, stereotypes, practices, and unquestioned assumptions that allow those who enact sexual violations to undertake their actions. Just as it takes a village to raise a child, it takes a village to rape a human being, and because of that, it's not really a single person who violates and a single person who gets victimized. Behind the one who violates are all the people who subscribe corporately to a conglomeration of beliefs and practices that allow a human being to undertake the act in the first place.¹⁸

Perhaps because of this banality, this normalization of sexual violations, I question whether the person who hurt me would even remember the night I'm describing or recognize any personal wrongdoing. It was, as I stated earlier, a very quiet affair. I've wondered, like many others do, what power I have to enact justice, to keep this person from doing the same thing to other people. Individually, I've discovered, the answer is very little.

In admitting this, perhaps I am proving myself an enabler (at best) or am putting others in harm's way (at worst). These are fair critiques. But I think it's more complex than that. As I stated earlier, this was a classic "he-said-she-said" case of sexual harm. It would not go to trial. It would not receive a conviction, rendering any kind of public accusation an emotional and expensive experiment in futility. Moreover, our justice system operates in such a way that it punishes an individual for what is considered to be an individually perpetrated crime against another individual. However, if what I propose in this book is true—that sexual harm is a collective and not just an individual problem—then it follows that our individual system of retributive punishment requires re-examination, because meaningful accountability is needed on the part of both the person who perpetrated the harm *and* the wider society that enabled it.

Throughout this book, I challenge the connotations of the words most commonly used to describe sexual wrongdoings. As preferable alternatives, I often use "sexual harm" and "sexual violation"—the term preferred by Linda Martín Alcoff—both because they're broader and less laden with stereotypes than others and because, as a baseline, a healthy or morally blameless sexual encounter should neither do harm nor violate.[19] As Chapter 2 offers a fresh definition of the word "rape," I employ that term in later chapters of the book, alongside "sexual violation" and "sexual harm." My hope is that these three terms, in concert with one another, linguistically capture the diversity and nuances of this kind of wrongdoing.

I am also cognizant that no single word or term can do the conversational work needed to communicate about such a tender topic, because those who need to speak require multiple ways of doing so to address the uniqueness of their experiences. While neutral terms like these help, those who have been victimized also need helpful dominant embedded beliefs and narratives from institutions that hold cultural epistemic authority, by which I mean institutions that influence how and what we know. Victimized parties also need safe spaces to tell their stories, allies who can listen, and creative forms of expression like music and art that go beyond language to richer, deeper forms of communication and connection. Put differently, being able to speak doesn't simply require discovering more helpful individual words. It also requires social support and more expansive ways of telling a story than language can provide.

The terms used to describe sexual harm are not the only ones that require a moment of consideration: "Victim," "survivor," "offender," "perpetrator," and "assailant" can also be problematic. For those who experience harm, the words "victim" and "survivor" can feel reductive. Critics of "victim" suggest it only highlights how agency was diminished in the act of violation while failing to acknowledge the agency that individual has in the aftermath. On the flipside, critics of "survivor" say that the word implies that harm has been permanently conquered and overlooks the depth of the violation.[20] Moreover, both conflate the person with the violation. I avoid these terms when possible, instead using personal names or language that avoids labeling, such as "a person who has been victimized" or "a person who has survived harm." I make the choice to keep the frameworks of victimization and survival because they represent a spectrum of experience. Those who have experienced harm often feel all aspects of this continuum, sensing both that something has been done to them and that they are recovering from it. As a result, both frameworks seem appropriate to employ interchangeably.

Many in the restorative justice community also express concerns about the terms that are used to refer to those who inflict harm because of the way that words like "offender," "assailant," and "perpetrator" reduce the totality of the person to the violation they inflicted. Scholars and practitioners such as Howard Zehr, Alissa Ackerman, and Jill Levenson rely on critiques of labeling theory to explain why these terms benefit neither those who have been victimized, the one who inflicted the harm, nor the wider community.[21] It causes victimized individuals to question their judgment, to ask how it was possible that they didn't see the harm coming, because people who are "perpetrators" are supposed to be identifiable in their difference from the rest of us. Likewise, it leaves the public believing that those who perpetrate are monolithic hunks of enfleshed evil who can be spotted from a mile away, so that if someone seems nice enough and another person makes an allegation against them, then the allegation must be false.[22] Finally, it causes those who inflict harm to become defensive—"I'm not that awful alien thing called a perpetrator!"—and, in turn, keeps them from engaging in meaningful accountability. For all these reasons, I will refer to this population using language like "the person who inflicted harm" when possible.

I will say more about my background and personal history in later chapters, but for now, it's important that you know that my first career was as a musician. As a child, I sang for a decade in a prominent girls' choir at an Episcopal cathedral, where I learned about the power of gender and conformity, the gift of community and allies, how music can speak into experiences that seem beyond words, and how important spirituality can be to a meaningful life. I continued to sing professionally through most of college and my early years in graduate school, complementing my love of music with studies in literature and psychology, both of which use different methods to enrich our understanding of who we are, how systems of power work, what harm looks like, and what hope and resilience mean.[23] My interest in theology remained prominent as I studied both of these fields, and eventually led me to doctoral studies in an interdisciplinary field known as practical theology. It was within this field that I felt I could draw these disciplines together in order to ask important questions about how individuals construct their identity, the role that relationships and social constructions play in the process, and who gets included and excluded from various communities due to individual and institutional sources of power. These interdisciplinary sources, therefore, all play an important role in this project.

Accompanying these disciplines were three books that profoundly impacted me as I went through this journey from being a musician to a theologian, all of which I discovered while I was in the early years of addressing the sexual harm that occurred in my life. The first was Judith Herman's *Trauma and Recovery*, a groundbreaking work in mental health that offers a primer on the history, political implications, and psychological reality of trauma in a person's life. Herman writes that meaning-making is essential to healing from trauma, and in that book, I began to understand the meaning of sexual trauma in my own life. The second book was Susan Brison's *Aftermath*, a work in feminist philosophy that considers how the self is relational, constructed, and profoundly impacted by trauma. Brison was able to name much of what I felt but couldn't find a way to explain, and it was thanks to her careful, honest, and brave analysis that I discovered that books could offer solidarity. Indeed, they could even become conversation partners that could help reconstruct the self. Finally, there was Kristen Leslie's *When Violence Is No Stranger*, a theological account of acquaintance rape. This was the first book I read in either pastoral or practical theology, and I found in its pages clear, accessible wisdom that helped me make sense of the spiritual dimensions of sexual harm. Together, these three works guided my own process of making meaning, helped me construct a new sense of self, and left me with the conviction that books can change lives. The words that these three scholars wrote became the reason that I am writing now.

Informed by these scholars and their fields, this book draws primarily on the contributions of scholars from psychology, feminist philosophy, and pastoral and practical theology. These are the fields that I found and continue to find most useful when it comes to understanding how sexual violations affect human lives, because all of these fields care deeply about what it means to be a human who can both suffer and flourish. All of them want to understand what sexual violations look like and why they matter, and each of them has something valuable to contribute to the conversation. I've included works from the wider psychological community because of the way these experts are able to identify common symptoms, biological processes, and ways to recover from sexual violations. Feminist philosophers care about what it means to be a self that exists among other selves with unequal degrees of power, and they also offer incisive analyses of sexual harm. Theology, perhaps, is the field that needs the most justification, especially for readers who may not be people of faith. Indeed, some scholars seem intent on seeing theology as a lesser discipline and faith or spirituality as forms of knowledge that exclusively cause sexual violations instead of also—and the term "also" is key here—contributing to healing.[24] In contrast to this oft-held view among academics, I believe the work of the best theologians is relevant to the public at large, because regardless of faith commitments, most human beings care about the kinds of issues that theologians dedicate their lives to, issues that I have often referred to as "2 a.m. questions" when teaching. These are the questions that wake us up at two o'clock in the morning, that press upon us, that haunt us. These questions are the bread and butter of a theologian's calling. They recognize that we are more than just ourselves, that we are fundamentally relational beings, bound together by something beyond the confines of our own bodies. Many contemporary leaders in the discipline—including Emilie Townes, Serene Jones, James Cone, and Kelly Brown Douglas—call out the role that power plays in our experiences and the ways that dominant sources of power often result in systemic forms of oppression. Other feminist theologians, such as Sallie McFague, wrestle with how words can shape our concepts of reality, often functioning as idols that serve the gods of misogyny or white supremacy. In short, whether or not one believes in God, theologians bring valuable insights to a more general analysis of sexual violations because of their attention to power, language, relationships, and transcendence.

Moreover, they are far more open to acknowledging the way that sexual violations instantiate not just physical and psychological but also spiritual suffering, suffering which can be especially relevant in cases of clergy sexual abuse.[25] Recognizing that sexual violations are also spiritual violations becomes even more relevant when one considers the landmark 2014 Pew Forum Religious Landscape Study, which found that while there was an increase in "Nones"—also known as religiously unaffiliated individuals—only 3.1% of adults who live in the United States define themselves as atheists.[26] It therefore becomes essential to acknowledge that when an individual attempts to speak about experiences of sexual harm, they may turn to frameworks from their faith life to cope, and they may also have questions that relate to spirituality. I incorporate relevant insights from theologians in this work, then, in an attempt to facilitate a richer and more holistic understanding of the causes of, responses to, and prevention of sexual harm, particularly in relation to language and narrative.

This book emerged as a result of experiences in my own life that caused me to spend twenty years thinking about both sexual violations and the words we use to describe them. I would do the reader a disservice were I to undertake this work without reference to those experiences. In this way, my method of writing differs from that of many academics, especially in fields like theology, where the standard is to refrain from using the first person, either because one believes it dilutes the scholarship or because one sees personal disclosure as distracting from addressing the needs of the reader. In addition, best practices in my own field of practical theology and pastoral care often discourage caregivers from disclosing personal experiences during a caregiving conversation. I agree entirely with this practice, as it refocuses the conversation on the needs of the caregiver, rather than keeping it on the care seeker. It also muddies boundaries, can emotionally flood the care seeker, and raises questions about whether the caregiver is asking the care seeker to keep a secret about the caregiver's life. However, pastoral theologians hold different points of view about how to navigate personal disclosure in their scholarship, as the relationship that exists between writer and reader differs from the relationship between caregiver and care seeker in a pastoral conversation. Some pastoral theologians refrain from talking about their personal relationship to the topic at hand, believing that it detracts from best practices in scholarship or puts the focus on them instead of the issues being discussed. Others do disclose or employ personal narrative in their work, because they feel that their personal experiences enhance the scholarship, because they want to be transparent about their relationship to the topic, or because they know that it helps to breaks down stigma and build solidarity.[27]

All three of these reasons impact my decision to disclose in this work. In particular, I began to think about disclosure differently when I learned that acknowledgment rates decline when survivor experiences do not align with rape myths, such that over 50% of victims are what Mary Koss refers to as "unacknowledged rape" survivors.[28] My story is therefore not the

Introduction   xxvii

anomaly. My story is closer to the norm, but it's a silent, insidious norm, which makes it that much more important to be a bit noisy.

In invoking the first person, I do not claim to speak for all victimized individuals, though I do use the first person when it appears that my experiences either have a degree of generalizability or make a concept concrete which otherwise might appear wholly theoretical. In addition, it's important to acknowledge that my identity impacts my experiences and perceptions of the world. In my case, I am a highly educated, middle-class white woman; I'm married to a man and have no physical or intellectual struggles that impact my daily life, though my father struggled with a rare, slow-moving form of Lou Gehrig's disease for twenty years, which gave me significant second-hand experience of disability. These aspects of my life impact how I perceive myself, how society interacts with and projects upon me, and the extent to which, with any kind of integrity, I can claim to speak for those beyond my social location with embodied expertise. Having said that, it is my hope that this book impresses upon the reader that language fails most at the margins. Those who experience multiple forms of marginalization typically also experience multiple forms of silencing. To diversify the voices in this book, I incorporate public instances of sexual violations in contemporary American culture to address the linguistic and social constructs we have established around sexual harm that ultimately perpetuate it.

Regarding the order and contents of what follows: Chapter 1 analyzes how various words in the English language fail to express the full spectrum of what sexual harm looks like and instead function in ways that linguistically and epistemically endorse rape scripts that perpetuate misogyny, racism, homophobia, transphobia, and classism. Chapter 2 suggests an alternative definition to the word "rape" that seeks to disrupt the power of these embedded beliefs and to re-shift the power this dominant word exerts in conversations about sexual violations so that it becomes a source of linguistic and epistemic resistance rather than linguistic and epistemic harm. The following two chapters consider the role that embedded beliefs play in the way that individuals speak about, conceptualize, and craft narratives about sexual violations, both at micro and systemic levels. The final chapter proposes that restorative justice may be an effective way to counteract the linguistic forms of injustice that prevent perpetrator accountability and the ability of someone who has suffered a sexual violation to speak and be heard.

There exists a persistent crisis of sexual harm in the United States. At times it is a vocal crisis, as it was during the outcry made by many survivors during the height of the #MeToo movement. At other times, it is quieter. But even at its loudest, there remains a haunting silence among those with experiences of sexual harm that occurs, in part, from a sense that there's no way to speak that others will understand.

These violations need to be voiced; otherwise we'll never build a safer, more just world. It's my hope, then, that this book presents ways of imagining and talking about sexual violations differently, so that those who feel voiceless might find the words they need to speak for themselves.

CHAPTER 1

Limiting Language

WHEN I WAS a child, still too young to read, my parents took me on an otherwise unmemorable vacation that stood out largely because my parents had an argument about Some Adult Thing, after which my father stormed off and my mother was left alone with me on a street corner. Not sure how to distract both of us and unclear when my father was going to come back, she bought us discounted tickets to see her favorite musical, *West Side Story*, without thinking much about the age appropriateness of the plot. I sat politely in the first row of the balcony, my feet dangling just over the edge of the seat, until the scene where Anita is almost gang-raped by the Jets.

At that point, I stood up on the chair and screamed, "You stop hurting her." My mother grabbed my arm, told me to sit down, insisted I be quiet. "It's not real." I screamed some more. "You're distracting the actors." I didn't stop. The people sitting around me began to look uncomfortable: What a poorly behaved child. That mother can't keep her own daughter in line.

"Be quiet or we're going to have to leave," my mother said. I sat down and didn't say another word.

I reflected often on this memory in the years after I experienced a sexual violation of my own. Why couldn't I stand up for myself if I had been able to stand up for a fictional character? Did I possess less wisdom as a young adult than as a four-year-old? Why had it become so hard to speak?

One of the reasons it was so challenging to find words is because the words themselves didn't seem to exist. Even now, after heightened awareness of the #MeToo movement inaugurated a public outcry concerning the prevalence of sexual harm, words shape what those who survive such events say and how they can say it. Put differently, words are an external source of categorization that we use to frame our understanding of right and wrong. We don't create them. We employ them. But they have tremendous power over how we understand our world. They impact how we perceive what constitutes a violation, delineating the boundaries of what ought to be considered harmful and what ought not be. The problem, however, is that the words we have do not line up with the actuality of harm, which means there's voiceless suffering that comes from the limits of the words that are supposed to describe it.[1]

In this chapter, I propose that the words we use for sexual violations fail to represent the scope of the problem, leaving survivors without easily accessible language to describe their experiences. This linguistic limitation affects their ability to both communicate and heal. I defend this thesis by undertaking a systematic examination of words that attempt to describe sexual harm, discussing their strengths and weaknesses, respectively, and I propose, as part of that examination, that the words we most commonly use to describe such violations—"rape" and "sexual assault"—are more effective in describing rape myths than they are at describing the nature of harm itself. Other words—namely, "sexual abuse" and "incest"—are effective but limited in their descriptive scope, while another cluster of words less commonly used to describe sexual harm—including "gender-based violence" and "criminal sexual conduct"—are problematic in their own right because of their limited circulation. I then turn to a discussion of "gray rape," which some scholars have proposed as an antidote to the problem. I close by discussing what is at stake for those who speak and those who listen in recognizing the role that words play in the process of recovering from sexual harm.

Why Do Individual Words Matter?

There are a variety of words available in the English language that can be deployed to describe forms of harm that are sexual in nature, with "rape," "sexual assault," and "sexual abuse" being some of the most common. Given that words already exist to describe these types of violations, it is not unreasonable to wonder what merits a discussion of their limitations. In what follows, I propose three reasons why such an analysis is important.

The first reason why this study is essential is because the words discussed below often mean different things in different contexts, their definition shifting depending on who is listening and what their epistemological priorities are. This linguistic instability places an additional burden on the person who survived the harm because if someone asks, "Were you raped?" the answer might well be, "That depends on who is asking."[2]

Here's an example of what I mean: In a therapeutic context, the role of the therapist is to provide tools that a client can use to reconstruct a sense of self and safety in the world following the traumatic event, and the goal is to help a survivor alleviate symptoms of discomfort and promote personal flourishing through a process of integrating the experience into the context of their life. The therapist is not interested in collecting evidence or corroborating testimonies as a means to validate the victim's assertions. Rather, it is more likely that a therapist would begin with an assumption that the person is telling the truth, and look to the presence of symptoms of post-traumatic stress, depression, or anxiety as signs of trauma or psychological discomfort that they could help alleviate. The therapist's role is, therefore, to start from a place of belief in order to help their client integrate the event and achieve psychological wellbeing. This process often involves giving the person who experienced the sexual violation autonomy to explain it in ways that make sense to them, instead of defining it against a prescribed set of criteria.

Here's an example of what this might look like in practice: I recall a session with my own therapist where I was going to tell her about what had happened to me, but when it came time for me to actually explain, I found that I didn't have the words to do it. I verbally froze, unable to speak, unable to say words like "rape" or "sexual assault" or even to offer a description of what had occurred. What I could do, though, was turn to music, the vocabulary of my childhood. I took out a compact disc player and turned on Samuel Barber's *Agnus Dei*, a devastating choral composition that begins as quietly as it is possible for singers to perform—*pianissimo*—and then escalates in tone and tension into a kind of collective vocal suffering. I had sung the piece many times, both before and after my own experiences of violation, and what a singer seems to communicate in the performance of it is the same thing I was feeling: a profound sense of aloneness, of hopelessness, of fear. It said what I needed to say better than any narrative could have. My therapist seemed to understand, and after that, I found that I was able to talk about my experiences a little more freely.

I am mindful that none of this would have happened in a police station or a judge's chambers. If a person alleges in a legal context that this thing called "rape" occurred, then it is the job of a judge, lawyers, or a jury to assess whether the narrative of the person alleging harm matches legal criteria such that the accused can be convicted of a crime. Lawyers in this context are not interested in whether survivors integrate trauma into their self-concept any more than therapists care about whether there is physical evidence of the crime. The legal system, therefore, burdens the survivor with the task of establishing credibility against a set of legally enforceable definitions that require the survivor to offer a consistent "snapshot," constrained not by the limits of their own story but by the limits of the law.[3]

Music, in that context, is silent.

Ironically, though the legal community is preoccupied with creating standards that delineate the contours of sexual violations, it does so inconsistently, with standards varying across the United States. In Arkansas, the penal code defines all forms of penetration of the mouth, vagina, or anus with any object—a sexual organ or otherwise—as "rape." Arizona law refrains from using the term "rape," instead criminalizing "sexual assault," which it defines as non-consensual intercourse or oral sexual contact, while Colorado uses the same term but defines it as either "sexual intrusion" or "penetration." Oregon's laws state that rape in the first degree only involves sexual intercourse with a person who is forced to engage when under 16 (in cases where the offender is a nuclear family member), under 12 (in all other cases), or when they are incapable of consent for physical

Limiting Language 5

or mental reasons. Washington DC and Iowa use only the term "sexual abuse" instead of either "sexual assault" or "rape," while Florida uses "sexual battery," North Dakota refers to "gross sexual imposition," and Michigan, Minnesota, South Carolina, and Guam utilize "criminal sexual conduct." California separates orally based sexual violations into a different crime—titled "oral copulation"—from those that involve intercourse.[4] Meanwhile, the Federal Bureau of Investigation (FBI) operates apart from state laws and has its own criteria for sex crimes. It defines rape as "penetration, no matter how slight, of the vagina or anus with any body part or object, or oral penetration by a sex organ of another person, without the consent of the victim."[5]

These types of legal inconsistencies instantiate confusion, especially when a person's experience might be categorized as rape in one context but not in another. For instance, a person who was vaginally penetrated with an object while passed out would, according to the State of Arkansas and the FBI, be said to have been raped, but the states of Arizona and Oregon would categorize this wrongdoing differently. So what exactly happened, and must the person who was on the receiving end of the violation change the language they use to describe this event as they cross state lines? The words employed by the legal community to describe sexual violations, in other words, create a certain level of unnecessary linguistic chaos for speakers and listeners alike.[6]

The second reason to consider the significance of the words we use for sexual violations is made clear by the statistics concerning how victims speak about it.[7] One meta-study found that only 39.6% of women who experienced an event that researchers defined as "rape" actually labeled it that way,[8] with the remaining 60.4% categorized as what Mary Koss terms "unacknowledged rape survivors."[9] Researchers estimate that acknowledgment rates are even lower on college campuses, where closer to 28.1% of women label personal experiences as rape.[10] Low rates of acknowledgment can be seen in men as well, with one study finding that while 20% of men had experienced an event that met researchers' definition of rape, "few men" (specific numbers not given) actually employed the term to describe their experience.[11] One study found that among bisexual cisgender men and bisexual trans individuals, rape acknowledgment dipped even further, to 17.9%.[12] That same study found that lack of acknowledgment correlates to significantly higher rates of PTSD, anxiety, and depression.

Rates of acknowledgment appear to be higher when physical force is utilized and when the person who enacts a sexual violation is a stranger, in other words, when the instance resembles rape myths, which are widely held assumptions about what constitutes sexual harm.[13] The power of rape myths pervades societal structures and practices. It affects which crimes the police view as worthy of investigation, how juries render a verdict, whether victims report, and even whether victims privately acknowledge that harm was done. Put into the language of the myth, then, what appears to constitute "real" sexual harm necessitates that a man attacks a woman using physical force, and, preferably, that man is a stranger. When these criteria do not align with personal experience, then survivors face both internal and external barriers to identifying harm, such that they are more likely to remain silent and less likely to seek resources available for healing. Given that victimization more often than not occurs in ways that violate the stereotype, this is unfortunate for survivors, though it is quite convenient for those who enact sexual violations.

The third reason is this: Listeners respond to a victim's story based upon their own understanding of what constitutes a sexual violation. This understanding may be informed by their own embedded beliefs—by their own background and prior sexual experiences, by their family's beliefs and their religious ones, by the norms they've inherited from the dominant culture, and so forth. Indeed, it takes a certain degree of self-reflexivity to be aware of what has informed one's framing of sexual harm, and yet, this self-reflexivity is essential, given that a listener's response often makes a profound difference in a survivor's recovery.[14] An evaluation of the words used to describe sexual violations merits discussion, then, because these words harken to what the instantiations of sexual harm demand of those who bear witness to it. When a person says a word like "rape" or "sexual assault," then that person causes the listener to step out of their comfort zone. Specifically, it demands that they step away from any denial they might have about the reality of sexual trauma. Susan Brison eloquently refers to this as "the myth of our own immunity,"[15] or the idea that we are socialized to believe that bad things happen to bad people—a useful defense mechanism that allows us to get through the day—because the truth of trauma's randomness might otherwise be overwhelming.[16]

One can observe the myth of our own immunity in some of the ways that society responds to sexual harm. In the criminal justice system, it is the accused who has a right to a speedy trial, not the victimized person because, presumably, it is the accused who has something significant at stake were the accusation to be false.[17] Culturally, we alternate between paying attention to the reality of trauma and turning away from it en masse, entering into collective denial because the prevalence of it is too difficult for us to face.[18] It is perhaps for reasons such as these that we prefer euphemisms to the words intended to convey what sexual violations are and what they do, and yet, effective, concise words are essential to express what occurred.[19]

By way of example, consider how former Baylor University president Ken Starr evaded use of the term "rape" during a period when numerous students brought forth claims, despite the fact that he seemed perfectly adept at speaking about all aspects of sex during his aggressive interrogation of Monica Lewinsky during Bill Clinton's presidency. For another example, theologian Monica Coleman recounts how her pastor avoided using the word "rape" in the church sanctuary, instead preferring euphemisms like "the experience of intimate violence," "deep personal pain," and "despairing conditions." Coleman suggests that he made this choice because people who come to church assume worship should involve "warm, fuzzy feelings" or because "Worship is supposed to be about praising God, and 'rape' does not make anyone want to celebrate."[20] Ironically, though, the Bible does not shy away from recording a number of horrific instances of sexual violations:[21] Lot offers his virgin daughters to a mob to violate (Gen. 19). Joseph is the victim of an attempted violation as well as sexual harassment (Gen. 39). Judges 19 describes the violation of a concubine by a group of strangers who is later dismembered by her master.[22] The prophetic books of Ezekiel, Isaiah, and Jeremiah all use "rape" metaphors,[23] and one New Testament scholar—who is either heretical, brave, or contentious, depending on who you talk to—by the name of Jane Schaberg even bucked Christian tradition and postulated that Mary's conception of Jesus was likely the result of rape and not of a mystical exchange with the Holy Spirit.[24] The texts that ground the tradition of Coleman's pastor, therefore, do not shy away from speaking about the horrors of sexual violations in nuanced, complicated, and political ways. The fact that Coleman's pastor and so many other Christians *do* avoid speaking of them, then, is less of a reflection of what the Bible says and much more a reflection of the caustic intermingling of the misogyny and trauma denial that all too often colors the lens through which Christianity is practiced and, in turn, the lens that normalizes American culture in its dominant form. Becoming cognizant of this lens and striving to remove it, therefore, requires the bravery to name the reality of sexual violations, even those that appear to defy what language represents.

One of the fields where scholars have been thinking for quite some time about how language performs and why that performativity matters is feminist theology, and some of the wisdom that researchers have gained about theological language imparts useful insights about secular terms. Sallie McFague, for instance, is concerned about how the male descriptors used for God—i.e., God as "Father"—reinforce patriarchal practices and other forms of systemic oppression among Christians, so that these words inform both ideology and action. Words for "God," she says, should be understood not as literal representations but rather as metaphors for a reality that can never fully be captured. In other words, no single word can fully represent God; each is a metaphor. She thus proposes that there is danger when a given metaphor becomes too dominant, thereby making it into a model which is either held with too much reverence (turning it into an idol) or does not reflect lived experience (rendering it irrelevant). The male model for God, she proposes, has come to function in this way.[25]

McFague does a compelling job of reminding Christians that the act of naming God has practical implications and that it can do real harm when terms support patriarchal agendas. The terms we most commonly use to talk about sexual violations run the same risk: As with the paternal model for God, many of the words discussed below have been constrained by patriarchal ideology, causing them to suffer from the problems of idolatry and irrelevance. This is particularly true of the words "rape" and "sexual assault." We all suffer because of the dominance of these words, just as we do when masculine language for God functions as an idol.

The ability to name in a way that does not invoke the problems of idolatry or irrelevance is a challenge for those who experience sexual victimization because so many of the English descriptors for these events—especially the most common ones—fall into these dual traps.[26] Either they are held up as idols—as infallible representations of harm—or they frame harm in ways that make it irrelevant. These two linguistic traps make it difficult to speak about the reality and scope of harm. And yet, the process of finding a way to communicate remains essential because speaking about sexual violations offers the survivor an opportunity to be known; to restore a sense of safety, community, and self; and to transform the meaning and power that the event has in their lives. In summary, speaking is more complicated than simply using the words already available to us because many don't represent the scope of sexual harm. Instead, they function as idols—representing scripts that do not align with reality—or are irrelevant.

"Rape" and "Sexual Assault"

According to Rose McGowan, the story goes like this: In 1997, Harvey Weinstein forced oral sex upon her in her hotel room at the Sundance Film Festival. Now fast forward to 2017, when *New York Times* journalists Jodi Kantor and Megan Twohey published an exposé about this accusation and others against Weinstein.[27] Kantor and Twohey recount an interview they conducted with a lawyer named Lanny Davis, who worked on Weinstein's crisis management team, in which he stated that:

> He [Weinstein] was aware that there were concerns, but not that she [McGowan] was accusing him of rape. So I'm making a bright line on the word rape. Anything below that line, he [Weinstein] was aware of feeling.... There's mental coercion that isn't physical coercion.[28]

The most likely reason why Davis would have avoided employing "rape" as a descriptor is that he did not want his statement to appear as an admission of guilt on behalf of his client. However, it is worth noting that McGowan's accusation would not necessarily have met a legal definition of "rape." Arizona law would have categorized the event as "sexual assault" because the state does not use the word "rape" in its penal code. In Arkansas, law enforcement officials would have had to find out whether Weinstein penetrated any part of the labia majora, because penetration is required to meet the definition of "deviate sexual activity" which is required to forward an allegation of either a rape or a sexual assault in the first degree. If the act did not qualify as "deviate sexual activity," then Arkansas law enforcement could have said the crime committed was "sexual assault in the second degree."[29] McGowan was actually in Utah at the time of the violation, where the state law limits "rape" to intercourse, meaning that Weinstein would have been charged with "forcible sodomy," since Utah's legal definition of sodomy includes oral sex.[30]

This example illustrates that the terms "rape" and "sexual assault" are sometimes used synonymously, creating confusion about what separates the two. The definition of each is also influenced by rape myths, such that these terms fail to convey the actuality of harm because they get equated with stereotypes about sexual victimization. These myths impact who can be perceived as a valid "victim" and who can be perceived as a valid "perpetrator," omitting large numbers of people in the process—the low acknowledgment rates cited above reinforce this point. In addition, intersectional oppression also plays into how these terms are heard in relation to the rape myths that define them: For instance, stereotypes about the promiscuity of Black women's bodies negatively impact whether others can see them as victims.³¹ Stereotypes about the sexual aggression of Black men construct them as what one might call ideal perpetrators.³² Those in the LGBTQ+ community are also not represented by these stereotypes: The idea that men inflict sexual trauma on women excludes the reality that same-sex violations occur, as do violations to members of the trans community. In short, those who are vulnerable to systemic oppression still have to speak about sexual violations using words that, by definition at least, do not represent them. In choosing to employ these terms—and thereby challenging the stereotypes embedded in them—they engage in acts of linguistic resistance. But given that these stereotypes are held by wide numbers of listeners, it also means that they may address a hostile audience who hears in the terms "rape" and "sexual assault" that a cisgender white woman's body has been physically attacked and sexually violated by a Black man who is also a stranger.

The Myths of the Ideal Victim and Perpetrator

One of the assumptions embedded in the terms "rape" and "sexual assault" is that there is an ideal victim of such violations. This ideal victim has some specific characteristics: She's a woman, specifically a white, cisgender, straight, economically stable, well-educated, non-promiscuous woman who was not drunk or provocatively dressed at the time of the attack.³³ Elizabeth Smart might be seen as an example of the ideal victim. She was a child at the time of her kidnapping and repeated rapes, and she came from a white, Mormon family that appeared to be not only loving but also well-educated and wealthy. Still, being an ideal victim didn't protect Smart from criticism, showing how even ideal victims face barriers when it comes to public support. Some questioned why Smart, a child at the time of her abduction, left her bed in the first place, why she didn't resist more or find a way to run away from her kidnappers and return to her family. In one well-publicized interview, Nancy Grace pressured Smart to explain whether she heard rescuers searching for her in the hours following her attack, implicitly judging her for not responding to them.³⁴

Smart also implied that the initial charges against Brian Mitchell did not include rape charges, which she felt was a sign that the government wasn't acknowledging "the worst things he did to me."[35] Being an ideal victim, in other words, provides no guarantee of either belief or support, with the likelihood of both deteriorating further if the victim deviates from the normed ideal.

Consider, therefore, some challenges faced by the individuals that those in American society commonly consider to be "unideal victims." Those who were drunk or dressed in a revealing manner at the time of their attacks are often judged for having provoked the person who hurt them, even if that person was a stranger. For but one well-publicized example of such judgment, see the case of Chanel Miller, an Asian American woman in her twenties who was fingered while passed out by Brock Turner on the Stanford University campus. Miller writes about reading public responses—including from lawyers—that judged her for her choice of clothing, for the amount that she drank, for being at a fraternity party in the first place. As she reflects, "They seemed angry that I'd made myself vulnerable, more than the fact that he'd acted on my vulnerability."[36]

But clothing and consumption aren't the only things that can precipitate public backlash. Promiscuity is a problem for victims as well. Though rape shield laws now prevent lawyers in the United States from grilling those who have been victimized about prior sexual experiences, this legislation has not eliminated negative judgment against victims. Perhaps the most obvious example of this is the way that sex workers are negatively judged if they bring forward a claim of sexual wrongdoing, because the public assumes that someone who has sex for a living is always up for another sexual encounter. There could be, we reason, no scenario to which they might conceivably object, although this logic makes little sense.[37] Just as a surgeon might not want to operate on his day off or object to doing a surgery he deems beyond his skillset, so a sex worker might object for any number of reasons to a sexual encounter; indeed, one study found that 68% of sex workers had experienced a sexual violation while working.[38] Yet, when was the last time you heard of a court case in which a sex worker claimed be a victim of a sex crime? Sex workers, therefore, face significant difficulty in getting others to believe their claims of harm, which is compounded by the challenges to accountability that they face because going to the police with a claim of rape would mean outing themselves and facing prosecution.

Here's another example of the negative consequences that arise when a person's identity doesn't match that of the ideal victim: Members of the LGTBQ+ community face barriers to public acknowledgment in the aftermath of a sexual violation because of widespread discrimination and misunderstanding of their identities. Some believe, for example, that lesbians are immune to sexual violations because women don't perpetrate sexual harm.[39] Others believe that members of the trans community are promiscuous or hypersexualized, such that their sexual appetites mean that they would never object to a sexual encounter. Both stereotypes ignore the constructed stigmatization that members of the LGBTQ+ community face that often results in increased vulnerability to sexual harm and not the reverse.[40] These structural barriers also result in low rates of reporting, as those who are victimized may be well aware of the barriers they face in regard to legal support or accountability.[41]

In addition to sexual and gender identity, race also affects the implicit credibility given to those who are victimized. In *Women, Race, and Class*, Angela Davis provides a historical overview of the rape of Black women in the United States in the antebellum and postbellum eras, documenting how rape was an accepted institutionalized form of sexual subjugation in both periods and was intended to eradicate the agency and personhood of Black women.[42] Concurrently, Black women became stereotyped as promiscuous and highly sexualized, rendering them essentially unrapeable in the eyes of the public, because one cannot rape a willing participant in a sexual encounter.[43] When Black women speak about their experiences of sexual coercion, then, they do so under social, legal, and linguistic structures that personify them as unideal victims.[44] Racism and economic oppression only increase the likelihood that a Black woman's claims will not be believed, thereby showing the power of intersectional systemic oppression.[45]

While Black women experience a unique form of intersectional systemic oppression when they attempt to make their voices heard following a sexual violation, the stereotype that they are always willing to engage in sexual activity is one they share in common with men and, in turn, a reason why men are also perceived to be unrapeable.[46] And while men are often believed to be a small subset of the victims of sexual violations, the rate of such sexual harm in prisons by both inmates and prison workers[47]—coupled with the alarming rate of incarceration in the United States—raises compelling questions about the underrepresentation of victimized men in the literature about sexual violations. In particular, it raises questions about the underrepresentation of victimized Black men, given their high incarceration rates.[48]

In summary, the way that rape myths embed in the terms "sexual assault" and "rape" has the potential to make speaking more difficult for anyone who does not fit the image of the ideal victim, including sex workers, members of the LGBTQ+ community, Black men, and Black women. As a result, it becomes more likely that the violation will extend itself beyond the act of sexual harm to the experience of trying to speak in its aftermath. Put differently, it's not just the experience of a sexual violation that attempts to silence victims; the words that are supposed to be tools for healing also contribute to the harm.

If there exists a myth of an ideal victim, there also exists a myth of an ideal perpetrator. Black men have historically embodied this stereotype in the United States, having been constructed to be the only individuals capable of inflicting sexual harm.[49] This myth not only allows for the continued subjugation of Black male bodies but also does not reflect the reality of who is committing sexual violations, if data on arrests are to be believed. In 2019, for instance, the FBI reported that of the 16,559 arrests made for rape charges, 11,588 of those arrested were white, 4,427 were Black, 249 were Native American or Native Alaskan, 276 were Asian, and 59 were Native Hawaiian.[50]

For a particularly well-publicized example of how the myth of the Black male rapist can affect a prosecution, consider the case of Trisha

Meili—more well known as the "Central Park jogger case"—in which five Black boys were tried and convicted of beating, tying, gagging, and sexually violating Meili. This bias toward Black men as ideal perpetrators affected the investigative and legal process so profoundly that the boys were convicted, even though they were innocent of the crimes. By way of contrast, in the case of Recy Taylor—a Black woman who was gang-raped by six white men in 1944—the myth of the Black man as ideal perpetrator caused two grand juries to decline to press charges against the white men who actually enacted the sexual violations, despite the fact that several of them confessed to the crime. These two examples illustrate how Black men are disproportionately labeled as assailants while white men—who appear to be the majority of those committing sexual violations—receive the message that the violations they perpetrate are permissible.[51]

The myth—or, in McFague's language, the idol—of the Black male ideal perpetrator therefore has the power to affect who a prosecutor files charges against, how a jury or judge rules, and how the court of public opinion sways. Perhaps the biggest challenge is how this myth impacts victims, including Black victims, as they interpret their own harm. Charlotte Pierce-Baker, a Black woman, acknowledges this when she writes about her own experience of a physically violent instance of sexual victimization inflicted by two Black men. As she explains it, even her interpretation of what happened to her was burdened by bias in a way that she resisted because she knew the stakes were high. As she writes, "I felt responsible for upholding the image of the strong Black man for our young son, *and* for the white world with whom I had contact.... I didn't want to confirm the white belief that all Black men rape."[52]

The Myth That Normed Sex Is Violent Sex

Normalized sex scripts only complicate the linguistic limitations of "rape" and "sexual assault," adding an additional layer of complexity once one recognizes that these are violent in and of themselves, in part due to the influence of hardcore pornography.[53] Indeed, a 2021 study found that 58%

of college-aged women reported at least one instance of being strangled during a sexual encounter; over 33% reported this happening more than five times. The study found a significant increase in anxiety, sadness, feelings of depression, and loneliness among those who'd experienced strangling (more commonly referred to as "choking").[54]

Let's rephrase this data for what it really signifies: Within the confines of a sexual encounter, over 50% of college-aged women have experienced an act whose primary purpose is to end life.

Or we could put it this way: Over 50% of college-aged women have experienced a sexual encounter in which "violence" and "sex" dangerously intermingled.

This kind of data, however, is not the only example of how violence and sex comingle. We describe men as "pursuing" women. Grabbing an arm, pulling a woman into an embrace, not taking an initial "no" seriously—all of these are insidious examples of ways in which a certain degree of violence has become socially acceptable within sexual encounters. With sex normed to include a certain degree of coercion or violence, the distinction between "rape," "sexual assault," and a socially acceptable sexual interaction disappears, as each begins to smear together like sidewalk chalk in the rain.

It becomes necessary, then, to derive standards of separation. Given the violence of sex scripts that are supposed to describe healthy sexual interactions, one must differentiate "rape" and "sexual assault" from a normative (or socially acceptable) sexual interaction. This is done through increasing the divide between normative and non-normative behavior, so that rape myths become based upon less common forms of sexual harm, such as a sexual violation inflicted on one person by another who is a stranger and utilizes extreme or bizarre forms of physical violence.[55] Violations involving an acquaintance or verbal coercion, then, become less exotic and thereby normalized.

How convenient for those who want to keep the status quo and for those who want to believe they are immune to harm, for if the concepts of "rape" and "sexual assault" remain exotic—here defined as "strikingly, excitingly, or mysteriously different or unusual"—then it allows individuals to more easily argue that such events are rare, outside of their sphere of reality.⁵⁶ Potential victims need not worry. All is safe and well. In concert, it allows those who benefit from the status quo—aka those who perpetrate harm—to continue to engage in violating behavior.

Catharine MacKinnon is perhaps the most well-known proponent of this perspective, asserting that sex has been normalized to be violent, such that the line between rape and sex is blurry. To reinforce MacKinnon's assertion, consider these psychological studies of college students, a group with a particularly high rate of unacknowledged rape. Heather Littleton and Danny Axsom conducted two studies with undergraduates to discover how this population scripted rape versus seduction. In the first study, students engaged in a free-writing activity where they described a scenario in which a rape occurred and a scenario in which seduction occurred. In the second, they rated elements—like whether a woman resisted a man's advances or whether the man complimented the woman—to determine whether they were elements of a seduction script, rape script, or both. The authors found that there was significant overlap between how students constructed rape and seduction scripts, including the acceptance that both involved male sexual coercion and a woman's discomfort with the sexual activity.⁵⁷ Here is one student's description of a rape, followed by another student's description of a seduction:

> The man would probably pick out a female who is either drunk or drinking. Their victim is probably someone they think is vulnerable.... The man would end up coaxing the girl away from the crowd. During the rape, the rapist is feeling control and sexual pleasure as he rapes his victim. Eventually, she will give up hope and just let it happen without fighting back. She is probably tied up or held by her attacker with ripped or torn clothing.⁵⁸
>
> A person who is going to seduce someone also knows that the other person is vulnerable and lonely.... You try to say "no" but the person persists and keeps giving you a disappointed look and keeps saying how beautiful you are.... You finally give in even

though you feel really uncomfortable.... The more you try to say no to his requests, you can't seem to say no to him, ending up doing things you don't want to do.[59]

Parallels between the two encounters emerge clearly: One person pursues and coerces in both. The other person objects in both. The difference between the two events, then, is not in the presence of violence but in the exoticness of it—torn and ripped clothing in the rape, "doing things you don't want to do" in the seduction. The rape script, as described by this first student, could make a dramatic film scene. The seduction might lead the director to say, "We need to heighten the tension."

Littleton and Axsom summarize their study by stating that:

> Given the traditional script of sexual interactions as adversarial, male-dominant, and rife with deceitful communication, such as token resistance, it would not be surprising to find that many instances of unwanted, forced sex are not interpreted as sexual assault or rape."[60]

This elision of rape scripts and sex scripts, then, makes it difficult to separate sexual violations from normalized sexual interactions, creating a slippery slope where some forms of violence—verbally coercing a woman to drink to intoxication before sex, pushing a woman against a wall in order to start hooking up with her—appear permissible, especially if the woman did not forcefully object.

This is the danger of allowing violent sex scripts to function as some kind of model for an appropriate sexual encounter. Masking as normal, they give carte blanche to those who inflict sexual harm to continue to violate others because they maintain the patriarchal structures that allow for it. Indeed, individuals may even come to assume that such scripts represent the way they *ought* to be acting in a sexual encounter, thereby creating the conditions for and the enactment of violations that might not otherwise have occurred had the scripts for sexual encounters been different.

On the Significance of the Myths

At stake in each of these myths is how we perceive the boundaries of sexual harm. Our cognitive constructions of "rape" and "sexual assault" have been skewed in ways that are profoundly limited, reflecting exotic forms of violence rather than the everyday enactment of it. Indeed, as Catharine MacKinnon points out, there is a fine line between what we consider "rape" and what we consider a non-violating sexual encounter because of the way that violence has become normative in sex. As she writes:

> Men who are in prison for rape think it's the dumbest thing that ever happened . . . it isn't just a miscarriage of justice; they were put in jail for something very little different from what most men do most of the time and call it sex. The only difference is they got caught.[61]

Assuming that MacKinnon is correct that normative sexual encounters possess a certain degree of violence within them, then they also enable future violations. In other words, because they remain unspoken as wrongs, they become tacitly socially acceptable, so that there is no wrong of which to speak. This thwarts the speech that is needed for both accountability and healing. The terms "rape" and "sexual assault," then, have come to signify instances that represent the minority of violations—times in which the violation includes exotic physical violence, a victimized party who is in a position of constructed vulnerability, perhaps because she is walking alone at night or because she is intoxicated to the point of being passed out, and an ideal perpetrator who is a stranger and likely Black. This sort of exotic rape script is required in order to maintain the dominance of a normalized sex script that allows for, perhaps even requires, a degree of coercion or violence. Misogyny and patriarchy benefit from this construction. Racism benefits from this construction. Those who actually inflict sexual violations benefit from this construction. Victimized individuals do not.[62]

As a result of the power of myths, I propose that "rape" and "sexual assault" encourage silence more than they empower recovery. They lead survivors to assess their own experiences against stereotypes that don't represent the full scope of harm. Instead, they send an implicit message to those who survived harm that there is a gold standard for what constitutes sexual wrongdoing and that this gold standard is measured not by impact but by a random set of pragmatic criteria that only represent a fraction of what actually causes harm. These words also allow those who bring about sexual violations to be left with an understanding that anything short of putting a gun to a white woman's head and forcing intercourse on her under threat of death is normal sexual behavior. Returning to McFague's vocabulary, then, these terms may be said to function simultaneously as idols that are also irrelevant to large numbers of survivors.

"Sexual Violence"[63]

The term "sexual violence" has been used as a complement to "rape" and "sexual assault," its history embedded in the anti-rape movement that took place in the United States during the 1970s and 1980s, when Susan Brownmiller asserted that the essence of rape was violence and not sex.[64] The benefit of this term is that there is truth to the statement that sexual violations are violent. Yet, this statement is still reductive. As I argue above, violence has become normalized in sex, such that sexual harm—especially in its less mythologized forms—becomes acceptable behavior.[65] Linguistically, then, the terms "sex" and "sexual violence" can become somewhat redundant or, at the very least, lead to the question of how to separate one from the other.

My second objection requires a short experiment with you, the reader. I would like you to take a moment to imagine something violent. Do not think long or hard about this. The first thing that comes to mind is fine. Now, what did you imagine—a man hitting a woman with a baseball bat? A gang fight that took place in a dark alley? One man taking aim at another with a gun? A teenager executing a school shooting? My guess is that the term "violence" conjured any one of an endless variety of physical harms, violations inflicted with objects that could cause bruising, bleeding, even death. It is, I suspect, less likely that one would envision harm of a cognitive, emotional, or epistemic nature—a man calling his wife derogatory names to humiliate her, a mother demeaning her daughter's self-esteem, a middle school bully body-shaming another child at lunch. All of these instances, I would argue, constitute violence verbally executed, but we often overlook these types of harm when we use the term "violence." Violence, for most of us, signifies a physical attack.

The term "sexual violence," therefore, runs into much the same problem as the terms "rape" and "sexual assault" do—it relies too heavily on myths about sexual violations, in particular, the assumption that a sexual violation is, by its nature, physically violent. This implicitly omits the role that verbal coercion and force can play in any episode of sexual harm, just as it harkens to the tendency in the United States to minimize the power of words. Perhaps nothing signifies this propensity more than the adage "Sticks and stones may break our bones but names will never hurt me." It seems like a childhood tradition to chant this saying on the playground, perhaps following a charged statement inflicted by the class bully. We commonly assume this phrase means that physical actions have more power than words, and so words cannot harm the child. Yet I cannot help but wonder whether this phrase is really intended to be an act of resistance, to say more about the child than the words because what the child is really saying is that words do have the potential to break a person just as much as sticks and stones do. In other words, the child acknowledges that yes, words do have the power to break a person—it's just that at this particular moment, in this particular slice of time, the child is insisting that words can't hurt *them*. The difference, the child seems to be saying, has more to do with how the child is constructing her identity, her autonomy, and her power over the person uttering the words. And while this may be an empowering interpretation of the maxim, it's not a common one, another example of how we've twisted words to minimize their impact. In this way, then, the term "sexual violence" suffers from the same problem that the terms "sexual assault" and "rape" do. Because the myth of physical violence heavily impacts this definition, it also suffers from the dual problems of idolatry and irrelevance because it exclusively privileges physical violence in the definition of sexual harm, thereby excluding those whose experiences of harm look different.

"Sexual Abuse" and "Incest"

Sexual abuse most commonly refers to sexual harm perpetrated by an individual in a place of power against another in a position of vulnerability, often over a period of time, such that sexual activity occurs within the context of a power differential that prevents the possibility of consent. Like sexual abuse, incest also involves sexual harm done to a person in a place of vulnerability, but it is more limited in its scope to scenarios in which the person who inflicts the sexual harm is a family member; incest, then, can be considered a subset of sexual abuse.

The benefit of these two terms is how they recognize that sexual violations involve a violation of relational boundaries. These boundaries are sometimes written down, such as when a psychologist has a client sign a contract for therapeutic services. At other times they are assumed, as in the case of the parent–child relationship, where the assumption is that the parent will meet the physical and emotional needs of a child entrusted to their care. "Sexual abuse" recognizes that a boundary violation occurred in the relationship, which can instantiate a crisis for the person victimized at multiple levels. The victimized individual may experience instability and confusion about what the nature of the relationship actually is and what the expectations for it are. In the case of clergy sexual abuse, the person victimized may also experience a profound spiritual crisis because their assumptions about the purpose of life and their understanding of God and organized religion no longer make sense. In cases where priests hold a high ontology—meaning that they are regarded as being different from other human beings, perhaps more like God than other humans—the crisis may involve the devious sense that God is actually authorizing the abuse, perhaps as a form of punishment for wrongdoing.[66]

In addition, the term "sexual abuse" recognizes that the inappropriate execution of power is a component in sexual harm.[67] As Pamela Cooper-White writes, recognizing the role of power in rape is essential to disrupting the narrative that rape is the natural consequence of "uncontrollable lust" that results from the "myth that men cannot control their sexual impulses once aroused."[68] The role of power in sexual abuse is particularly evident in instances where the person who violates has power over the victim, as in cases where those who were sexually violated are a member of a vulnerable class, including when they are elderly, a child, or have a disability. Authority or professional status may also function as a source of power over the harmed party, as when the one inflicting the sexual harm is the victim's doctor, therapist, teacher, or faith leader. In each of these scenarios, the person who is sexually victimized is unequal in power to the one who does the victimizing.[69] The terms "sexual abuse" and "incest," therefore, recognize that sexual harm requires misused power, what might be characterized as power-over (power exerted over another) rather than power-to-do (power that allows for the healthy enactment of agency).[70]

However, in their common understanding at least, "sexual abuse" and "incest" do not claim that all forms of sexual harm are forms of misused power, but rather implicitly separate out certain enactments of it and assert that these particular instantiations qualify as misuses of power. What these terms fail to account for, then, are violations that occur between individuals who appear, at face value, to be peers or equals. This would include, but not be limited to, one-time violations that occur between romantic partners, friends, or spouses, instances in which a profound part of the wrongdoing is the violation of the assumed peer status that occurs during the sexual enactment of power over another.

These words are effective insofar as they name the experience of a subset of individuals who suffer sexual harm, particularly those who were harmed by those in positions of power, including by clergy, by a family member, or by an older individual.[71] However, they also exclude the experience of many survivors, making these words, in McFague's terminology, to some degree, irrelevant.[72]

"Gender-Based Violence" and "Violence Against Women"

The term "gender-based violence" entered public discourse through the United Nation's *Declaration on the Elimination of Violence Against Women*, which employed it as a way of clarifying what constituted violence against women. The writers of the United Nations document therefore intended the terms "gender-based violence" and "violence against women" to be synonymous. As stated in Article 1 of that document:

> For the purposes of this Declaration, the term "violence against women" means any act of gender-based violence that results in, or is likely to result in, physical, sexual or psychological harm or suffering to women, including threats of such acts, coercion or arbitrary deprivation of liberty, whether occurring in public or in private life.[73]

The document then proceeds to define the term "violence against women" as:

a. Physical, sexual and psychological violence occurring in the family, including battering, sexual abuse of female children in the household, dowry-related violence, marital rape, female genital mutilation and other traditional practices harmful to women, non-spousal violence and violence related to exploitation;
b. Physical, sexual and psychological violence occurring within the general community, including rape, sexual abuse, sexual harassment and intimidation at work, in educational institutions and elsewhere, trafficking in women and forced prostitution;
c. Physical, sexual and psychological violence perpetrated or condoned by the State, wherever it occurs.[74]

The definitions for "gender-based violence" and "violence against women" highlight how seemingly individual acts of violence perpetrated upon individual women are not isolated or scattered events but rather acts that emerge out of social structures that permit or encourage them.[75] The harm inflicted upon one woman is, therefore, harm done to all women because of the way that it signals a given society's overarching value of them.[76]

There are two problems with these terms: First, they assume that violence against women is violence undertaken by men. While the statistical majority of sexual harm *is* harm inflicted by men, these terms fail to give voice to harm that is perpetrated by women, thereby raising the question whether a woman who rapes another person has committed an act of gender-based violence or whether she has committed something that ought to go by a different name. The second locus at which these terms fail is that not all sexual harm is harm done to heterosexual, cisgender women. The recognition that individuals who are members of the LGBTQ+ community also experience sexual violations requires a recontextualization of these terms if they are to represent the true scope of harm.

One might respond that it is possible to argue that sexual harm done to members of the transgender and non-gender binary communities represents instances of gender-based violence because they too are part of the non-dominant gender. Likewise, one might object on the grounds that trans women *are* women. However, the term "gender-based violence" has not historically been employed this way and instead has been used primarily to describe violence enacted upon the body of a cisgender, heterosexual woman. The issue, therefore, is how the history of this term affects how it is heard. Its history—while well-intentioned—has all too often caused us to hear "gender-based violence" as a form of violence affecting only heterosexual, cisgender women. The realities of non-cisgender sexual violations, therefore, raise the question of whether to work harder to extrapolate or widen the term "gender-based violence" to include LGBTQ+ individuals or whether to coin another term that would encompass their systemic oppression. Such a question warrants more extensive input from how survivors in this community would prefer to speak about their experiences.

It appears that the terms "violence against women" and "gender-based violence" are useful insofar as they contextualize heterosexual harm inflicted upon a cisgender woman by a cisgender man. However, both of these terms conform to assumptions about sexual harm insofar as they assume that cisgender, heterosexual women are seen as ideal victims and cisgender, heterosexual males are ideal perpetrators. For those individuals whose experiences fail to conform to this stereotype, these words may pose barriers to being heard, such that "gender-based violence" connotes a kind of idolatry that takes the form of assuming that only cisgender, heterosexual women are victims. This connotation may also render the term linguistically irrelevant for other victims who do not fit the dominant stereotype.

"Gross Sexual Imposition" and "Criminal Sexual Conduct"

North Dakota is among the states that criminalize sexual harm using the term "gross sexual imposition," while South Carolina, Michigan, and Minnesota utilize the term "criminal sexual conduct." There are two benefits to these phrases: First, of all the terms discussed in this chapter, they, perhaps, most appropriately encapsulate what sexual harm is: It is, literally, a terrible, crass, or vulgar sexual imposition, just as it is sexual conduct that is so unwanted that it warrants a societal response. Second, these terms are broad and less burdened by stereotypes, therefore opening the possibility that they could be used to describe a more diverse set of harms than other terms do. However, the difficulty with both of these is that they're jargon. Outside of the legal sphere, no one uses them. Most people have never even heard of them before, and because we're not familiar with them, they feel unnatural, inaccessible. It's hard to imagine uttering them in a conversation.

These words remind us that language can't be meaningful without collective buy-in; otherwise sounds are just nonsense or syllables smushed together. So for a specific word or a specific language to do any kind of substantive conversational work in society at large, it can't just be the property of one individual or a small set of individuals. The general public must agree that a new word exists and agree upon its meaning in order for that word to become part of the public's linguistic consciousness. As it stands now, the terms "gross sexual imposition" and "criminal sexual misconduct" function this way only among a subset of individuals—namely, those in the legal profession—but they are not the conversational property of the general public. These words, therefore, are less prone to the problems of idolatry but more exclusively prone to be irrelevant because they do not have collective buy-in from English speakers.

A Note on Gray Rape

Terms like "gray rape," which are designed to address the supposed ambiguity in some instances of sexual harm, have been proposed by scholars as a productive way to move through the linguistic stalemate.[77] Linda Martín Alcoff suggests that:

> Young activists and victims have introduced the term "gray rape" to capture the complexity of some events. This has helped, I believe, to enlarge the scope of the discussion and make it possible for more voices to come forward. The idea that rape is a simple, straightforward matter actually works to dissuade many victims from coming forward who feel that their own experience had complexity and ambiguity, and it inhibits the vitally necessary process of being able to discuss one's experience with others. Acknowledging "gray rape" thus becomes a way to respect the perspective of survivors themselves.[78]

While Alcoff is right to widen the scope of voices who can speak about their experiences of harm, I harbor concerns about using a term like "gray rape" to do so because it doesn't put pressure on culturally embedded beliefs and those who support them to widen the scope of what constitutes sexual harm. "Gray rape" is not so much essentially ambiguous as constructed to be as such, and so what need to change, then, are the constructions and what gets included as "real" harm. Put differently, the term "gray rape" suggests that there is a line that exists between "real" and "ambiguous" violations, with the gold standard being those that reflect rape myths, while the gray forms are somehow a standard deviation less valid and therefore a standard deviation less awful. But it's hard to quantify or rank harm—as I'll elaborate later—and so instead of attempting to do so, I can't help but wonder if it would make more sense to dismantle the assumptions about normative sexual encounters that include violence and to become more cognizant of the role that rape myths and stereotypes play in our constructions of harm. With those dismantled, what appears to be ambiguous may become easier to name for the wrong that it was and the harm that it did.

On Linguistic Gaslighting

Perhaps the most concerning takeaway from the analysis above is the way that the words that are supposed to give victimized individuals a voice can effectively function as a type of linguistic gaslighting, preventing those who have experienced a violation from naming or categorizing it as such.[79] This is most obviously a danger when the pragmatics of the violation stray from rape stereotypes—when the victimized party is minoritized, a man, or transgender; when the party who inflicts the harm is white and an acquaintance; when the person on the receiving end of it fails to represent the ideal. It makes sense, then, that so many survivors do not identify themselves as such, given that they're left out of the words and the stereotypes that define them.

If you don't see yourself included in the language, then what is there to say? Because those who survived harm live within linguistic discourses, they may also self-gaslight, becoming unable to categorize harm that they might have named had they been exposed to different epistemic constructions of it, by which I mean that they might have thought differently about their own experiences if they had been exposed to different ways of constructing the knowledge related to it. This can lead to denial, cognitive dissonance, and confusion as the survivor tries to explain their own experiences in relation to the available labels, depriving them of narrative agency, and thwarting their ability to communicate and to heal. Moreover, even if survivors can privately label wrongdoing, they may be hesitant to do so outside of the privacy of their own minds, knowing that language is a collective enterprise, and that what a survivor labels "rape" may not be received by a listener the same way. The inability to categorize and to speak, then, can function as a kind of linguistic rape, harkening to the first, in which the sexually violated person was unable to exercise a different type of agency.

To the extent that those who use language tacitly participate in this gaslighting, the collective culture becomes responsible for the survivor's inability to name, speak about, and address the harm done. In this way, society at large becomes responsible for harm inflicted upon an individual victim through its collective unquestioned assumptions about what constitutes a sexual violation. Put differently, any individual violation is not undertaken in a vacuum but rather is the culmination of a lifetime of socialization as well as a lifetime of participating in linguistic discourses that fail to acknowledge the full scope of harm. For the victimized party, then, part of what can turn a sexual violation into a sexual trauma is that society does not categorize it as such, and so the definitional gaps that we as a collective overlook functionally become part of the violation inflicted upon the individual.

Practical Consequences

Trauma experts have long recognized that speaking about trauma does something to the way that the brain processes it, breaking the cycle of symptoms that cause distress to the person who survived the harm.[80] Language accomplishes this because it facilitates the construction of narrative around the traumatic event, which, in turn, helps the person to understand the trauma within the context of their life. Meaning-making, identity construction, and the rebuilding of trust through relationships built with witnesses who hear the trauma narrative all become positive byproducts of speech.

I will say more about this in later chapters. However, what is relevant at this point is that if healing from trauma requires the ability to use words to communicate it, then one might reason that healing would be more complicated when descriptors are not readily available or when terms embody stereotypes that do not reflect someone's experience. Moreover, when the legal establishment subscribes to definitions of sexual violations that align with societally upheld rape myths, then those who are on the receiving end of a sexual violation may be less likely to utilize the criminal justice system to address their claims. The impact of this is significant in terms of legal accountability: While a slim number of accusations ever go to trial or receive a conviction, and while those who do embark upon this process often criticize it as being retraumatizing, they may feel disempowered to even approach the criminal justice system—which represents the State—because they are aware that it may not even categorize the pain inflicted upon them as prosecutable. It is, therefore, as if the State is saying that a person's experience and response are false, invalid. This, in turn, perpetuates silence. In the remainder of the chapter, I would like to briefly highlight several consequences that emerge from the limits that words impose upon our constructions of sexual violations, consequences that I will develop more in future chapters.

First, if we accept that the terms most commonly used to describe sexual violations fall short of encompassing the scope of harm, then this affects not only how victimized individuals speak but also how listeners hear. Those who listen to testimonies of those who experience sexual violations may be unaware that the linguistic choices they make may cause the person who shared so vulnerably to feel misrepresented or discredited, and thus cause a listener to inflict unintentional linguistic harm. It may, therefore, be useful for listeners to ask the person who experienced the violation what words feel most authentic to the experience, and to mirror that language as a sign of solidarity. This, of course, is not easily done in all conversations, given that some contexts may impose linguistic constraints. A legal conversation is one such example. But it is possible in other circumstances—in a conversation between friends in a dorm room, between a professor and a student, between a therapist and a client, between a chaplain and a care seeker. In each of these scenarios, the listener's words matter, and if the listener can speak in ways that meaningfully reflect and validate what that other person is trying to say, then those words are more likely to perform in ways that heal.

Second, speaking about a sexual violation may be uniquely challenging for someone whose experience does not correlate with rape stereotypes. Consider the following reflections from philosopher Susan Brison as an example:

> One was the best kind of rape, as far as my credibility as a victim was concerned. The other was the worst.
>
> In one, I was 35, on a morning walk in France, when a stranger jumped me from behind, beat, raped, repeatedly choked me into unconsciousness, hit me with a rock, and left me for dead at the bottom of a ravine. I reported it, spoke out about it, and wrote a book about it. My account of what happened was believed, and my assailant, who would have been prosecuted even if I hadn't pressed charges, was found guilty of rape and attempted murder.
>
> In the other, I was 20, asleep in my dorm room in England, when a man I knew knocked on my door. I let him in and he raped me. I didn't tell anyone. Afterwards, I stopped going to classes and, when I didn't get my period for two months, I thought I was pregnant and became suicidal. I never reported it, told no one about it until many years later, and, even then, didn't call what happened "rape." I didn't talk about it publicly until three years ago, and haven't published anything about it until now.[81]

In Brison's case, one sexual violation clearly aligned with rape myths. It was physically violent; she was nearly killed; the person who sexually violated her was a stranger who acted in broad daylight; she was not intoxicated and was dressed in baggy jeans and a sweatshirt.[82] The second event did not correspond with rape myths: The violating party was an acquaintance, she let him in, and, presumably, the man did not use measurable physical force. In reading her account of both ordeals, the reader understands why one event resulted in a conviction and why she did not speak publicly about the other for years. One event fit the myths of what rape is supposed to be. The other did not. For those who witness others' trauma, then, it is important to recognize that when an individual's experience does not fit rape stereotypes, that individual may feel disempowered to use the vocabulary provided by the English language. Those who lived through sexual harm may also feel that, absent a word, they are absent a violation. This may result in feelings of guilt or shame because that person feels suffering but also feels that the suffering is not warranted.[83]

The limitations of words used to describe sexual violations, therefore, impose a linguistic burden placed on those whose experiences do not align with rape myths. This, in turn, becomes an obstacle in the healing process, given that trauma experts have demonstrated how important speaking about trauma is to healing from it. If an individual lacks the words to speak, then that individual faces an additional barrier to healing. This is not to say that trauma is inexpressible (I do not agree with Cathy Caruth's assertion on this), but it is to say that communication becomes more difficult.[84] When someone speaks about an event that deviates from rape myths, therefore, it takes significant grit and bravery to do so.

Finally, given the limitations of words, it may be that non-linguistic forms of communication, such as art or music, can be a more effective means of communication. In the years after my own experience of harm, I found the greatest source of healing wasn't in speaking or telling the details of my story but rather in the choral singing I had done since childhood, often in professional contexts. Though I never spoke with anyone in my choir about the details of what happened, I regained enormous trust through our ritual of coming together, gathering around a piano or in church choir stalls, and singing our respective parts, our voices blending together, our breathing measured. The ritual was a form of group regulation. It was reassuring, comforting, trust-building, and the act of both sharing my own voice and blending together with others modeled what it meant to be part of a community—it required that I be a self that simultaneously had agency and that participated in close relationships with others.[85] Singing also became a model of life-affirming touch: When a person sings, her vocal cords emit sound waves that resonate into the body of the listener, and when individuals sing together, those sound waves travel from one body to another. They resonate—they harmonize—in one another's bodies. Creating that embodied harmony was restorative in a way that no form of speaking ever was, nor in a way that speaking is designed to be. Speech, in other words, is not our only communicative tool, and at times, it may not be the best one, but it nonetheless remains an important one that could be further enhanced were the limitations imposed on it by social forces to be addressed.

* * *

In her book *Believing*, law professor Anita Hill writes that those who survive sexual violations face multiple obstacles to their credibility. These may be most profound when an individual's identity doesn't match the ideal victim's or, put differently, when their identity has been constructed in ways that marginalize them. This makes it difficult to speak, to be believed, and to seek accountability. Writing with reference to the #MeToo movement, she explains that,

> Women in Hollywood did a great public service by coming forward and sharing stories of the rank abuse they experienced. Their vulnerability was made obvious by revelations of an industry culture of silence. Ultimately, though, public enchantment with a depiction of a harassment victim as a glamorous starlet, in part based on the rape myth of the perfect victim, did a disservice to

those who were featured in the initial #MeToo stories, as well as many others, such as service workers. The term #MeToo was coined in 2006 by Tarana Burke, an African-American activist, to help Black and Brown girls who'd been sexually assaulted, as Burke was. It's a shame that the narrow representation of sexual assault and harassment coming out of the #MeToo movement left out Burke's intended survivors as well as lesbian, gay, trans, queer, and bisexual people's broad range of experiences.[86]

Hill's observations are sobering for individuals who seek to strengthen the credibility of those who've experienced harm. Even more sobering is that the vocabulary available to speak about sexual harm reflects the stereotypes about survivors that Hill identifies. As this overview of individual terms suggests, the words available to discuss violations are often embedded with assumptions about who is a legitimate victim that don't reflect the reality of who's actually affected. This benefits those who perpetrate harm as well as those who have a vested interest in maintaining systemic oppression for their own benefit. It does not, however, support those who need words for the purposes of accountability and healing.

But perhaps most insidiously, we don't question these terms. We don't look at who they represent, who they leave out, and how our very use of them makes us complicit in wrongdoing. Instead, we assume that words represent reality and reality represents truth when what we really need to do is to look into our linguistic gaps for who is left out and why. We need to recognize that language is collective, just as the perpetuation of sexual harm is.

This last point may be counterintuitive. After all, what most of these words—excepting gender-based violence—share in common is the assumption that sexual harm is individual harm inflicted by one person onto another. And, of course, it *can* be individual and private, but to say that it's only that is reductive. Human beings don't just wake up one day and sexually victimize others out of the blue. The harm inflicted in one moment of time is the result of a complex process of power-based socialization that primes some people to perpetrate harm and others to be the victims of it. It teaches girls to be silent objects and men to be aggressive subjects. It promotes a system of sex education that fails at many levels, including by failing to teach a proper understanding of consent.[87] It allows hard core pornography to go unrestricted and thereby define the boundaries of appropriate sexual behavior.[88] It adheres to a justice system that reassures those who inflict sexual harm that sex crimes will receive a blind eye, and all of these practices are upheld by a system of language that fails to adequately represent the scope of the violations themselves. The result, then, is that those who speak about sexual violations struggle to find and use words in a culture that is systematically intent on silencing victims.

I close with a thought experiment to summarize what is at stake: Imagine that there was no word for manslaughter. Any crime that went to trial could only be tried as murder in the first degree, meaning murder that was premediated and undertaken with malice, otherwise known as deliberate intent to kill. The law only recognizes premeditated murder as a crime; it sees manslaughter as an accident, one that shouldn't be punished with a court trial, with jail time, with the press raking over the murderer's reputation. It was, after all, an accidental death—that was tragedy enough. And if harm occurred, it wasn't intended, and after all, wasn't it possible that the deceased played a role in their own demise? The person might even have wanted to die and created a scenario that ensured their death—like a car crash—at the expense of the murderer.

We would think differently about what it meant to take a life if the term "manslaughter" did not exist. We would have a different framework for understanding when such taking required accountability and when it did not. Moreover, one might assume that there would be a rise in manslaughter, given that society did not label it as a wrong. And if there was no accountability, then it would be easier to undertake the act.

One sees the parallel with sexual violations here. As long as we fail to recognize the diverse forms that sexual violations take, neither those who inflict sexual harm nor those who are recipients of it will have words to represent the experience. Moreover, they will not have words that can perform in ways that will facilitate their own healing, nor will they perform in ways that will hold those who inflict sexual violations accountable. What we need, then, is a collective commitment to linguistic transformation, a transformation that involves both finding more words and also redefining the ones we use most often to talk about sexual violations.

Interruption

Here we pause for an interruption. It's unscheduled and undesired, and it would be more convenient to avoid, but sometimes we don't get to choose what stalls the story, what traps the narrative.

Here we stop to speak of the ones who inflict harm, because those who perpetrate sexual violations interrupt. They stop their victim's story and insert themselves as a character in a plot, like an extra in a film who decides to speak without being written into the script. This person's identity, their physical traits, their height, their smell, their strength, their name, and the word "perpetrator" become irrevocably part of the victimized party's story line, leaving them to figure out how to speak not only of the harm but also of the one who enacted it. For the survivor to speak about their experiences, then, can be challenging because they must speak about at least one other human being—the one who brought the harm about. This task of speaking about the one who caused the wrong is complicated both because of the words we have to describe the individuals who inflict harm and because of practical concerns, many of which relate to safety. Sometimes, then, it becomes easier for someone not to speak of that person—or persons—at all.

Most of the time, the victimized party cannot speak about the person who violated them the same way that they speak about other people, especially if that person hasn't been brought to trial and convicted. The practical thus becomes the dictator of speech, as those who experience sexual violations may fear physical, emotional, or economic retaliation by the person who harmed them. So they calculate the benefits of words versus the cost of them and determine that their own safety is more valuable than naming the person who violated them, or maybe even than naming the harm itself.

Then there is the second limiting factor—the law. The law prescribes what those who experience a sexual violation can and cannot say about the person who caused it without risking a defamation lawsuit from the person who hurt them. Free speech, in other words, is not so free for those who experience sexual violations and is constrained by legal codes that can protect those accused of inflicting harm.

This would all be unfortunate in a country that doesn't pride itself on the value of free speech, but it's ironic in a country that does. Still, ideological irony is, in and of itself, another luxury for those who have experienced sexual violations, especially if they lack the financial means to fight the force of a defamation suit. So again, those who have an embodied experience of being sexually violated must do a calculation, weighing their own safety against the value of speaking a name, and when they deem the cost to their own survival to be too great, they remain silent, precipitating protection for those who cause harm in an effort to protect themselves.

Can you blame them?

I don't.

There is, therefore, a luxury to naming not only the violation itself but also the violator that not every victimized individual possesses because of practical constraints. Recognizing this challenges the assumption that victims have a predetermined responsibility to publicly identify and press charges against the person who harmed them, because an individual who chooses not to do so may well be making a calculated, informed choice based upon resources and likely outcomes. In other words, if we can't protect victimized individuals, then we can't expect them to take on the responsibility of seeking accountability or protecting others who might be harmed in the future by the same person.

The rub, however, is that speaking about individuals who commit sexual harm is important, even if deeply challenging, because it helps both the person who was victimized and the wider community to better understand what sexual violations look like, why they matter, and what recovery entails. Those who attempt to write about their violations, however, often do so with either scant reference to the party who inflicted the harm or none at all, as if they are attempting to keep that person as a peripheral character in the story rather than affording them a central role.[89] Sometimes they make the choice to protect themselves physically or from the threat of legal actions. Sometimes they make it as a way to reclaim agency in the narrative. Sometimes they find the person's name despicable. All of these reasons make sense—they're as practical as they are strategic.

I am no different in this regard: You will read nothing in this book about the details of the person who was on the inflicting end of the violation against me. I've conscientiously avoided identifying physical features, where the person lived, what their interests and professional aspirations were, whether they had a sense of humor, what the details of our relationship were like, and my age at the time. On the whole, this seems wise: Their identity, in many ways, doesn't matter, because given the rates of sexual violations, if it wasn't this person, it could well have been someone else.

But here's what gets lost with the vagaries: If you were to read about this particular human being, you would observe nothing special.

"Ordinary" is an apt descriptor. I imagine most people who manifest sexual violations are like this, which is part of what's so stunning about the whole thing. One expects that someone who inflicts this kind of harm is different from the rest of us. That he's got to have an evil twinkle in his eye, some kind of tell. That's how it is in the movies, anyway, and so shouldn't it be like that in real life? Shouldn't we be able to know and, in turn, take steps to avoid getting hurt?

Turns out that it's not as simple as that. If it were, of course, there'd be fewer people hurt, especially given that many women are socialized, as philosopher Ann Cahill notes, to be pre-victims, meaning that they engage in regular practices derived from the assumption that rape is a

Limiting Language   39

real possibility in their lives.[90] Such practices include keeping an eye out for potential danger, for some indication that a given characteristic—a raised eyebrow, a scar, the color of one's skin—might be the telltale mark of danger. The rub is that those who sexually violate others don't wear signs on their foreheads advertising what they're capable of or planning to do, and indeed, sometimes the person appears to be not only normal but charming, talented, even exceptional. Consider Brock Turner as a prime example. Turner's father told Judge Aaron Persky at sentencing that Turner was likable, hard-working, and had "a smile that is truly welcoming to those around him."[91] All of these characteristics may belong to Brock Turner, and none of those necessitate that he's incapable of harm.

You see, it's possible for the same person to get A's on tests, to win swim competitions, and to stick a finger into a passed-out woman's vagina. These are not mutually exclusive sets.

In other words, the public seems to have inherited a belief wherein they conflate the ability of a person to make poor choices with an overall poverty of character. This is reductive—because people are complex—and ignores how community constructs character from an early age.[92] This hyper-focus on essential character also distracts the public from focusing on choices, asking what the available choices were for that person at the time, what actions they decided to take, and what informed that decision-making process.

The language around both perpetration and victimization does little to challenge these embedded beliefs about how character takes priority over available choices and actions. Terms like "victim" and "survivor" reduce the person who has experienced a sexual violation to the sum parts of that event, while "perpetrator" and "assailant" reduce the identity of one who inflicts the harm to their wrongdoing. This language shapes public perception of the scope and nature of sexual wrongdoing as well as the type of person who might enact it. It is also insidious language, incapable of being avoided unless one wants to consistently engage in multi-worded descriptions or create new jargon that might not be recognizable to a wide audience.[93] Indeed, the pervasiveness of this language causes it to function as a kind of systemic and epistemic misorientation which most of us, including myself, are guilty of perpetuating.[94] In other words, the words we all tacitly agree to use around sexual violations construct knowledge in ways that result in linguistic reduction that doesn't fully recognize the scope of sexual harm. In turn, such linguistic reduction prevents us from challenging these embedded beliefs, from recognizing that most human beings—even including those who perpetrate harm—are nuanced and complicated. A person can charm, coach your daughter's basketball team, be married and professionally successful, publicly advocate for women, and still pin down a girl on a bed against her will, cover her mouth, and attempt to have sex with her. This is possible, though many believe it is not. For but one example of those who believe that positive actions are incompatible with the negative ones, see the editorial that Brett Kavanaugh released a week after his public hearing with Christine Blasey Ford, in which he tries to defend the anger he exhibited at the hearings and sway the reader that he could not have done what Blasey Ford alleges because he coaches his girls' basketball teams, has had female clerks, and is a "pro-law judge."[95] Regardless of Kavanaugh's innocence, his argument about why he couldn't have done what Blasey Ford alleges essentially boils down to the fact that he made good choices on other occasions and therefore could not have made a bad choice on this one. What Kavanaugh seems to have missed, however, is that action is not universally consistent over time—we'd have a lot more perfect people if it was.

Circling back to words: When we reduce an individual to a "perpetrator," then we become cognitively tempted to conflate character and action, to search for a universal character essence that determines the universal moral value of their actions. If we can figure out their character, then we can judge whether they might have undertaken a given action. This reduces complicated, constructed human beings to flat, underdeveloped characters. Put differently, it's not realistic, and it doesn't benefit anyone: The individual who inflicted harm may feel that the word "perpetrator" is not an accurate representation of their full character and, in turn, may become more defensive or unwilling to accept the consequences of their actions. Individuals who were violated may be left trying to reconcile how it was possible for someone to appear to be kind while also inflicting harm, and wider society becomes unable to support either party because they have a reductive view of what perpetration looks like and, in turn, wind up enabling the former group of people while dismissing the latter. The language of "perpetrator" is, therefore, problematic because it conflates a person's actions and a person's identity when these two things are not the same.

Individuals who experienced victimization may deride my proposal because they've seen firsthand how devastating the actions of those who instantiate harm are. I understand their instinct. I've done the same. But we can still ask someone to take accountability for their actions without seeking to make a broader argument about their identity, especially given that doing so might make them more defensive—or ashamed—and therefore less likely to accept responsibility.

My concern with reducing individuals who perpetrate to the sum of their worst actions is that it's not pragmatic. It encourages the community to assume that those who inflict sexual harm are easily identifiable because they are essentially evil, which causes victims and outsiders alike to look only for those people who appear to fit ideal perpetrator stereotypes, which, in essence, means looking for Black men. Moreover, when someone who has been sexually violated makes a claim against someone who doesn't fit the ideal perpetrator stereotype, then it becomes easier not to believe the person who was victimized or, at the very least, to blame them for not preventing harm. It also discourages us as a society from focusing on the complex forces that turn a person into one who perpetrates harm, because while one single individual made a very damaging choice, that person didn't make the choice in a vacuum but rather made it while marinating in a system of beliefs and experiences related to sex, relationships, and gender norms in which we all participate, which means that until those embedded beliefs are restructured, we are all, to some extent, responsible for the harm inflicted upon a victimized person.

Beneficially, however, terms like "assailant" and "offender," allow writers and speakers to create distance between the person as perpetrator and the problem of perpetration. I've often felt that the identity of the person who perpetrated wrongdoing in my own life was largely *adiaphora*—indifferent to the issue at hand—because sexual harm would likely have entered my life by another means because of how embedded beliefs about misogyny and the permissibility of sexual harm intersect with my gender. In that way, the individual who inflicted the harm may have interrupted the narrative I was constructing about my life, but the specific person is more of a peripheral character than a central one. The central character, the one that demands development and attention, is not a person but a system of beliefs of various kinds that precipitate and enable the practices of sexual violations. To that end, I agree with Chanel Miller when she explains in the introduction to her memoir, "I will use Brock's name, but the truth is he could be Brad or Brody or Benson, and it doesn't matter."[96]

And then, finally, there is the matter of speaking for another. Those who survived a sexual harm have suffered because of the ways that others have spoken for them, crafting their stories in ways that violate how they might label or contextualize their experiences.[97] Are those who experience sexual violations doing the same when they speak of the people who bring them about, especially when those who inflict the harm are the only other people who remember what happened? Indeed, they may be the *only* person who has a memory of what happened if the victimized party wasn't conscious, the only one who could tell a different story about what happened and why it is significant. They are also the only ones who could, with any experiential credibility, convince a listener that the victim's interpretation is incorrect.

This argument only works if we agree that there's a single story with truth-value, *and* we simultaneously assume it's possible for an individual to discern and identify all aspects of that truth. But maybe the story is more complicated than this. Maybe both the story and the truth are not singular but multiple and constructed such that there are ways to tell the story that are patently false (as in the case of a person who says consent occurred when it did not) and also ways to tell it that are inconsistent and conflicting but that nonetheless contain an element of truth. Perhaps this is what happens when someone creates an interruption—they take what the pre-victim assumes to be a coherent narrative and fracture it, shattering the pieces along with their own. The challenge is, therefore, to not only stop the interruption and to rebuild the narrative of the self in a way that honors one's identity but also to speak in a way that recognizes the presence of the one who interrupted while not giving them the power to write the rest of the story.

CHAPTER 2

Reclaiming Rape

THE 2017 #MeToo movement focused public attention not only on the magnitude of sexual violations in the United States but also on the nebulousness of them. As victims brought more and more claims of harm forward, calling out high-profile men ranging from Matt Lauer to Elie Wiesel, Americans began to discuss whether the perception of victimhood was contagious, whether women, in an attempt to become part of the frenzy, were mistaking regret for wrongdoing. Indeed, in 2018, one year after the #MeToo hashtag surged, more than 40% of Americans felt that the movement had become exaggerated and melodramatic. They were concerned that the lives of the accused might be destroyed by the complaints filed against them, and they worried that making a claim had become trendy, causing individuals to level allegations when the event in question did not rise to the level of wrong. One participant in the survey, a fifty-three-year-old Texan woman summarized the fear with these words:

> I feel like in the last year, that girls are like, "Oh yeah, me too!" ... I feel like some of the girls want the sympathy and the attention. And I feel like that really, really takes away from the girls that it really happened to.[1]

This Texan woman's words appear to assume that there is some benefit to victimhood that makes it desirable, so desirable, in fact, that a person would manufacture or exaggerate an experience of harm in order to gain attention or fame. They also appear to assume there's an objective way to measure harm, even though it can be difficult to assess what "really happened to" someone if language and socially constructed narratives fail to represent the scope and impact of wrongdoing. This undermines victimized parties in ways that make it challenging for them to be understood.

In this chapter, I develop the first of several constructive suggestions for how to create more space for those who have survived a sexual violation to speak and for their words to be received. Here I propose a redefinition of the term "rape," which I offer for two reasons. First, "rape" remains the most common word to describe sexual harm, and while currently fraught by myths and stereotypes, its definition has evolved significantly over time. With societal support, there is no reason it couldn't change again or return to something more like its earlier definition. Also, "rape" remains the most recognizable—the most powerful—way to describe sexual wrong. As Lacy Crawford reflects, "Say *rape*, and people get it."[2]

For far too long, English speakers have attempted to create gradations of harm based upon the pragmatics of the act done rather than the impact on the individual or group that the individual represents. The English language's current definition of "rape," so laden with false stereotypes, has only exacerbated this tendency, with the result that those who have been violated feel unentitled to speak. Still, to throw away the word would be to linguistically throw away an opportunity to acknowledge the actuality of pain, pain that deserves a word strong enough to represent it. Reclaiming the word "rape" also acknowledges the need to create some kind of definition for sexual harm that individuals can more incisively use in order to speak and have their suffering acknowledged by the wider community. The trick, however, is to re-fashion the term in a way that is nimble enough for individuals who have experienced sexual harm to see themselves within it.

The goal of this chapter is to propose such a definition. Specifically, I propose that "rape" be defined as an act of power, using sex, that violates agency, body, and desire. I hope to accomplish two things by proposing this definition: First, I seek to offer a definition that disrupts the power that rape myths have in defining the contours of what we perceive to cause harm, and second, I seek to lessen attempts to gradate harm. But first, I begin with a historical overview of the term "rape" and consider what is at stake for those who experience sexual harm if we do not reevaluate the way we identify about it.

A Brief History of "Rape"

Derived from the Latin *rapere*—which means to grab or snatch—"rape" in its initial English form meant "to kidnap," either with or without a sexual component. One of the earliest surviving English documents with the word in it actually concerns Geoffrey Chaucer, author of *The Canterbury Tales*, who was accused of rape—or "raptus"—by a woman named Cecily Chaumpaigne in 1380.[3] The document nowhere clarifies whether Chaumpaigne was charging Chaucer with a sexual violation or platonic kidnapping,[4] leaving scholars to theorize about exactly what happened and why she withdrew the charges in May of that year.[5]

This early English employment of the term "rape" implies that something was taken, either that the person who experienced the harm was physically taken from her house and family, or that something was taken from her sexually, such as her virginity, all of which could be lumped together under English law because the law constructed women as property that could be taken—physically or sexually—from a man. This construction conveniently represented the interests of those men who were in power, though it does not mean that men were not harmed by rape. (One need only refer to Geoffrey Chaucer's father, who was abducted by his aunt because she wanted him to marry her daughter, by way of example.) Still, this definition of rape, in conjunction with the status of women, explains the historic lag in codifying marital rape as a crime because, if rape is the taking of something, then it is impossible to take what a person already owns.[6] The same logic was used to justify why it was permissible for slave owners to rape and breed slaves against their will without any repercussion.[7]

This platonic use of the term "rape" persisted in English long past the medieval period and into the 1700s, where it can be found in Alexander

Pope's *The Rape of the Lock*, a satirical poem about a suitor who cuts off a lock of a woman's hair without her permission. As late as 1960, it was prominently featured in *The Fantasticks*, a musical in which the character El Gallo sings, "I know you prefer abduction, but the proper word is rape . . . a pretty rape, a literary rape." *The Fantasticks* eventually became the world's longest running musical, and by the time the anti-rape movement became prominent in the 1970s, lyricist Tom Jones began to receive pushback about the song's lyrics. He eventually changed them, in recognition that audiences heard the word "rape" in a way that conflicted with his platonic intent.[8]

Though the platonic use of the term "rape" persisted into the twentieth century, the FBI framed "rape" as a sexual crime as early as 1927, when it defined the term as "the carnal knowledge of a female, forcibly and against her will."[9] This definition relies heavily upon the understanding that rape is a crime inflicted exclusively on women and that it is not just a sexual crime but also a physically violent crime, yet, to the casual reader at least, it leaves the parameters of force unclear. I looked up the FBI's definition of "rape" decades later when I began to address what happened to me, and remember being befuddled by this definition—what on earth was "carnal knowledge?" How much force was needed to count as "forcibly"—did being physically picked up and moved against one's will count? Were abrasions sufficient or were ligature marks required? What about force that left no marks, such as forcible words? Much as Chanel Miller had to Google the terms "foreign object" and "digital" to find out that Brock Turner inserted his finger into her vagina, so I found myself Googling exactly what "carnal knowledge" and "force" did and did not include.[10] What I found didn't help. Definitions were either reductive or contradictory, which led to more cognitive dissonance on my part because I continued to distrust my own experience and the impact it had had on me. Because I couldn't find clear epistemic validation in the law—because the law's way of knowing didn't appear to be a form of knowing that could constructively address what I was experiencing—I also fought against the idea of talking about my experiences with others, largely because I did not want them to think I was lying.

The FBI eventually revised its definition of "rape" in 2012 in an effort to address concerns like mine—concerns that the definition as it stood did not reflect the reality of the crime because it excluded those who were not women and relied too much on vague language to describe physical force as the defining factor of whether harm occurred. As it currently stands, the FBI now defines "rape" as "The penetration, no matter how slight, of the vagina or anus with any body part or object, or oral penetration by a sex organ of another person, without the consent of the victim."[11] Notably, this definition expands the types of events that might qualify as "rape," makes the crime gender-neutral, and removes force entirely as a criterion, replacing it with consent.

What this short history of the term "rape" reveals is that the term has evolved significantly over time, much as other words in the English language have. There is no reason, then, that it couldn't continue to do so, transforming into a more inclusive term to describe sexual harm. The new FBI definition began this expansion, showing that this kind of linguistic conversion is not impossible to accomplish. It has been done before. But it will take a commitment from those who are able to speak and those who are able to listen to make the shift, as every time an individual uses the term "rape" in a more inclusive way, it becomes an act of linguistic resistance against the stereotypes currently associated with it.

Redefining Rape

Given my concerns with how these multiple definitions can be both idolatrous and irrelevant, I want to step back and propose a new definition of "rape" that shifts the emphasis away from practicalities and refocuses it on impact. To that end, I offer the following definition, which I will parse out in the remainder of the chapter: Rape is constituted by acts of power, using sex, that violate agency, body, and desire.

Parsing the Definition: Power

Feminists writing about rape in the past have often attempted to postulate the reason these violations occur, with Susan Brownmiller profoundly shaping the course of the discussion with her argument that such forms of harm are not about sex but about power, namely, that they are "nothing more or less than a conscious process of intimidation by which *all men* keep *all women* in a state of fear."[12] Brownmiller's assertion was intended to press against the assumption that sexual violations originate out of uncontrollable lust in men or that women arouse men in such a way that they cannot be held responsible for the exercise of their desires. As Pamela Cooper-White summarizes:

> Sexual assault is an extreme form of violence precisely because erogenous zones of the body are experienced as the most intimate and vulnerable; however, the primary purpose of sexual assault is not to discharge sexual tension, but to conquer, humiliate, and violate. The victim of sexual assault is not an "object of desire," but a literal object of domination and dehumanization.

However, Cooper-White also acknowledges that it may be reductive to suggest that rape is only about power, because if such were the case, then the solution to sexual harm would be to educate those who violate about the abuse of power, which has had limited success.[13] She concludes it may be more helpful to say that rape—the term Cooper-White employs—is simultaneously about "power, and sex," "power, using sex," and "power, gender, and race."[14] While Cooper-White is right to trouble an overly simplistic understanding of the origins or motives of rape, her complexification leads to the further question of what *kind* of power enables the perpetration of harm. Here I propose that it's important to acknowledge how power operates both individually and collectively in any sexual encounter and how both forms of power are misused in rape.

Individual Power
Power, at its broadest, is the ability to either facilitate change or avert it. It is not, in and of itself, essentially negative in sex because, as Cooper-White recognizes, some exercise of power is required in any sexual act to ensure that the encounter occurs. If participants are entirely passive, then nothing will happen. A given sexual engagement, then, requires that at least one participant is not passive, meaning that at least one participant must have the ability to pursue their sexual desire in order to manifest the sexual act.[15]

Cooper-White proceeds to distinguish between what might be termed "assertive power" and "aggressive power," meaning that while all sexual encounters require the exercise of power, whether or not the act is harmful is dependent on the type of power used.[16] The distinguishing factor between a healthy sexual encounter and a violating one, then, is not *that* power is used but rather *how* power is used. Here, the distinction between understanding power as "power-over" and the exercise of power as "power-to-do" can be of use.[17] When individuals exercise power in ways that are aggressive and deprive others of agency—as occurs in sexual harm—then they exert power over the person who eventually gets labeled as "the victim." In contrast, individuals who exert power in ways that support the agency of others enable them to act of their own volition—they give others the power-to-do. Power-over, therefore, aims to reduce the agency of other human beings by exploiting their vulnerability in order to enhance the power of those who inflict sexual harm. This form of power exertion is not always easy to recognize in the moment: Though physical power-over might leave marks, those who experience domestic violence might believe they deserve the injury because of how the person harming them gaslights and employs verbal abuse. Psychological power-over—often exerted through language—can, therefore, be so sly that the vulnerable party isn't able to identify it as such.

Here's one example of what this looks like. While conducting research for this book, I had a chance to speak with several women who are part of the Thistle Farms community in Nashville, Tennessee. Thistle Farms is a nonprofit social enterprise for women who have experienced trafficking and prostitution, founded by The Reverend Becca Stevens, an Episcopal priest who herself was sexually abused as a child by a member of her church shortly after her father, who was also a priest, died in a car accident.[18] It first provides a two-year healing component in a stable, safe, and beautiful home shared with several other women, along with healthcare, counseling, and trauma therapy to aid in their recovery, all free of charge. It also assists with family reunification, community education access, and legal advocacy. Graduates are eligible to receive job training and employment at the eponymously named company, which manufactures healing products like lavender candles and eucalyptus mint lotions. This gives graduates a financial alternative to returning to the streets, as many have criminal records that make it difficult for them to otherwise obtain employment.

Becca and I had crossed paths several times over the past decade, as we were both Episcopal priests committed to ending sexual exploitation. It was one of those friendships that had emerged from a number of mutual colleagues saying, "Let me introduce you to Becca, because you two should really know each other." We'd shared stories over beer, toured the Thistle Farms manufacturing facility, and through her, I had met several of the program's graduates, all of whom were models of bravery, fortitude, and optimism.

One of the graduates I spoke with was a woman named Amanda.[19] We talked on Zoom early in the COVID pandemic, and she had the video off, so that all I saw of her was a photograph—a static image of a vibrant woman with a beaming smile. But behind the picture was a dynamic, gritty voice, tinted with a Southern accent. Amanda described growing up in a small town in a broken home, with a mother who had untreated mental illness and a largely absent father. At the age of twelve, she began to do drugs, including intravenous ones, eventually landing on meth as her drug of choice. Then, she began to date, as she explains it:

> The dope boys, and I did things that I didn't want to do because of my addiction, and I just—you know—I did them because I wanted to stay high and get high, and, um, a lot of times I was forced to

do things just because I was there because I thought that he loved me or, um—there's lots of reasons, really, but mainly because of the addiction, you know. We do things—a lot of things—that we don't want to do when we're high to get and stay high.

When I asked her how she labeled these experiences, she explained that she didn't think that she was being exploited or that what was going on counted as "prostitution" at the time, even after years of being forced to have sex with multiple men in order to get drugs from her pimp. As Amanda went on to say, "Honestly, I didn't know that I had been prostituted until I got to the program [Thistle Farms] because I didn't realize that using my body for financial gain [to get drugs] was a form of prostitution."

When I then asked Amanda if she considered these sexual violations to fall under the label of "rape," she said:

I don't use the word rape. I don't look at it as being raped because I was willing. I mean I don't necessarily—it's kind of borderline because it's not that I was willing, and it's not that I was forced really. It's that I didn't necessarily want to do certain things, but I did them because I wanted to get high. So it's like I wasn't raped, but like I didn't necessarily want to do it either.

Throughout the interview, Amanda described a cycle of physical, emotional, and psychological abuse—including gaslighting—by her pimp, who practiced power over Amanda, eradicating her agency for his pleasure and financial gain. So this was not a level playing field. It was one in which Amanda was rendered vulnerable by her addiction, and her pimp exploited that addiction. Moreover, because she received drugs instead of money for sex, her pimp disguised the wrong by moving it one degree away from the dominant script we have for prostitution, one in which a woman receives cash—not drugs—for sex. In this way, her pimp not only practiced power-over but did so in a way that made the wrong more difficult to label.

Now, one might say that Amanda was a willing participant because she received the drugs she wanted in exchange for sexual acts, but this assumes that Amanda was in a place to give consent and that the consent was freely given, neither of which makes sense to argue when one considers how Amanda was rendered vulnerable to her pimp by her addiction. Drugs, as the FBI recognizes, inhibit a person's ability to give consent. Moreover, given Amanda's dependency on her pimp for drugs, it is reasonable to ask whether Amanda could freely give consent even if she wasn't actively high—when such a power imbalance exists, then freedom to enact agency correspondingly decreases or, at least, becomes more challenging. Put differently, her pimp benefited from using power-over to attempt to rob Amanda of subjectivity, and that enactment of power-over was more difficult to identify because of how it deviated from rape and prostitution scripts.

Systemic Power
Power enacts at an individual level during the act of rape itself, but it also plays out in how systemic structures, including language, precipitate and respond to it. As Catharine MacKinnon writes:

> Having power means, among other things, that when someone says, "this is how it is," it is taken as being that way.... Speaking socially, the beliefs of the powerful become proof, in part because the world actually arranges itself to affirm what the powerful want to see.[20]

Elsewhere, MacKinnon explains the way in which language functions as a tool for the social construction of power:

> The world is not entirely the way the powerful say it is or want to believe it is. If it appears to be, it is because power constructs the appearance of reality, by silencing the voices of the powerless, by excluding them from access to authoritative discourse.

> Powerlessness means when you say, "this is how it is," it is not taken as being that way. This makes articulating silence, perceiving the presence of absence, believing those who have been socially stripped of credibility, critically contextualizing what passes for simple fact, necessary to the epistemology of the powerless.[21]

Systemic powerlessness and language, therefore, intersect in rape. As I discussed at length in the prior chapter, a significant number of individuals who experience sexual violations experience events in which the pragmatics do not correlate with the rape myth and with the current connotation of rape, thereby depriving them of easy access to language to describe the event. Absent a word, they may feel that they are absent a violation. Absent a word, they may not communicate the violation to others. Absent a word, they may not even admit it to themselves.

Additionally, when a listener hears someone talk about their experience of rape, they may listen and respond in a way that is designed to discredit and thereby cause that person to question their own assessment of the event or to recontextualize the meaning of it. By way of example, Susan Ehrlich documents how news headlines in Canada tend to humanize the accused party, lessening their agency—and, in turn, their responsibility—while simultaneously dehumanizing the harmed party by erasing them from the narrative.[22] Ehrlich goes on to explore how defense lawyers used language in Canadian courtrooms to undermine claims of wrongdoing. In particular, they employed "subtle and insidious linguistic expressions of mitigated and obscured agency" in reference to those who were accused,[23] and in trials where the accused party was an acquaintance, they tended to take advantage of that conflation, using the language of "consensual sex" to undermine any assertion that sex was inappropriate.[24]

Outside the courtroom, those with power to craft dominant cultural stories use language to reframe the experiences of those who experience sexual violations, thereby robbing them of agency in what we might consider to be a narrative rape. Susan Brison, for instance, observes how the United States government used reports of Iraqi soldiers raping Kuwaitis to justify the Gulf War, just as it used the threat of Mexican men raping white women to support the building of a border wall.[25] Likewise, Linda Martín Alcoff writes about how the George H.W. Bush administration tried to justify the invasion of Panama by publicizing incidents in which wives of soldiers were sexually harassed by Panamanian Defense Forces.[26]

If these kinds of rhetorical mind games motivate international policy, matters are no better domestically. Brison describes how transphobic politicians frame the trans body in terms of danger, arguing that trans women should not be allowed to use the women's bathroom because it could enable the rape of non-trans women. She also describes how political leaders marketed Jim Crow laws as a way to protect delicate white women from getting raped by deviant Black men.[27] Language, then, exerts systemic power in sexual violations not just because it delineates the contours of words like "rape" and "sexual assault" but also because it is a tool that can be wielded to facilitate our entire understanding of what harm is, who is culpable, who is innocent, and what the response to it should be. As Alcoff summarizes:

> Part of the manipulation here is to displace causal agency and deflect blame: the old story of blaming women for going into the room, or to the car, or the woods for a walk, as if these choices were tantamount to consent. Manipulators are aware that it is difficult to express a preemptive distrust of people in your social circles, or men you work with. This difficulty may be exacerbated where there is an implicit expectation of racial solidarity against a racist society that portrays men of color as predatory.[28]

The examples that Ehrlich, Brison, and Alcoff offer involve individuals in places of authority—namely, government officials and lawyers—wielding rhetorical force to influence public perception of sexual harm in ways that deprive victimized parties of narrative agency. Slut-shaming and cyberbullying on social media often function the same way.

Case in point—the documentary *Audrie and Daisy*, which dives into the ways that these speech acts bear down on the lives of those who have lived through sexual violations, complicating their healing process, in profound and often negative ways. The first girl profiled in the documentary, Audrie Pott, died by suicide after her attackers texted photos of her unconscious body, onto which they had written sexually explicit comments. The second girl profiled, Daisy Coleman, also died by suicide and was one of two girls who were part of a high-profile rape case that occurred in Maryville, Missouri, back in 2013. Coleman was fourteen when a high school senior named Matthew Barnett took her into a bedroom, had sex with her while she was severely intoxicated, and then drove her home, leaving her on the front lawn in sweatpants and a t-shirt. It was 22 degrees outside. She lay outside for three hours before her mother found her clawing at the front door, took Daisy to the emergency room for a rape kit, and discovered that she must have been close to comatose at the time of the sexual encounter.[29]

During the investigation, Coleman experienced in-person and online harassment, as students in her high school questioned the authenticity of her allegation, and the harassment only increased after the Nodaway County's prosecuting attorney dismissed felony charges against Barnett.[30] Social media posts and hashtags sprung up following the exoneration with messages such as the following:

> #matt1daisy0
> #daisyisaliar
> #ihatedaisy
> Hope she realizes this just made her look stupid, and not get sympathy
> They ARENT rapists #whore
> She was a liar. Why do you think her Dr. Phil show never aired?
> I think she did go back on her story
> Yeah the evidence is her story. Her drunk story
> Daisy is a dumb slut who just wanted attention. Don't compare any case to hers if you think the other is even kind of true. Know your shit before posting.[31]

The impact that the social media posts left on Daisy was profound, as she reflects in the documentary:

> You begin to believe that all these bad things they're saying about you are actually true. So your image of yourself completely changes and you kind of become a shell of yourself. You almost see that, you know, doing away with yourself is the only way to fix things, which isn't the truth at all, but it's all you can truly see when you're sitting in a dark corner and you're not looking around at the light.

Coleman's quotation intimates to the audience that there is a performative element in slut-shaming and cyberbullying, meaning that the use of the troll's words isn't just symbolic. The words *do* something, actually changing the victimized person's self-concept. In this way, speech performs to enact further harm. Susan Brison, therefore, remains correct when she says that "*Saying* something about a traumatic memory *does* something to it," though Brison was making the argument that saying something about trauma has the potential to transform the memory in ways that facilitate healing.[32] It is just as true, though, that saying something can make the trauma worse, especially when the speech comes from hostile listeners. In Coleman's case, the slut-shaming that she experienced essentially functioned as a form of linguistic rape, an abducting of her narrative agency that caused her to question her identity, purpose, and goodness, leaving her so despondent that she made repeated suicide attempts and died by suicide in 2020.

When we fail to acknowledge the insidious ways that language performs to enable rape culture and thwart healing, then we create more opportunities for harm, not just for those directly victimized by rape but for the culture at large. Those who survive sexual violations lack narrative agency. Those who cause them are not held accountable. Opportunities for further victimization appear because perpetration becomes normalized, acceptable behavior. The effects of the violation go unquestioned.

Language can, therefore, function as a slippery slope, its harm not immediately obvious, its effects seemingly insignificant as it gaslights victimized parties via the courtroom, the media, the internet, and conversations with friends, family, and leaders in places of authority, including ministers and higher education administrators. In this way, words can perform a linguistic rape that robs a person of their agency by attempting to shape the narrative of their life, even as it attempts to do the same to the culture at large, robbing the collective of ways to shape their views about what the contours of sexual harm really are.

Parsing the Definition: Sexual Act

The legal system has a tendency to assume that heterosexual intercourse is the pinnacle of sexual activity, as if reflecting the hierarchy of the tween "base" system, where a "home run" is the end goal, the highest form of sexual achievement. We see this reflected in sentencing guidelines, which generally reserve the highest penalties for unwanted intercourse, thereby creating a hierarchy of harm that correlates with a hierarchy of punishment. In contrast, I propose that it may be more beneficial to have a more expansive definition of "sexual act" that includes not only heterosexual intercourse but also other forms of sexual activity, including oral sex—per the FBI's current definition—as well as the touching, photographing, and visual or written representation of sexual body parts. I suggest this for two reasons: First, it is difficult to objectively quantify the scale of harm when referencing only the pragmatics of the event; one has to understand the impact to the harmed party. Second, it can be difficult to establish when a sexual act begins and ends.

Problematizing the Hierarchy of Harm

Consider two sexual violations. In the first, a teenage boy slides his penis into the vagina of his best friend's girlfriend while she is drunk and passed out.[33] In the second, men suck a lactating young woman's breasts while she is wide awake.[34] Which is the greater violation? Perhaps the first example is worse because intercourse was involved, or perhaps the second is worse because it is such a diabolically unexpected form of betrayal. Maybe it is less harmful to be attacked while asleep, because the person will not have to remember the attack, or it might be that it is more harmful because that person is so vulnerable. At any rate, this comparison shows the futility of attempting to quantify harm based only on the practicalities of the event.

The assumption that certain unwanted sexual acts are worse than others has periodically arisen in well-publicized cases of sexual harm, particularly in regard to the distinction between oral sex and intercourse and the way in which forcing the former might be seen as less problematic than forcing the latter. Perhaps nowhere was this distinction more widely discussed than in New York's criminal prosecution of Harvey Weinstein, where Mimi Haleyi and Annabella Sciorra both accused Harvey Weinstein of forcing oral sex upon them. Their claims were some of the more tendentious against Weinstein, in part because of the nature of what they were accusing. Cunnilingus is, after all, the one form of sex in which the woman is theoretically the sole focus of pleasure such that it becomes difficult to argue that the woman didn't "want it" when she is the only party whose body is being aroused. And yet, being forced into intimacy, even forced into orgasm, is its own form of violation.[35] As Lisa Taddeo writes in a *New York Times* opinion piece about her own experience of unwanted oral sex:

> Here's one sick part: I don't feel good using the word "assault." Part of the reason is my feeling of complicity. Part is my humiliation. And finally, there's the thought that someone reading this will think that it's not "as big of a deal" as intercourse. That I am being overly dramatic. That the poor guy was just trying to make a sad girl feel better.
>
> But that, in fact, is the worst part. The blur.
>
> For some women, the way it feels for someone to force himself on you in a nearly emotional way carries with it a certain diabolical confusion.[36]

The "diabolical confusion" that Taddeo writes about appears to emerge from the disjunct between her own experience of violation and her embedded beliefs—inherited culturally—about what it ought to look like. In other words, rape myths drive the cognitive dissonance. Or, put differently, since the act appears to violate rape myths, appearing to lack violence *and* theoretically done in the service of Taddeo's own pleasure, then it becomes significantly harder to communicate the source of the injustice to a listener. This inability to communicate is further exacerbated if one assumes that forced intercourse is essentially a worse infliction of harm, perhaps because of a presupposition that more physical harm could be inflicted during the act.

Such constructions again reduce rape to myths and to the pragmatics of the act itself instead of considering other aspects of the event, including perceived impact. Forced oral sex on a woman, for instance, may make all the diabolical sense in the world if someone specifically wants to inflict the illusion of pleasure in the service of control. This appears to have been the case in the Weinstein trial as well as in the rape of India Oxenberg by the NXIVM cult leader Keith Raniere. Raniere repeatedly ordered Oxenberg to engage in forced cunnilingus as an exercise in social coercion designed to perfect her submission to him. Oxenberg, for her part, did not identify the act as any form of violation at the time and believed that it was being done as part of the group's commitment to self-improvement.[37]

The Boundaries of Sexual Acts
A second reason to avoid delineating the exact contours of sexual harm is because it can be unclear where the sexual act begins and ends. Consider, for example, the experience of fifteen-year-old Audrie Pott, who attended a high school party back in 2012, during which she was sexually violated by multiple teenage boys while passed out. The boys took pictures of the event, which they shared on social media and via text.

Pott hanged herself eight days later.

In a documentary about the event, Audrie's father, Larry Pott, reflects that:

> I didn't know anything at the time, but they used indelible markers to completely cover one whole side of her face, lifted up her bra and her panties, drew on her private parts, wrote nasty things on her body, and then sexually assaulted her.[38]

I am particularly curious here about the term "and then" in Larry Pott's statement because of how it signals that the act of writing lewd messages on Audrie's body—including parts of her body used for sex—is separate from the act of "sexual assault." Pott may have been unaware of the way he separated "sexual assault" from the act of writing, or he may have been reflecting the legal epistemology that might have separated out each of these acts into different crimes: Writing on a person's body would be considered battery, fingering a passed-out girl would be considered, legally, the act of sexual violation, and the photographs/videos taken would be considered child pornography. But either way, Pott made a distinction between the drawing, the photography, and the penetration, when he could have perceived this as one continuous act of sexual violation that began with the act of writing on her body and continued with the dissemination of the photos.

That Pott distinguished between "sexual assault" and other forms of violation illustrates how we as a culture assume that such distinctions make sense, perhaps because of the epistemic power of the legal profession. Yet, as Catharine MacKinnon argues, there is a certain arbitrariness in trying to separate forms of sexual harm from one another, as each serves the same purpose, which is to maintain the power and pleasure of the powerful through the continued subjugation of those whose bodies are constructed to be less powerful. Thus, it becomes possible to argue that sexual violations extend into pornography. As MacKinnon argues:

> Sex and violence are inextricably interwoven in the harm of pornography. They are interwoven in the material itself. Pornography makes sex into a violation and makes rape and torture and intrusion into sex. The sex and the violence are interwoven on every other level of the pornography's social existence as

well. Over time and exposure, many viewers respond sexually to violence against women whether it is sexualized or not. It therefore is sex, behaviorally speaking. . . . Subjection is always violating, but it is not always violent; even less often is it perceived as such.[39]

When considering what constitutes a sexual act, then, it is not simply a matter of separating penetrative acts from non-penetrative ones, or drawing age-based lines in the sand to delineate statutory rape from other forms of harm, or saying that there is something worse about physical coercion than psychological manipulation. Sometimes, as MacKinnon recognizes, a sexual act that causes harm is not perceived to be either traumatic or sexual in nature, which is problematic because, in failing to recognize the scope of sexual harm, we become collectively complicit in it. And when we overlook the real pain caused by some forms of sexual harm, then it becomes more permissible to overlook others as well.

Here's another example.

In September of 2020, lawyers filed a lawsuit alleging that refugees detained at the Irwin County Detention Center in Georgia had received hysterectomies without their consent. The whistleblower, a nurse by the name of Dawn Wooten, stated that she repeatedly observed women receiving hysterectomies who either lacked the English-language skills to consent to the medical procedure or who were lied to entirely. One immigrant interviewed as part of the proceedings described the Immigration and Customs Enforcement (ICE) facility as "an experimental concentration camp."[40]

This was not a unique occurrence in the history of the United States. Approximately 40% of Native American women were forcibly sterilized in the 1960s and 1970s because doctors—who had been influenced by systemic racism—believed they lacked the intelligence to properly use other forms of birth control.[41] About 30% of Puerto Rican women were sterilized during the mid-twentieth century.[42] The so-called "father of gynecology," Dr. J. Marion Sims, performed experimental surgeries on multiple enslaved women without anesthesia, assuming that they had higher pain thresholds, while medical schools in the South performed unnecessary sterilization procedures on Black women in what became known as the "Mississippi appendectomies." In the United States, such procedures became legal in 1927, when the Supreme Court ruled in *Buck v. Bell* that it was permissible to sterilize individuals without their consent. The case originated because Carrie Buck—a "feeble-minded" young woman—was placed in an asylum after she became pregnant, and when doctors wanted to forcibly sterilize her, she alleged that she was being denied essential procreative rights. The Court ruled against her 8–1, with Oliver Wendall Holmes Jr. writing that "The principle that sustains compulsory vaccination is broad enough to cover cutting the Fallopian tubes."[43]

Of note: Buck became pregnant because she was raped by the nephew of her foster parents. When they learned of the pregnancy, they placed her in an asylum. This is why she was considered "feeble-minded."[44]

When I hear the story of Carrie Buck or the many other stories of forced sterilization that pepper the history of the United States, I cannot help but ask exactly where the sexual violation ended and some other form of violation began. In Buck's case, did the sexual violation end after the harm done by her foster parents' nephew or after she was placed in an asylum? After she was deemed to be "feeble-minded" or after the Supreme Court ruled against her? A similar argument might be made in relation to the forced sterilizations of Black and Native American women as well as refugees detained at ICE facilities, some of whom may have had a prior history of sexual harm which led them to flee their countries of origin in the first place. My fear, therefore, is that in separating out each of these events and labeling them as distinct entities or injustices, one runs the risk of failing to see how what appears to be a single act of violation can actually be part of a larger and longer narrative of harm that is covertly, if not overtly, sexual in orientation.

Finally, the way that an individual who has lived through a sexual violation structures narrative and creates meaning around violations also complicates attempts to clearly demarcate the end of a sexual act from an objective perspective. As Charlotte Pierce-Baker writes about a hysterectomy shortly after a rape:

> I still have difficulty separating the rape from my hysterectomy. I believe that the rape trauma contributed to the urgency of my surgery. My body was crying out for itself. *Scoop out the putrid mess*. It seemed like further punishment—or maybe a purging.[45]

Even here, where a hysterectomy was done for reasons unrelated to the initial violation, one sees how it becomes possible to create meaning from the event in a way that relates back to the sexual violation so that the two become interwoven in meaning, conflated into a single story rather than into distinct events.

Parsing the Definition: Agency

If power gives the ability to facilitate or avert change, then agency offers the capacity to do so or, put differently, the capacity to act as a subject. Power and agency, therefore, have an intimate relationship to one another, and as Ann Cahill recognizes, the attempted eradication of agency is often an essential component of sexual harm:

> A fundamental part of the violence of rape is that intersubjectivity becomes a one-way street, rather than the dynamic engagement that embodiment calls for.... The actions of the rapist eclipse the victim's agency in a particularly sexual manner. Because it renders impossible for that moment the victim's intersubjective agency, rape is a bodily, sexual assault on a woman's underlying conditions of being.[46]

Cahill is correct in asserting that one of the most devastating aspects of any act of sexual harm is that a person's agency—which is so integral to the self—is rendered ineffective.[47] It is somewhat reductive, however, to say that a person's agency is entirely thwarted in sexual harm. Perhaps excepting a case where someone is violated in their sleep, the person experiencing the sexual violation does assert agency of some kind. They may fight back, scream, or try to reason with the person hurting them, and even in the seeming absence of doing—as in cases where the victimized individual freezes or dissociates—what is really happening is that this individual is doing what it takes to psychologically and physically survive. The damage done to agency is thus not necessarily the eradication of it during the attack but rather the message received because of the *attempted* annihilation: Your agency does not matter in relation to this more powerful person and the structures that this person represents.

The attempt to eradicate agency during the violation itself can also extend well beyond it, into what is often termed the "second rape" that comes when someone attempts to speak about what happened. The use of slut-shaming and cyberbullying in the Coleman episode provides a concrete example of how attempts to eradicate agency continue long after the initial act of harm seems to end. Prosecutorial attempts to discredit those who experience sexual violations as they navigate the legal process offer other examples, as Charlotte Pierce-Baker reflects when she writes:

> The trial that was supposed to be in my favor violated me again and again, and I was given no time to prepare for a fight. I had been tempted many times to let it all go—to drop the charges. Was it worth all the agony? David [her husband] never let me give in.[48]

Pierce-Baker's reflection on a trial that ultimately incarcerated one of the men who raped her is but one of many examples of how the judicial system performs a "second rape" on those who bring charges and whose cases go to trial.[49] Such acts function to continually cause someone who survived a violation to question their own truth, their own power, and, in turn, their own agency, so that language and power collide to perform in ways that are designed to shame, gaslight, and diminish. And yet, to say that agency is totally eradicated is again reductive. Many who have endured sexual violations do persevere on the stand, finding creative and thoughtful ways to answer questions to which they should not be subjected. They also write down the stories of their experiences, exerting narrative agency as they give meaning to the events of a trial.[50] And when they feel as if they themselves cannot exert agency on their own, they—hopefully—receive the support of allies. Sometimes, as in the case of Charlotte Pierce-Baker, these allies are spouses and friends and family. Pierce-Baker writes of a friend named Bessie, who accompanied her to her trial for support, and of her parents and in-laws, who provided childcare for her son during the trial and who also found ways to show her kindness and gentleness during the trial.[51]

But other times, they may be strangers. Around the time I spoke with Amanda—the graduate of the Thistle Farms program who I mentioned earlier in this chapter—I spoke with another woman who had gone through the program and who asked to be anonymous. She spoke of how the residential treatment component of Thistle Farms saved her life, as well as how strangers who donated to the program made her healing possible. As she recounts:

> Like when I first got there [to the residential treatment program], like I didn't really have any teeth left in my mouth, you know, they were rotten. They provided me with everything that I needed. They gave me a place to heal. You know, being able to get my mouth fixed, being able to smile again, like that right there was—like I walked around talking like this all the time [puts hand in front of mouth], and when I was laughing I put my hand up to my mouth. But like a lot of women . . . would tell you, just being able to smile with teeth in your mouth, it's just unbelievable.

This kind of agential restoration reinforces—through reference to lived experience—how sexual violations deprive human beings of agency in complex and nuanced ways, from the inability to fight during the attack to the inability to speak freely on the stand to the inability to smile. These acts of agential deprivation are created by others, by both the individuals who directly inflict them and by the systems that enable them. Conversely and fittingly, though, restoration of agency also requires community support, be it in the form of a spouse or a friend or a stranger. As this same graduate summarized, "There's people in this world that truly do love the stranger, you know, and that want to help."[52]

Parsing the Definition: Desire

To desire something is to recognize a lack or deficit of what is and then seek to fill that void. It is impossible for humans to survive a day without some desire—the desire for safety, food, shelter, heat or air conditioning, distraction, or fulfillment. Sexual desire has become a benchmark for understanding whether sexual harm occurred for scholars like Ann Cahill, who see it as a possible antidote to using consent as the determinative factor of a non-violating sexual encounter. However, Cahill questions whether desire ought to be a determinative factor, given that research has shown that sexual desire in women is often responsive rather than spontaneous, meaning that sexual desire in women tends to arise in response to a sexual stimulus rather than in anticipation of it.[53] As Cahill writes, "The attempt to have desire take the role of consent, as a necessary precondition to an ethical sexual interaction, now appears to be a decidedly masculinist strategy, one that mistakenly adopts a masculine norm as a gender-neutral one."[54]

As an antidote, Cahill suggests that healthy desire could be intersubjective desire, by which she means that desire functions as a "phenomenological experience that arises (or does not arise) in the context of a given interaction . . . something that a sexual interaction can itself bring into being."[55] However, Cahill worries that this too might be problematic, since it raises the question of how to consider a sexual encounter in which a person does not desire to participate but willingly does so out of generosity, as an other-directed gift. She concludes that in an ethical sexual encounter, what matters is not the presence of desire so much as whether a lack of desire goes unobserved by the other party.

This seems to be an oversimplified view of what desire would mean in such an encounter, given that there is a difference between what I term the desire *to do* something and desire *within* something. I might desire to get a seasonal flu shot (desire *to do*) because I recognize my own lack of immunity to the virus but experience no desire *within* the act of getting it, no pleasure, no interest in having the needle in my arm longer than necessary or in repeating the puncture the next day. A similar argument could be made for sexual desire, in which one partner might have a desire to participate in an encounter but experience no desire—spontaneous, responsive, or otherwise—during it. Instead, the initial desire to participate was present because of the nature of their relationship to the person involved, perhaps because of the intersubjective dynamic that exists external to the one-time sexual encounter.

What, then, constitutes this healthy intersubjective dynamic of desire? Here I agree with Cahill that the distinction between sexual harm and a just sexual encounter—to invoke terminology that Cahill draws from Nicola Gavey—is that the former tries "to transcend or eradicate the intersubjectivity at the heart of the human condition."[56] In such an encounter,

> the assailant ... attempts to replace an intersubjective encounter with a tyrannical one, one where the only salient factors are the assailant's desires and intentions. In such instances, the victim's subjectivity was temporarily eclipsed, and her ability to affect the interaction—an ability that is central to her dignity as a person of moral worth—was thwarted. Yet I also argue the rapist's attempt to eliminate intersubjectivity ultimately fails, precisely because the rapist needs the victim to have a subjectivity that must be thwarted.[57]

What distinguishes a healthy sexual encounter from a harmful one, therefore, is whether one person recognizes the desire—or lack thereof—of the other to participate in the activity both prior to and during it.[58]

However, even this view of desire may be overly simplistic once one recognizes that humans possess more than one kind of desire.[59] The first, which I term "root desire," is defined by the desire for self-preservation and may include the desire to have one's bodily needs met as well as the desire for social belonging, safety, esteem, self-actualization, or self-transcendence.[60] The second form of desire, what I term "projected desire," stems from these root ones and functions as the specific ways in which individuals seek to have their root desires met. People seeking social belonging, therefore, might join a chess club or a choir, but they might also join the Ku Klux Klan. Those seeking to meet the root desire for physiological wellness might commit to running outdoors three days a week, but they might also go on a fad diet. An individual trying to meet the root desire for esteem might write a novel in order to see their name displayed prominently in their local independent bookstore, or they might engage in cyberbullying because the number of likes they receive for trolling offers a surge of power that they mistake for pride.

Projected desires, therefore, can be beneficial to the individual and community, or they can go horribly awry if they project in the wrong direction. Oftentimes, a given individual's misdirection develops not in a vacuum but because of misorientations within the culture, misorientations that are guided by harmful dominant embedded beliefs and constructions that do not bring about the dignity of every human being but rather set up power structures that superficially benefit some while damaging others. When thinking of how desire operates in sexual acts, then, it becomes important to parse out the kind of projected desires that cause individuals to feel they desire—or, just as importantly—do not desire a given sexual encounter. It also becomes important to parse out what embedded beliefs and values guide those desires, as well as how those desires get voiced in a given sexual encounter.

A Brief Note on Consent
Consent has most widely been used to determine whether or not a person actually desired to participate in a given sexual act—if they verbally consented, then the act was desired. If they objected, then it was not. Feminist philosophers, however, have troubled the notion that consent is so clear-cut. Some, like Susan Brison, state that it simply makes no sense to assume that consent should be the standard used to judge harm:

> We do not call theft "gift-giving without consent." Why not? Because that is a contradiction in terms. Something not freely given does not count as a gift. So why does penetration of some sort without consent count as sex? Why is it that we see no contradiction in this?[61]

Brison continues that consent is not only an unreasonable standard by which to judge sexual harm but also an epistemically reductive one because of the way in which it frames the entire event from the perspective of one party but not the other. Again using theft as a model, she continues:

> If the one who has the right to give the gift does not consent to giving it, there is no gift-giving—even if the recipient of the item that changed hands takes himself to have received a gift. So why call rape "sex without consent"? . . . To the person who hands over the money (note this *is* an action), it is neither gift-giving nor charity, it is theft—*and what the victim says goes*. We do not privilege the mugger's take on it by calling it gift-giving without consent.[62]

Reinforcing Brison's assertion that consent is an illogical way to assess desire, Linda Martín Alcoff also critiques consent on the grounds that verbal consent does not necessarily align with internal desire. Drawing on consent during sex work, she queries how structural forces of systemic oppression might cause a sex worker to verbally consent to a sex act in which they genuinely do not want to participate because "that encounter may have been made possible by extreme conditions of privation, psychological abuse, and the unequal capacity to find wage work."[63] Alcoff also turns to literature about childhood sexual abuse to describe the ways that children may verbally consent to a given action not because they desire to participate but because they trust or idolize the adult in question, because they are dependent on the adult, or because they fear the repercussions if they do not consent. To that end, Alcoff acknowledges that "Resisting can be incredibly difficult; I have a dear friend who managed to fake appendicitis as a pre-pubescent child as a means to get into a hospital and away from her father's repeated rapes. She actually underwent the surgery."[64]

The problem that both these scholars harken to is that consent has gained something of an epistemic monopoly in conversations about rape, becoming not one of many indicators that something has gone awry in a sexual encounter but the *sole* indicator of wrongdoing. This monopoly causes individuals to overlook that sexual harm is more complicated than that, that it cannot be reduced to the absence of a two-letter word: "No." What might be more appropriately said is that saying "no" is a worthy indicator of a lack of consent, but saying nothing or even saying "yes" is not an entirely foolproof indication of desire because of the way that consent can be manipulated into being, coerced through a person's ability to convince another that engaging in the sexual activity is the best of all possible choices. What is needed, therefore, is not so much the eradication of consent as a benchmark for evaluating whether harm was done but a skepticism of its strength and a mitigation of its monopoly.

Parsing the Definition: The Body

Rape occurs on bodies. This seems like an obvious claim, potentially indisputable. So it makes sense to recognize the body's presence in a definition of rape. Yet what exactly does it mean to say that rape gets inflicted on the body? Here, I would like to make two claims: First, that any act of rape is inflicted upon the body in a way that manifests both as discursive and beyond discourse. Second, I'd like to claim that "the body" can also represent a wider group of human beings.

Ann Cahill argues in *Rethinking Rape* that sexual violations are always enacted on bodies, but that there is no "universally experienced and imposed wrong of rape" because bodies are discursive sites.[65] Cahill is correct that the way individuals might name, interpret, and construct meaning around a sexual violation is at least to some degree constructed and informed by larger embedded beliefs. I would argue, however, that there are also limits to seeing the body as an exclusively discursive site. Consider, for instance, the presence of bruising, scratches, or strangle marks on someone's body. The names or the meaning given to these physical injuries could be said to be difficult to interpret apart from the embedded beliefs in which they are enmeshed, but their presence seems somewhat more objective, something akin to fact.[66] Even if this were not the case, though, the body still plays an essential role in any rape—it is the site on which the violation occurs, the place where harm is experienced, and often, continues to be re-lived long after the event itself ends.

If rape is enacted upon an individual body, though, its effects nonetheless impact the bodies of others.[67] It inflicts harm on the larger community, on loved ones, parents, partners, and spouses who may have to put their own needs aside to care for the victimized party, on the friends with broken hearts, on the individuals whose relationships with the victimized party end because they do not believe or because they say and do harmful things in the aftermath of the violation. The sexual violation also inflicts harm on a broader community of bodies, especially in cases where an instance of harm goes unnamed or unredressed. Consider, for instance, the numerous instances of clergy sexual misconduct in the Roman Catholic Church, in which accused clergy were not defrocked, given therapy, and asked to engage in meaningful accountability, but moved to a different parish, their conduct brushed aside by those higher up in the Church's hierarchy. The leaders who failed to report and hold a given clergy member accountable not only failed to enact justice for the person who experienced the harm but also tacitly made it permissible for other priests to engage in the same behavior. The entire body of the Church, therefore, felt the impact of a single priest's misconduct in ways that ranged from additional rapes occurring to moral injury on the part of leaders who failed to enact accountability to secondary trauma to loss of faith.[68] Without acknowledgment and accountability, then, the effects of a single act of rape ripple, the waves sometimes clearly visible and sometimes barely able to be seen, their impact so widespread as to become dangerously insidious.

On Linguistic Resistance

There is, of course, one major challenge to the definition of rape that I've proposed in this chapter: It is not a shared definition.

Language requires collective buy-in. Naming is a corporate act in which both the speaker and the listener must agree upon the definition of terms if one is to be understood by the other. Indeed, this is one of the gifts we have been given as humans—the ability to not only name but to have our naming understood by others. Little will change, then, without a great deal of systemic, grassroots education about the reality of sexual violations and the importance of redefining the term "rape" to align with the scope of them.

Until that happens, the definitional gaps that exist in matters of sexual harm will continue to function as forms of linguistic violence done to the individual by the collective. This linguistic violation becomes just one more component of the rape, one more way in which the person's body, agency, and desire get disregarded, resulting in a toxic, symbiotic relationship between individuals and the collective in regard to the sexual harm done. By way of example, the individual who sexually violates a woman hurts the class of "women" because of the message that the violation sends about women's subjectivity as a group. That person's act makes it more permissible to treat other women in demeaning ways because of their gender identity. In turn, the lack of validation that the woman receives through the language and narratives available to her to express the violation becomes a form of harm inflicted on the woman by the larger culture who collectively subscribe to them.

A cynic might argue that a more expansive definition of "rape" will result in more false accusations, more libel incurred upon innocent individuals accused of perpetrating wrongdoing. This may be the case, though I find it unlikely, given the bias in favor of the accused and the institutions they represent. I think it is far more likely that those who have experienced sexual harm might feel relief in finally being able to describe the hurt with a simple, monosyllabic, commonly used word. What is at stake, then, is the possibility of giving people a way to concisely conceptualize their experiences and communicate them to others in ways that lead to solidarity, strength, and healing.

Mary Gaitskill summarizes this well in her essay, "On Not Being a Victim," in which she describes two personal experiences of sexual violation. One event aligned with rape myths; the other did not, and she found herself more able to conceptualize the former than the latter. She explains her difficulty in speaking about the second violation this way:

> I didn't understand my own story until I described it to an older woman many years later, as a proof of the unreliability of feelings. "Oh, I think your feelings were reliable," she returned. "It sounds like you were raped. It sounds like you raped yourself." I immediately knew that what she said was true, that in failing even to try to speak up for myself, I had, in a sense, raped myself.
>
> I don't say this in a tone of self-recrimination. I was in a difficult situation: I was very young, and he was aggressive. But my inability to speak for myself—to *stand up* for myself—had little to do with those facts. I was unable to stand up for myself because I had never been taught how.[69]

So many of us were "never taught how," and we only discover what we didn't know after the violation as we begin to question how we categorize and how we speak.

But then, sometimes, something happens, perhaps in a moment or perhaps slowly over time, and the center cannot hold, and things fall apart. This happened for me one afternoon when I was a graduate student reading an article that defined the word "rape" in accordance with stereotypes. I do not remember who wrote the article or what the overall perspective of it was, but I perceived the article as an indictment of what I said happened in my own life, which I was only just beginning to try to understand.

That afternoon, I emailed a pastoral theology professor named Kristen Leslie who researched sexual harm. Kristen was formidable, confident, an expert in her field. I was a graduate student at the university where she taught at the time, and I remember thinking that emailing her was a bit audacious on my part because I wasn't in a class with her, and we'd never spoken before.

"She's probably too busy for me," I thought, immediately regretting I'd sent the message at all. But instead of ignoring me, she responded a few hours later saying that she had time later that afternoon and was happy to talk. When I got to her office, the sun had begun to set over New England, leaving the air chill and dark, and I kept my coat on for the whole conversation, which was a consequence of my own discomfort and not her office heating.

In my core, in my gut, I felt frozen.

She asked me why I wanted to meet with her, and I launched into a lengthy complaint about language: "The word 'rape' in this article only describes the times when a football player pulls a cheerleader into a dark alley by the hair and then beats her and unzips his pants while she screams and tries to fight back. Is that the only thing rape is? Is that the only thing that counts?"

"Is that all you think it is?" she said.

"I don't know," I shrugged, and she paused.

"Is there something else you want to talk about? Something that happened to you?"

This stopped me in my tracks, and for a moment, I was silent. Here was a stranger who was hearing not just the words that I said but the substance of what I was omitting, the question lurking under the surface that I was unwilling to speak into being. That Kristen was someone I barely knew somehow made it easier to imagine saying something, and yet I had told only one other person at that point, and I had felt such tremendous vulnerability that I couldn't imagine going through the process again. It felt like vomiting up some kind of toxic sludge that needed to get out of my system, but it certainly wasn't a pleasant process. The memory itself felt raw and fragmented and painful, loud and angry in my head, and I hated talking about it, just as I was afraid of the judgment that might come from telling a story that sounded so quiet in comparison to the hypothetical cheerleader's screams.

"I don't know," I said.

Kristen paused for a minute and then spoke again. "This way you're doing things—not talking—is it working?"

I shook my head, and she shrugged. "Then maybe it's time to try something else."

"Well shoot," I thought to myself. "That sounds like very good advice."

So I began to speak. But the process wasn't easy, despite my best efforts at eloquence. Midway through the story, I started shaking, pulled my legs to my chest and found that I couldn't get words out of my mouth. Speech felt halting at best, which blindsided me, like I was trying to push a boulder across the street, and even with respectable muscles, it wasn't budging. My body felt icy and my mouth felt paralyzed, and I remember being surprised by this. I had always prided myself on my skill with language: I had been an English major. I paid my way through college and graduate school as a choral singer. Words and speech were my areas of expertise, but when it came to talking about this time in my life, I experienced something like selective muteness, which arose from fear and shame and intimidation. I did not know how to describe that night in a way that another person could understand, and it seemed like the only way to explain was to describe the whole ordeal in detail, which I did not want to do, but which seemed unavoidable. Kristen, for her part, remained calm and steady, not unnerved by anything I said, and when the muteness set in, she stepped in to tell the story with me, offering words for body parts or emotions, asking if one of those was what I meant. I would nod or shake my head, and when I finally finished, she looked me straight in the eye and said, "What you described sounds like a rape."[70]

I had a viscerally negative reaction to this word: Even though she tried to reassure me otherwise, I believed that if I appropriated that word for myself, then I was a liar because my experience did not fit the stereotype of it, and if I didn't appropriate it for myself, then I couldn't label that night as a violation, even though it was causing such persistent suffering. But I also remembered her question: Is your way of doing things working?

And again, the answer was, "No."

I needed a label, so I considered the possibility of labeling the experience of that night as "rape" in my mind, but the idea of using that word publicly in relation to it still felt confounding. If I used it, the listener would likely have a different understanding than what I intended. I now understand that psychological studies show what I intuited: Listeners have strong stereotypes of what constitutes a "real rape:" Those who experience sexual violations are more likely to be believed when the person who inflicted it is a stranger and when they themselves were not intoxicated, were conservatively clothed, have white skin, physically resisted, reported the rape immediately, and were subject to physical violence that resulted in obvious injuries.[71] When someone's story does not align with this stereotype, the credibility of their claims is more likely to be questioned. It wasn't, therefore, just a matter of me speaking; it was a matter of how the word "rape" would be heard by others, and I knew that.

In the years that have passed, I've come to realize that what Kristen saw in me was different from what I saw in myself. When I look at that meeting through her eyes, what I see now is a young woman at a crossroads in her life, who was trying to figure out what to trust more, her own body and its memory or the words she had to describe them. In coming to Kristen, what I was really looking for was validation, a sign that I wasn't crazy, that I was a reliable narrator of my own story, that I was believable. Kristen, for her part, heard that, so she made an important choice when she used the word "rape" because even though it was and remains an imperfect word—as all the words for sexual violations are—it did the conversational work of showing that she believed me. In using it, she was saying that what I remembered, and was reliving on a daily basis, should rightly be categorized as a wrong.

Today, I also see her use of the word "rape" as an act of linguistic resistance that challenged stereotypes and widened the expansion of this word so that it aligned more closely with the contours of what harm actually looks like. Individuals who take on the task of linguistic resistance can have a profound impact upon victimized parties because they take language—and those who craft it—to task, bypassing a call for linguistic accountability and instead taking the initiative to instantiate it. The difficulty with these singular acts, however, is that language is a communal endeavor. Kristen's adoption of a more expansive definition of rape was meaningful to me; however, the act of linguistic resistance she undertook on my behalf was the act of a singular human being, and it will take a village to change the meaning of the word "rape."

Just as it takes a village to rape a human being.

CHAPTER 3

Speaking as a Narrative Self

Why Our Stories Matter

DURING THE FIRST conversations I had about my own experiences, I felt no warm fuzzies or purifying insight when I spoke, even though the people listening were kind and gentle. Instead, I had this sense that someone had dumped a bucket of sludge over me, and I needed a shower to wash it off. I called the feeling "slimed." As I wrote years later in a journal, my experience of the person who harmed me,

> was like being in those amusement park cups that spin around—I couldn't orient myself, and it wasn't very enjoyable, but to get off the ride seemed boring, a disappointment, a letdown, so I paid another token and stayed on for one more round. Maybe this time, I wouldn't wind up feeling nauseous at the end.

When I would talk about that particular night or other experiences with this human being more broadly with my therapist and trusted friends, speaking about the violations that were integral to them only delivered the nausea back to my front door, complete with a side order of guilt, confusion, and blame. Then I would feel shame because the talking process that was supposed to make me feel better was only making me feel worse. I was grateful in those days for other individuals with similar experiences who had perspective I lacked, especially one who had spoken publicly about an extended experience of clergy sexual abuse. When I shared my guilt about how speaking never felt cathartic, about how I hated telling people what happened because I was afraid of the burden I was imposing on them and the way it might shape their view of me, she laughed. It was a counterintuitive reaction that I experienced as comforting, a sign of empathy, that she had been where I was, had developed wisdom that I didn't have yet.

"Oh boy, do I remember that feeling," she said. "It's terrible, but it'll pass. One day, the trauma won't own you anymore. It'll just be a story, a prior chapter in the book of your life."

In retrospect, I wish someone had warned me that speaking would initially feel like I was immersed in a pile of sludge, and I also wish I had known that the slimy feeling wouldn't last forever. It did go away, and speech became much easier. I say this knowing full well that I was one of the lucky individuals who had a support network ready to catch her: I had access to a university therapy program that operated on a sliding scale, a group of kind and generous friends, and a set of professors and religious professionals who were open to discussions. Unlike many who talk about their violations, rarely did I encounter disbelief.

When I was ready to speak, they listened, and I received only belief in kind for my confession. Even so, I initially felt no better for the telling. I sensed instead an incisive dissonance between how they saw me—as someone who was fundamentally good, the victim of a wrong—and how I perceived myself as a willing accomplice in my own demise. I don't feel this way anymore, and I wish I could say that it was because one of those individuals said something magical that suddenly shifted my perspective—something I could share with you as I write—but it wasn't one comment so much as the sheer repetition and unorchestrated consistency of their reflections.

Over and over again, they listened.

Over and over again, they believed me.

Over and over again, they said the fault didn't lie with me, until one day, as my friend promised, the trauma lost its power.

Why Our Stories Matter

The stories that we tell about rape are as important as the stories that we get told through our inherited narratives, what Carrie Doehring refers to as "embedded beliefs."[1] We often fail to question the authority of these stories or even to notice they exist and, because of that, do not consider the impact they have on how we narrate our individual stories or how we speak about our own experiences. I'll explain more about why this is and the impact that it has on the processing of traumatic events like rape in what follows.

We are embodied stories, each of us becoming an author with our first cries. But we do not pen this story alone. Infant vulnerability limits the ability to independently construct a self, and it places the burden of self-construction on parents and daycare workers and nannies and grandparents and siblings who will hopefully try to label the young human's needs and desires for what they are—the desire for love, the desire for attachment and social belonging, the desire for safety, the desire to be known.

At this stage of life, our embodied vulnerabilities and the inability to speak mean that we need not only physical and emotional support but also narrative support. We are not—nor can we even pretend to be—autonomous selves.[2] That illusion emerges later, as we learn to fear dependence and defenselessness, as we mistake the luxury of agency for the self's autonomy.[3] Still, while none of us are sole authors of our stories at any point in our life's journey, we participate in the writing process from the start through our desire for survival, for food and sleep and attachment. Most of us make those desires known by crying and kicking and screaming and only later employ the sophistication of words—nouns, then verbs, statements about being, followed by descriptions of doing.

The agency we exercise in our infancy helps draft the earliest chapters of the stories of our selves, but it's those with more agency and power who flesh out the rough plotline we offer. We rely on caregivers to interpret the cries and kicks and colic and give them meaning. Even our names, the very signifiers of our identity, are not of our own choosing but are monikers given by parents who can only hope they suit their children.

As humans grow, they play a more active role in the self's construction. The ability to effectively express opinions becomes more sophisticated as words become sentences, paragraphs, and stories, increasingly creative and increasingly informed by our settings and embedded beliefs. The process of constructing the self, therefore, becomes one in which children play a more active role as they grow and gain the ability to communicate through the exercise of agency. One way that children craft this story is within the context of relationships with their peers, relationships which may be friendly or hostile. As Anita Hill notes, school culture can be an early driver of community as well as gender-based violence, since "cliques" and "popular groups" often elevate straight white men to the top of the school's popularity food chain. This separates children into "insiders" and "outsiders" which, as Hill writes, "creates a perfect template for bullying and harassment."[4]

In addition to this sorting process, play becomes crucial to the task of crafting a narrative self, as it gives children an opportunity to temporarily try on new selves, to imagine what it might be like to be a construction worker, a parent, an artist.[5] Play functions as something of a variation on Pascal's famous wager, which states that it is preferable to act as a Christian and to try to convince oneself of Christianity's truth than to live as an atheist, because the good that is potentially gained from faith (an afterlife) outweighs the potential loss to the atheist (eternal damnation). Children too make a wager through play, aspire to a particular self-construction for thirty minutes or so and see how it feels, discover how others respond, and assess whether the gains are worth the losses. This process allows children to draft and redraft the emerging story of the self.[6]

Yet even though children exert more agency in the process of self-construction, the effort remains communal. Here are some examples to explain what I mean: Around the age of eight, my parents introduced me to *Murphy Brown* (a 1980s sitcom about a journalist), and I went through a phase where I would walk around with a legal pad and jot down news stories that I would then recite to my mom and dad using my very best newscaster voice. At thirteen, I had a writing teacher who introduced me to the word "feminism," and I hung up posters of Rosie the Riveter on the wall and began wearing red bandannas and overalls to symbolize my commitments. In college, I skipped over the classes listed in the women's studies section of the course catalog because I had absorbed the belief from some of my professors that anything with the word "feminist" was a lesser form of scholarship.

In all three of these examples, my attempts to embody a particular aspirational self did not appear in isolation but rather emerged from sources that others in my setting considered authoritative—a popular television show, an empowering image of liberal feminism, the views of a group of people with doctorates. Shaped by these stories, I tried on aspirational selves to see how they fit, motivated by my own evaluation of them as well as the evaluation provided by my parents, teachers, friends, and culture at large. Sometimes the feedback affirmed my own instincts. I received a very positive response to my *Murphy Brown* phase because my father was an English teacher who insisted that I learn to write, and both my mother and grandma affirmed my Rosie the Riveter phase, since my grandma had lived Rosie's narrative, entering the workforce for the first time during World War II. However, that initial affirmation conflicted with the postfeminist messages I received in college: Women like me were students on campus, after all.[7] Wasn't that evidence enough of our inclusion? And women's wisdom was included in my English and religion syllabi, albeit as token classes, as the "woman's" week that inevitably occurred toward the end of the term when everyone was too tired to complete the reading.

I didn't want to be a token, so down came the Rosie the Riveter poster.

Time to donate the bandannas and overalls.

When confronted with two contrasting cultural narratives—the narrative that it was important to fight for women's rights and the narrative that the fight had already been won—my grandma's liberal feminist lived experience had nothing on the postfeminist ideology privileged by the loudest voices in my academic setting. So the latter narrative trumped the former, both because the latter came from a seemingly more authoritative source and because it appealed to me.

I preferred to believe that I was living in a world in which the battle for my body's equality had been won.

I found out the hard way that I was wrong.

I offer these examples to illustrate how the self's construction is not a linear process or an autonomous one in which the self gradually and clearly develops into some predestined end. Sometimes the aspirational selves that cultural narratives present as options contradict one another, and sometimes the feedback we receive shifts the narrative. A best outcome of aspirational self-experiments is that external confirmation aligns with internal confirmation. Consider, for instance, a toddler who shares a toy in preschool. Sharing is not the most natural of habits to develop, as any parent of siblings has observed, and indeed, the instinct against sharing makes sense: Humans live in a world with limited resources, and they give away a resource any time they share, which makes them more vulnerable than they were before. After all, the very thing that they give away might be the thing that could be essential for their survival. Still, the toddler does this amazingly counterintuitive act of sharing and finds, surprisingly, that they don't regret it because sharing brings about this new experience called "generosity," and it makes them feel warm and kind. The toddler likes the feeling. Meanwhile, their teacher praises them for giving up the toy, further affirming that what their instinct says is true: They are a generous self.

If one potential best-case scenario is when personal and external affirmation aligns, then one of the least positive outcomes occurs when they don't. This leads to cognitive dissonance at best and suffering at worst. Consider, for instance, a young Black boy who believes that he is worthy of love. That instinct may be affirmed by his parents, but then he enters school and for some reason that he does not understand, the teacher seems to single him out for wrongs he didn't commit. The other kids respond to the teacher's assessment by refusing to play with this boy during recess. He begins to notice that the parents of the other children stare at him and his family as if there is something wrong with them all, as if there is something wrong with him, as if he is not the inherently good self that he thought he was.

This is but one hypothetical example of how the societal stories we tell impact an individual's self-concept, one in which the story that the boy's parents tell is hitting up against powerful stories told by the dominant culture. Others include, but are not limited to, instances where parents refuse to recognize the gender identity of their children, when friends abandon a member of their group who came out of the closet, when a boss discriminates against a worker on the basis of sex, and when children mock a differently abled youngster on the playground. In all these examples, the person receives the message from others that their perceived sense of self lacks value, resulting not in mutual self-construction but in confusion and, potentially, the destruction of self-concept.[8]

Though self-destruction is often a negative experience, it can also be of positive value under the right circumstances, such as when the self changes due to the gentle and constant influence of time rather than interpersonal or systemic forms of oppression. Indeed, the self can evolve in such profound ways with time that there is sometimes little relation between, say, a given person's sense of self at age four and that same person's sense of self at age twenty. The self can, therefore, experience radical twists and shifts and disjuncts, with the result that people routinely say things like, "I don't recognize that version of myself," or "I am nothing like I used to be." Trauma is, therefore, not the only force that causes a rupture to the self (unless one conceives of trauma as a more general epistemic evolution—an evolution in ways of knowing—that can occur as a byproduct of existing in time).

The very experience of existing within time can also bring about the same process.[9]

Memory's relationship to time is also significant to evolving narrative self-construction. Time can shift the memory and, in turn, shift the meaning given to it and the role it plays in the narrative construction of the self in such profound ways that the self does not necessarily continuously evolve so much as it gently dismantles and reconstitutes.[10] As the person continues to co-write the story in community, these twists and turns get written and rewritten within a narrative that continues to develop within the shifting context of memory. Trauma and time can, therefore, instantiate radical twists in the plotline and characterization that are central to the overarching story known as a person's self-concept.

In a sexual encounter that is not violating, individuals agree to co-write a story together. Perhaps it is the story of a one-night stand or a lifelong love, but either way, each agrees to contribute to the narrative by participating in the initial encounter, which might be said to be a first draft of the story. Over time, the draft gets revised and rewritten as the participants assess and reassess its significance so that sometimes the lover becomes a main character, while at other times, the lover becomes an extra in the larger narrative structure of a life. What remains from the original encounter, then, is the agreement made on the night that each individual became part of the constructed memory of the other, so that what unites them is not simply the time spent during the sexual encounter itself but also the commitment to be a self that includes the other person as part of the narrative.

One of the differences between a violating and non-violating sexual encounter, then, is that the victimized party is denied co-authorship, so that the person who causes the violation alone writes the key plot points, overexerting narrative agency in a way that attempts to write the victimized person's story and have a lasting impact on that person's self. What separates those who inflict sexual harm from those who are on the receiving end of it, then, is that the latter group did not consent—irrespective of what they said or did not say during the encounter—to becoming the selves that the former tried to narrate them into being.

Victimized individuals are thus left with the question of how to acknowledge the ghostwriting of their stories. Chanel Miller—who was violated by Brock Turner while unconscious—describes this phenomenon when she writes about the moment in the hospital when she began to recognize that one of the things that happened during the attack was that her identity had been constructed without her consent:

A stack of papers were set in front of me. My arm snaked out of the blankets to sign. If they explained what I was consenting to, it was lost on me. Papers and papers, all different colors, light purple, yellow, tangerine. No one explained why my underwear was gone, why my hands were bleeding, why my hair was dirty, why I was dressed in funny pants, but things seemed to be moving right along, and I figured if I kept signing and nodding, I would come out of this place cleaned up and set right again. I put my name at the bottom, a big loop C and two lumps for the M. I stopped when I saw the words Rape Victim in bold at the top of one sheet. A fish leapt out of the water. I paused. No, I do not consent to being a rape victim. If I signed on the line, would I become one? If I refused to sign, could I remain my regular self?[11]

Not every person who survives a sexual violation is given a piece of paper and told to sign onto their new identity at the dotted line, but in some way or another, they contend with the consequences of having a new identity thrust upon them. They must figure out how to reclaim narrative agency when they didn't write the story in the first place. They must discern how to understand their relationship to a story that they never wanted to be theirs. They must find a way to tell the story not just of the event but also of the self that emerged in the aftermath of it.

Trauma theorists across disciplines established decades ago that reclaiming narrative agency is essential to the process of recovery, as Susan Brison summarizes when she writes, "*Saying* something about a traumatic memory *does* something to it."[12] In other words, speaking plays a performative role in trauma recovery, meaning that speaking doesn't just describe the trauma. It also changes it somehow. To best understand *why* language works this way, it is helpful to understand the mechanics of *how* it works. Bessel van der Kolk explains that trauma compromises the brain's ability to speak: Flashbacks deactivate one of the speech centers of the brain—known as Broca's area—and light up another region known as Brodmann's area 19, a part of the visual cortex that serves as an entry point for visual images that get transferred to other parts of the brain for processing and meaning-making. From the perspective of neurobiology, then, one of the reasons why it is so difficult for someone who has experienced a traumatic sexual violation to narrate their experiences is because those experiences have compromised access to the part of the brain that manages speech.[13] Likewise, the thalamus, the part of the brain that collects information from our senses and integrates them into memory, also tends to stop working properly in the aftermath of trauma. As van der Kolk summarizes, this "explains why trauma is primarily remembered not as a story, a narrative with a beginning, middle, and end, but as isolated sensory imprints: images, sounds, and physical sensations that are accompanied by intense emotions, usually terror and helplessness."[14]

Experts in the mental health community have developed various therapeutic techniques to help the brain regain the ability to process the traumatic event linguistically, and these are part of an overall process of regaining safety, meaning, and a sense of self that reintegrates into a community. Judith Herman, who first proposed these three stages, explains that while the first and most fundamental step in trauma recovery is to create physical, psychological, and spiritual safety,[15] the most intensive therapeutic work is often done in the second stage, when individuals engage in a process of remembrance and mourning that involves constructing the meaning of the traumatic event through rebuilding a narrative sense of self. This process involves not just a narrative exploration of the trauma itself but also an exploration of that narrative self prior to the trauma, as the embedded beliefs that framed that narrative impact how a person might initially and subsequently interpret the violation.[16] Having established that context, Herman explains that the next step is to be able to talk about the facts of the traumatic event and then to give those facts narrative structure, feeling, and meaning because in such a process, individuals gain an opportunity to explain how the trauma destroyed previous beliefs and assumptions about the world.[17]

This process involves an implicit—though perhaps unintended—assumption that the very act of speaking can immediately make someone who has been traumatized feel better, as if speech is not only performative but also quickly cathartic. We see this all the time in media representations of both trauma specifically and conflict more generally. A character feels they can't speak, avoids trusting other people, but then, just when they're at their breaking point, they trust another person enough to speak and—voila! Problem solved.[18] These media representations of how speech functions assume that the transformative power of speech happens quickly. If speakers don't immediately feel better, then they might assume something went wrong or that they've incorrectly understood their own story. Perhaps they shouldn't have spoken at all.

I wish that we more frequently named this assumption about speech so that we could nuance it, because while speech does enact a transformation, the transformation may not be quick or flashy. This is why social support, grounded in a hermeneutic of belief, is so essential for those who experience these kinds of violations. But practicing a hermeneutic of belief—by which I mean a way of listening that starts with empathy and assumes belief—is itself countercultural when the story society tells about those who lived through a rape is that they're histrionic, they want attention, they want to destroy the people who hurt them because they have personal vendettas, or they simply regret having sex and are calling regret "rape." It's the hermeneutic of *dis*belief that prevails, a hermeneutic that only intensifies when the victimized party does not match the ideal victim stereotype of a white, cisgender, heterosexual woman who is sober, unprovocatively dressed, economically stable, and normatively abled. For instance, when the victimized party is Black, they are pit against the culturally dominant embedded belief that Black women are promiscuous and Black men are rapists and both have insatiable sex drives that render them unrapeable.[19] When listeners see and hear them, when they impose inherited narratives about their skin color and sexuality upon them, then they continue the process of violation. A hermeneutic of belief is therefore both countercultural and an act of resistance that is essential for someone's recovery, especially in cases where intersectional systemic oppression plays a role.

Even in cases where the victimized party more closely matches the ideal victim stereotype, though, it can be challenging for someone who survived a sexual violation to speak when they don't feel as if words capture the nature of the violation. Case in point: Lacy Crawford was a fifteen-year-old boarding school student when two boys proceeded to force their penises down her throat. It was the early 1990s. Bill Clinton's sexual escapades hadn't yet raised the question of whether oral sex "counted" as real sex, and Crawford felt confused by the nature of the wrong because "rape"—as she understood it and as the law defined it at the time—required heterosexual intercourse, and if the boys hadn't raped her, then what had they done? As she writes, "I envied the monosyllabic force of the word *rape*. Say *rape*, and people get it. People know the telos of the encounter (intercourse) and the nature of the exchange (non-consensual). Whereas I had no label."[20]

Crawford goes on to write that one of the reasons she initially refused to use the term "rape" in relation to her own experience was out of respect for others who she felt were the rightful owners of it. That protective instinct on her part is rich in empathy because she seems to be saying that she did not want to distill the force of their experiences. It also signals that she knew there was not a hermeneutic of belief within her community. At St. Paul's—the elite boarding school she attended—students called her a "slut" and a "whore" instead of a victim.[21] Faculty were aware of what happened but declined to report the incident or pursue a disciplinary case, and the head chaplain at the school, rather than engaging in an empathic or an other-directed response, helped her pack her bags and sent her home.[22]

When someone who experiences a sexual violation lacks a label or doesn't feel safe enough to use it, then she has to get creative about how to express herself. Self-harm becomes a tempting option, though not one that can be recommended by any who have tried it. But there are other, more constructive, possibilities. Chanel Miller traveled across the country to Rhode Island to take a print-making class after Brock Turner fingered her while she was unconscious. Maya Angelou refused to speak for five years after she was raped as a child because her attacker was murdered when she identified him, and she believed herself responsible for his death. She used this mute time to read every book in the library at her school so that, "When I decided to speak, I had a lot to say and many ways in which to say what I had to say."[23] In Lacy Crawford's case, she met a different school chaplain who recognized the wrongdoing for what it was. The chaplain provided lifegiving support by supervising an independent project Crawford wanted to do on biochemical depression and creative genius, by offering her a safe and secure space where she could go on-campus, and by letting Crawford take care of her dog, Radley, who became a source of stability.[24] In these ways, the chaplain functioned as a listener and a self-affirming ally without ever using the word "rape" in their conversations, exemplifying what pastoral theologians term a "ministry of presence," rather than a ministry of dogmatic words.

At various points, I have told my own story through song and ritual and therapy, as well as through journal entries and fragments of narrative knit together in poetry, raw lists of loss and lament, and stream of consciousness exercises meant for no other eyes but mine. Later, I completed a master's thesis on the theological implications of the language used for sexual violations but never mentioned my own experiences in the writing or to my adviser. While words were central to many of these forms of expression, I did not rely on them exclusively. Indeed, some of the embodied practices I adopted were just as important as the spoken ones. I returned to my previous job as a professional choral singer, rekindling the safety in music that had sustained me as a child. I also began practicing yoga, which scholars like Bessel van der Kolk have found to be effective for treating posttraumatic stress symptoms.[25] The grounding exercises and emphasis upon deep breathing in yoga have been found to directly counteract the heightened cortisol and shallow breathing of trauma, and the way that yoga safely allows an individual to re-engage with a somatic relationship to their own body becomes central to healing from events in which the body is so outside of control.

Yoga, in particular, does not require words, but that doesn't mean that the body's own actions can't become part of the self's narrative. Indeed, the body is a central component of the self, essential to its story. I recall, for instance, a yoga class I took during graduate school with a teacher who asked us to do Simhasana, also known as lion's pose. Part of completing the pose involves making a sound that resembles a lion's roar, and for the life of me, I could not do it. The teacher came over and sat next to me while other students practiced, and asked what was getting in my way of completing the pose. But I couldn't seem to explain that either, certainly not in the middle of a yoga class.

"I understand," she said, without my speaking a single word at all. "It happened to me too."

Then she showed me how to do a restorative pose instead, a pose designed to ground and calm. What I remember from that moment was that my blood pressure lowered, my muscles relaxed, and I felt somatically safe. Some of that occurred because this teacher was so reassuring, but some of it was also the pose she helped me into, one designed to create a sense of safety and stability. Neither words nor language were involved, and yet the somatic memory became central to the narrative that I inhabited about the trauma. Finally feeling safe, my sense of time began to shift. No longer was time static because I felt stuck in the trauma. No longer was my body trapped by the trauma's sensations. For a moment, my system recalibrated itself, and once my body had that recalibration in its memory, it became easier to reset it to that state of calm in the future, until the symptoms of the trauma subsided in both frequency and intensity. In being able to inhabit both time and my own body, I was able to move from a place of permanent stuckness to movement, and being able to move had narrative consequences. It allowed my sense of self to unclench itself so that the process of narratively constructing the self—a communal process that is so essential to who we are as humans—could resume.

Speaking about a personal violation can also be challenging for someone who has been victimized, because talking about the event necessitates talking about someone else—the person who perpetrated the harm. No one wants that link, that enduring connection to this other human being, and many try to distance themselves in as many ways as possible: They sever their relationship with the person who perpetrated the harm, avoid naming them or going to places that bring back the memories.

Who can blame them?

All of these strategies create some distance, but they don't erase the story—they can't delete that particular human being from that particular moment in time when wrong was done. So there's denial, of course, and attempts to forget. But these strategies don't work for the long term and are a cruel reminder that the one thing the violated party most wants—to remove the offending party from the narrative of their life—is the one thing that cannot be done.

The realization that this person who raped me will remain in my memory until my memory is no more tends to make my chest tighten—it signifies the limits of my agency. I may have enough of it to write, edit, and rewrite a narrative that changes the significance of their presence, but I lack the ability to hit the delete button over and over again until I've erased that chapter from my life. The ultimate narrative insult, then, is inability to control the story, and that admission is one of the reasons why I remain uncomfortable writing about my own experiences, because it requires that I acknowledge that another person authored a story on my body that I did not want to have written, and while I have the power of interpretation over that story, I cannot undo it in a way that removes the offending character entirely.

Yet I also recognize that my instinct is ironic, in a way. Because as much as I wish I could erase this singular human being from my memory, I also recall the ways that this person tried to erase me.

I refuse to return the favor, as an act of resistance.

Those who experience sexual violations sometimes sense intuitively that those who inflicted the harm deprived them of narrative agency, but at other times, that knowledge is produced through reflection, through intentional challenging of the initial interpretation of one's story. It takes time. So I want to trouble the assumption that this robbing of narrative agency is always obvious and easily identifiable both to those who directly experience rape and to their communities. Shame, fear, social control, confusion, and systemic justification theory—the idea that people tend to believe the status quo is fair and therefore refrain from challenging it—all impact perception. Because it can be easier to blame oneself than to admit one's vulnerability to the randomness of horrors, it becomes tempting to interrogate the event in an effort to locate one's own agency. Victimized individuals may, therefore, first imagine themselves as co-writers or, at least, ghostwriters who had at least some agency or subjectivity in the encounter to maintain a sense of control or a sense of protection. Maybe they genuinely believe that's the most accurate representation of the event. Put more colloquially, they are prone to blame themselves. And while psychologists often label this as denial, I'm not sure it's always as simple as that—sometimes people are wrestling with the significance of events using competing ways of knowing (or epistemologies), which resolves into cognitive dissonance and the feeling that one is assembling a puzzle, but the events that make up the pieces do not fit together to create a coherent picture. That's not denial. That's turmoil.

Kate Elizabeth Russell offers an in-depth exploration of this form of wrestling in her novel *My Dark Vanessa*, which offers the namesake's account of a sexual relationship she had with her high school English teacher, a relationship she refuses to acknowledge as abusive despite external pressure to do so. Vanessa narrates one sexual encounter late in the relationship, when she is a young adult, in which she is keenly aware of the ambiguity of the encounter:

Between breaths, he says, "I want you to come."
    I want you to stop, I think. But I don't say it out loud—I can't. I can't talk, can't see. Even if I force my eyes open, they won't focus. My head is cotton, my mouth gravel. I'm thirsty, I'm sick,

I'm nothing. He keeps going, faster now, which means he's close, only a minute or so left. A thought shoots through me—is this rape? Is he raping me?[26]

Several pages later, Vanessa explains to the reader that she was not victimized then or at any other point in her relationship with Mr. Strane because, "I've never wanted to be [a victim], and if I don't want to be, then I'm not. That's how it works. The difference between rape and sex is state of mind. *You can't rape the willing, right?*"[27]

Part of the reason Vanessa has such a difficult time admitting that Mr. Strane abused her has to do with the inherent power dynamic—she was a child. He was an adult. He was worldly. She was vulnerable. He was a teacher. She was a student. But another reason that Vanessa struggled to identify the abuse was because Mr. Strane gave her gifts, told her she was special and beautiful, and for whatever negative feelings he elicited in her, he also made her feel desired and loved. The dual—or dueling—narratives that victimized parties can tell themselves about offending parties make admitting to the existence of the violation within the context of an ongoing relationship diabolically torturous.

I know this firsthand. Because the person who raped me was someone I'd had a relationship with at many levels, I often felt that my mind had been split in two and that I was engaged in a mental courtroom where half of my brain had mounted a defense with memories of compliments and kindnesses serving as evidence, while the other half of my brain was prosecutorial, presenting evidence of times when I had been grabbed and pressured, coerced and manipulated. All of these memories painted an incongruous picture, like Picasso's *Weeping Woman*.

How could someone who hurt you also say you were smart and beautiful?

Which set of evidence was real?

I felt stuck. If I ruled in favor of the defense, then I was ruling against the reality of my own suffering. But if I ruled the other way, then I would have to admit to complications and vulnerabilities that I was, as yet, unwilling to accept. The story I choose to believe now is that there's truth to both sides of the argument.

On Subjectivity

The culturally dominant embedded beliefs that color the interpretation of sexual violations also shape someone's ability to identify how their subjectivity was robbed: When people are raised to believe that rape is somehow othered, then they possess an unrealistic understanding of their own inviolability. This is different from saying that these individuals are not pre-victims or do not believe themselves to be as such. Indeed, it is possible to see oneself as a pre-victim while simultaneously being convinced that one will never experience a sexual violation personally.

Here's an example of what I mean: One of my closest childhood friends went to college a few hours away from me, and so I took the bus to visit her for a weekend during my freshman year. I recall walking into her dorm room, which was bright and sunny, and saw her roommate sleeping on the couch. My friend then whispered in my ear, "She was raped a few weeks ago at a frat party."

I remember thinking to myself, "Well, I don't go to frat parties," which wasn't a way of blaming the girl so much as it was a way of protecting myself. I knew that human beings didn't deserve to be violated because they put their bodies in a particular space, but I also assumed that if *I* didn't put my body in that same, supposedly unsafe, space, then I could guarantee my own security. And so my friend and I went nowhere near the row of fraternities and sororities that weekend—we visited a local coffee shop and ate in the dining hall. We studied in the library and walked across campus in the bright midday light. We stayed up late and talked about new boyfriends and profound philosophical revelations in her bedroom. We restricted our movements to spaces where we knew that our bodies had permission to be—the clear lighting of the coffee shop, the public solitude of the library, the privacy of her dorm room. Ironically, we were acting like pre-victims of rape—like women whose safety was only guaranteed because we took the proper precautions—while simultaneously believing those actions liberated us from being pre-victims of rape. We believed that we could maintain our subjectivity if we only did the right thing, while failing to acknowledge that limiting the space we felt we had permission to occupy was an attack on where we could function as subjects.

Subjectivity—the idea that a person can exercise agency and do things—becomes even more complicated when one considers how it functions during a sexual violation itself. For instance, the illusion that one has subjectivity during rape is complicated further when the person who perpetrated the harm is known and trusted, a friend or a lover, because then the person who experienced the violation has additional data points in the form of memory that may contradict the data provided by the attack. The person may remember times when they did have subjectivity in the relationship, when they were able to make choices and when those choices were respected. The violated individual may also remember times when the person who inflicted the violation was kind or expressed deep, abiding love, offered gifts, made verbal commitments, cooked dinner, picked up the kids from school. At best, these memories can provide some nuance, a recognition that relationships can be complex and the people in them equally so. But these memories at their worst can paint individuals who rape in a very different light and act as a counternarrative that they can exploit or that the harmed party can inadvertently use to self-gaslight.

Sometimes, the memories make more sense when one can interpret them from another's perspective. I recall, for instance, that when I was involved with the person who raped me, my roommate was dating someone who was abusive on many levels, including sexually. I loathed her boyfriend and took to writing multiple angry entries about it in my journal, complaining about how my beloved friend deserved to be treated so much better than she was. But I never told her what my fears about the relationship were, even though I thought of her as a sister. At the time, I thought that telling the truth would end our friendship. I think I also believed my words didn't mean much—I probably couldn't convince her to end things, so I said nothing.

She ended the relationship on her own.

When I was going through my old journals recently, I found what I had written and texted her screenshots of my words.

"I'm so sorry," I wrote. "I should have said something."

She responded seconds later. "I never said anything about how much I hated that person who raped you, but I'll say here and now that we were all so glad when you two stopped talking."

How ironic, I thought, that we were so clearly able to see hurt and harm in each other's lives but not in ourselves, that we were willing to name it in the privacy of our own hearts, but not say the words out loud. We both imagined that we had more subjectivity than we did, but then again, we were invested in those relationships, and we wanted them to succeed or to at least give the appearance of succeeding because then we wouldn't have to experience the public shame of what we perceived to be our own failure. Add system justification theory and family systems to that and it all makes sense—humans are attracted to homeostasis like a child to an ice cream truck because homeostasis is stability and stability feels vital for survival. This is part of why individuals stay in abusive relationships and believe themselves to have more agency than they do. The relationship may be coercive, but to leave it is to enter the unknown, and sometimes it feels wiser to maintain a known lack of safety than to seek out what lies beyond. Because whatever the beyond is, it involves a different life with a different self. And that can be both impossible to imagine and even more impossible to speak about.

CHAPTER 4

On Dominant Stories

DURING MY FIRST year of graduate school, I knocked on the door of Siobhán Garrigan—a confident, incisively intelligent professor with a keen commitment to social justice—because I had some questions about language, and I wagered she could answer them. Siobhán taught courses on ritual, performativity, and gender, and language was central to her work. Indeed, her commitment to language was what I knew of her at the time. As the Dean of the school's chapel program, she was in the process of teaching the student body about why it was important to remove the exclusively masculine language for God that was the norm in Christian worship spaces. Some students felt that the move to shift the language for God was tantamount to heresy, while others felt that the language was not only outdated but exclusionary, but what I observed in their reaction was how impactful that three-letter word—God—could be, how it bore within it history and politics and how people projected upon it everything from memories of their first church service to experiences with their parents. Put differently, what Siobhán's work showed was that words were not only symbols for concepts but also political, change agents, and sites of wrestling.

On that day I knocked on her door, though, I wasn't interested in talking about that three-letter word. I was interested in talking about a four-letter word: rape. My reasoning was that if Siobhán knew so much about the word "God," then she might have some insights to share on the word "rape" as well. I wanted to know why this word felt so hard to say, and what forces shaped the boundaries of how I and other English speakers in the United States heard it. I had gotten better at talking about my own experiences by this point, no longer curled in a ball and unable to speak, but still, I stumbled when I tried to name, succinctly, what had happened and why I was in her office.

"I'm sorry," I said, "I just can't bring myself to say—" My voice trailed off, and there was a pause, a space in the conversation.

"I was raped," Siobhán said, filling in the words for me, taking away the burden of language so I didn't have to carry it alone. She sighed. "You know, sometimes the hardest words to say are also the most important ones to say."

I squinted. "The problem is that I don't feel I belong in that word."

"Why's that?" she said.

"Because 'rape' is something that happens between strangers, maybe between a football player and a cheerleader in an alley," I said. "And that's not what happened to me."

"Because you knew the person," Siobhán said, and I nodded.

"I don't even know the person who did this to you, and I'm angry at them," she said, and her voice, rich with an Irish lilt, intensified. "You know, we're all responsible for what happened to you. When we only see in the word 'rape' one thing—a stereotype—then you're the one who suffers for it, and it shouldn't be falling to you alone to try to explain. Your experience deserves to belong in the words, and we all need to make space for it."

Up until that point, it had never occurred to me that sexual harm wasn't just harm that occurred between individuals, but in that moment, I learned from Siobhán that what appears to be an individual violation is actually the culmination of a number of systemic wrongs. That conversation also became my introduction to thinking about how the words we say and the stories we tell are both individual enterprises *and* collective ones that we all, to some extent, participate in and shape. Scholars have at times labeled these overarching stories differently—as "discourses," "embedded beliefs," or what I refer to as "dominant stories." While these concepts aren't synonymous, they share in common the idea that ways of knowing are able to be passed along between individuals and groups, often without us even noticing. When I speak of "dominant stories," then, what I mean is that we often inherit stories from the dominant culture. These stories impart ways of knowing that affect the assumptions we make and the way we interpret what we hear. They're also often wide-reaching, insidious, unchecked, and passed from generation to generation. What I'd like to do in this chapter, then, is to consider some of these dominant stories that shape our collective interpretation of rape, specifically Christianity's use of masculine language and its emphasis on purity culture, the way that the mental health field constructs posttraumatic stress disorder, and the way that journalists frame stories of harm through the use of evidence. I will address another dominant story—the one told by the legal community—in this book's final chapter on restorative justice.

Christianity's Complicity in Sexual Harm

Back in chapter 1, I discussed how the embedded belief that God should be represented by masculine language causes that language to be either idolatrous or irrelevant. This is one example of a powerful embedded belief within Christianity that ultimately causes epistemic harm to many, including those who have experienced sexual harms. This epistemic harm—a form of harm that relates to how we construct knowledge—occurs because such language intimates that certain bodies are more like God (more *imago Dei*) and certain bodies bear less of a resemblance. In practice, such language winds up privileging normative male bodies at the expense of others. However, language is not the only place where Christianity privileges masculinity in a way that directly creates epistemic difficulties for those who experience sexual violations. Purity culture and male-dominated leadership within denominations are two other examples of such practices.

The Loud Speech of Christian Purity Culture

Purity culture is a prominent part of evangelical Christianity in the United States and proposes that Christians—especially women—should refrain from sexual contact outside the context of heterosexual marriage in order to maintain purity. This faith commitment emerges from a literal interpretation of Thessalonians 4:3–8, in which Paul writes that Christians should control their bodies and refrain from sexual immorality because God judges individuals based on their purity. It results not just in ideological commitments but practical actions, including purity pledges (pledges taken by teenagers and young adults in which they promise to abstain from sex before marriage), purity rings (worn to symbolize the pledge taken), and purity balls attended by fathers and their teenage daughters, in which fathers often sign pledges where they promise to be examples of purity.

In practice, purity culture winds up penalizing women not just for sex outside of marriage but also for sexual acts that occur in violating situations, because the movement tends to make no clear distinction between desired and undesired sex acts. As a result, women who hold purity culture as an embedded belief, a cornerstone of their faith, may feel that a sexual violation renders them spiritually impure.[1] Their communities may as well. Case in point: Elizabeth Smart—who has become widely known as someone who drew heavily on her Mormon faith as a positive coping source during her nine-month-long kidnapping—criticized the role that purity culture plays in the lives of individuals who experienced sexual harm, drawing upon her own memory of sitting in a high school Christian education session (called "Seminary" in the Mormon faith) after returning from her captivity. She remarks that the teacher told her and the other students in the class that "You're like this beautiful fence . . . and you hammer these nails in, and then every time you have sex with someone else, it's like you're hammering in another nail. And you can take them out, you can repent of them, but the holes are still there."[2]

After the class, in which the teachers did not know that Smart had been raped while in captivity, Smart states that she thought,

> This is terrible. Do they not realize I'm sitting in class? Do they not realize that I'm listening to what they're saying? Those are terrible analogies. No one should use them, period. . . . Especially

for someone who's been raped, they've already felt these feelings of worthlessness, of filth, of just—of just being so crushed, and then to hear a teacher come back and say, "Nobody wants you now"... You just think, I should just die right now.... Statistically speaking, I'm not the only girl that's ever been raped. And those kinds of analogies, they stick with people.[3]

Smart's analysis of what happened in her class emblematizes that purity culture can often function as a source of harm within the Christian community because the commitment to sexual purity winds up enabling beliefs about personal responsibility, guilt, and shame among those who have been raped.[4] Moreover, even if women and girls do not have direct experiences of sexual harm, the power that purity culture has in their own lives may lead them to believe that they're responsible for the harm done to others because of the way that purity culture constructs their bodies as temptresses to insatiable male desires.[5] In practice, this means that when a man sexually violates a woman, it is the fault of both the woman who was harmed *and* women who may have tempted the man at other points in time.[6]

In the end, purity culture both endangers the epistemic resources available to those who experience sexual violations *and* promotes practices that enable sexual violations in the future. In particular, the belief that women inherently tempt men's sexual desires encourages misogynistic embedded beliefs and practices, most notably the belief that women should be subservient to men both within church settings and within the household. This kind of hierarchical gender essentialism sets up the conditions for sexual violations to occur by priming women to both see themselves as lesser than men while simultaneously teaching women that they are responsible for men's unhealthy sexual urges so that when they are on the receiving end of a violation, they can find fault with no one but themselves.[7]

Critics of Christianity might argue that this is precisely why organized religion should be outed as a primary perpetuator of systemic oppression, including misogyny, rather than as any kind of positive spiritual resource.

However, this kind of critique is reductive on two counts. First, it is theologically reductive, given that a primary belief of many Christians is that all human beings, not just men, are made in the image of God (Gen. 1:28). Additionally, it ignores the ways that Christianity can offer positive resources for coping with difficult events if those resources promote meaning-making, connection, and belief in a non-punitive God.[8] The issue, therefore, is not so much with Christianity on the whole but the extent to which certain Christians have coopted the narrative of what Christianity is such that—to invoke the words that Senator Dianne Feinstein spoke to Amy Coney Barrett during her Supreme Court nomination hearing—the dogma of this segment of Christianity speaks loudly.[9] This loud way of speaking Christianity violates so much of what Jesus himself said about honoring all human beings, especially the marginalized and victimized. Yet purity culture is not the only place where this kind of distorted dogma speaks loudly. It also speaks loudly in denominations where individuals are excluded from leadership positions on the basis of their bodies.

The Loud Speech of Christian Male Leadership

Sallie McFague was one of the first theologians to voice concerns about how the language used to describe God reinforces patriarchal practices in Christianity. Historically, the Christian vocabulary for God has been dominated by male identifiers and pronouns, like "He" or "Father."[10] These emerged for complex reasons ranging from the way that many—but not all—of the Hebrew pronouns to describe the Divine are masculine to Jesus's description of God as "Father." Christians who had the power to shape the central embedded beliefs of the faith—who were, up until recently, almost exclusively men as well—interpreted these pronouns to be signifiers of reality rather than reflections of linguistic and social constructions.[11] The dominant masculine language used to describe God has, therefore, been used to justify masculine dominance within the faith at large, leading to practices including exclusively male leadership in churches to the idea that men ought to be the spiritual heads of families or the belief that only men are made in the image of Jesus (and therefore God).

McFague does a compelling job of reminding Christians that the act of God-naming has practical implications and that it can do concrete harm when terms support patriarchal agendas. In many instances, the patriarchal practices that have been justified by the theological conviction that God is male have been used to subordinate women and to justify or cover up the sexual violations that have occurred both inside and outside of church walls. This is perhaps most paradigmatically illustrated by the extreme levels of sexual harm enacted by leaders of the Roman Catholic Church, a church body that only ordains men, in part because of their theological conviction that the essentially male identity of Christ was also an essential part of his identity at large. That—coupled with the Roman Catholic Church's commitment to natural law—allows the Church to conclude that only men can represent Christ (be *Alter Christus*) as priests because they are the only ones who share Christ's maleness.[12]

The consequence of these constructions of gender is that many victimized Catholics were taught to see the male body—specifically the ordained male body—as ontologically superior to other bodies. Indeed, this is something Roman Catholic priests have exploited, with many victimized individuals stating that one reason they did not report the harm was that the priest who abused them justified the harm in reference to their identity as a priest. They might have said something to the effect of, "This is God's will" or "This is a way for you to enact penance for sin." Additionally, victimized individuals often felt that what happened to them couldn't count as abuse because someone who'd been called to represent Christ was incapable of wrongdoing. Such spiritual manipulation is an example of how the construction of male bodies enables rape and leads to guilt, shame, and distress in victimized individuals.

The construction of gender within an organization like the Roman Catholic Church not only contributes to epistemic struggles for victims but also cashes out in structures that seem incapable of hearing what victims say when they do dare to come forward with a claim of wrongdoing.[13]

Indeed, numerous news articles have documented how the Roman Catholic Church's hierarchy has all too often refused to believe victims or responded by simply moving the priest to another parish, as if removing the victimized person from the priest's daily life would prevent future harm. Others have said their claims were not taken seriously because they had no credibility as a woman or child speaking up against a man who was a priest.[14] Such denial within the church hierarchy was enabled by the embedded beliefs about gender and God within the organization itself.

What instances like the scandals that have rocked the Roman Catholic Church demonstrate is that the construction of bodies can perform in ways that enable harm at an individual and systemic level. It becomes reductive, therefore, to blame only individual priests for their sexual wrongdoings when those acts were also supported by beliefs in the church about God's gender and reinforced by a hierarchy that benefited from it. Put into Sallie McFague's terms, maleness in Roman Catholicism came to function as an idol that male bodies with power (aka priests) could exploit to enact sexual harm. The language used for God only further authorized such wrongdoing, because the exclusively male identifiers prevented other kinds of conceptions of divinity, which might have been feminine or gender-neutral. So while it would be reductive to say that the male language for God alone caused this and other sexual harms within Christian denominations, it does seem appropriate to suggest that the embedded beliefs about gender that manifest in the dominant words used to describe God in Christianity have performed in ways that impact how Christians, violators, communities, and victimized parties have interpreted the harm done.

The Construction of the Traumatic Event

The mental health community has been essential to shaping the public understanding of rape, including the scope of wrong and the consequences of it. And while the mental health community's efforts have undoubtedly been critical to alleviating suffering and destigmatizing sexual harm, their work has also emerged from and within dominant culture and its embedded beliefs. This has, in turn, affected how this community has framed the nature and scope of wrongdoing, and how the public perceives it. One way this evidences itself is through the history of posttraumatic stress disorder (PTSD) and the shifting ways it defines the contours of traumatic harm. That shift has had a hand in crafting what I will call a post-rape script that affects how the mental health community and public define who is a legitimate rape survivor.

Mental health experts had been studying how humans responded to trauma for close to a century before the diagnosis of PTSD finally appeared in the third edition of the *Diagnostic and Statistical Manual of Mental Disorders* (*DSM*)—the diagnostic manual used by mental health practitioners—in 1980.[15] Back in the late 1800s, Charcot proposed that both men and women could suffer from trauma-induced hysteria. Pierre Janet observed that dissociation could arise from traumatic events and thwart a person's mental wellbeing, while the German neurologist Hermann Oppenheim proposed that the nervous system—and not hysteria—caused the symptoms we now associate with posttraumatic stress.[16]

In 1952, the American Psychiatric Association released its first iteration of the *DSM*, the manual that first provided a comprehensive classification of psychological illnesses. PTSD was not mentioned in that edition. Rather, the American Psychiatric Association described something called "Gross Stress Reaction," which was believed to occur among "more or less 'normal' persons who have experienced intolerable stress."[17] Interestingly, the manual suggests taking an etiological, rather than a phenomenological, approach to the disorder, meaning that it defines the disorder through an originating event rather than through symptoms alone. In other words, this form of psychiatric illness did not just arise out of thin air. It emerged because of a precipitating event. In this way, the disorder is unique among psychological illnesses in that it requires the presence of an etiological agent—an originating event—that causes the symptoms. Indeed, in the current *DSM-5*, trauma and stressor-induced disorders remain the only disorders to include etiological rather than exclusively phenomenological criteria for diagnosis.[18] But remember that the etiological event can't just be *any* event. It must be a specific *type* of event, the kind that the mental health community believes will precipitate the reaction.

Rape wasn't included in this early version of the *DSM*. Instead, the manual suggests that this kind of reaction is most likely to emerge following military combat or a "civilian catastrophe," such as bearing witness to an explosion or waking up to a fire in one's home.[19] The researchers believed this reaction would be short-lived, that it was "transient" and would most likely clear quickly with treatment, and if it didn't, then the manual encouraged clinicians to consider a form of neurosis.

Of note here is who is included in the originating event and who is not—by suggesting that the primary driver of this kind of reaction was combat, it limited the scope of who might be diagnosed to men. It was justifiable, then, when these symptoms appeared in their bodies, but a woman who was raped was an entirely different story. Recall that well into the twentieth century, spousal rape was legal in many jurisdictions, both within the United States and abroad. England, for instance, allowed spousal rape under the system of coverture, which proposed that upon marriage, a woman lost any legal rights of her own, making her sexual violation permissible. Similar laws existed in the United States, with spousal rape remaining legal in at least some states until the 1990s.[20] Rape inside of a marriage was therefore permissible, but trauma on the part of the raped woman was not. Rather than being seen as traumatized, a woman who exhibited the same symptoms as a man in combat due to rape would have been dismissed or labeled as hysterical. This was most paradigmatically evidenced decades earlier in the case of Louise Augustine Gleizes, a French woman treated by Charcot long before the first *DSM* was released. Charcot—one of the earliest and most significant trauma researchers—labeled her symptoms as hysteria, despite a history of childhood rape which he failed to acknowledge and treat. Gleizes was eventually placed in solitary confinement when she refused to be photographed by

Charcot and the colleagues who visited to see her hysteria in action. She later disguised herself in men's clothes and ran away from the hospital where she was being held, never to be seen again. Charcot, meanwhile, became famous for his treatment of her, as well as for the work he did to establish trauma reactions in men. Yet he never did connect the dots that women could be trauma victims or that rape could precipitate a posttraumatic stress reaction.

As it relates to the first iteration of the *DSM*, then, the exclusivity of the originating event meant that individuals who experienced rape—most of whom were women—found no legitimacy of their posttraumatic symptoms through a diagnosis. This made it easier to vilify the woman's character rather than the harm for her behavior in the aftermath of rape, which, in turn, made it easier to maintain systems of misogyny that benefited from women's denigration. Hence, it was convenient to say that women were not traumatized—they were out of control, dramatic, unreliable narrators of their own story, and liars. Rape was not the cause of their symptoms because rape was a harm that lacked legitimacy. The problem, quite simply, was them.[21]

Matters did not improve when psychiatric experts revised the first edition of the *DSM* in 1968. In that edition, they removed the disorder known as "Gross Stress Reaction" and replaced it with something referred to as "Transient Situational Disturbance," which was described as temporary psychological distress emerging from a stressor among individuals "without any apparent underlying mental disorders." As in the first iteration of the *DSM*, this edition suggested that the symptoms should last only for a short period of time—regardless of their severity—and that clinicians should look to alternative diagnoses if they persisted.[22] But what is perhaps most worth noting about the *DSM-II* is that it maintained that this form of psychiatric illness did not just arise out of thin air; it arose because of exposure to a potentially traumatic event, and yet, rape was not named as a potential trigger.

In 1980, the American Psychiatric Association released the *DSM-III*, codifying posttraumatic stress disorder under that name for the first time. Just as the manuals before it, the criterion for the originating event reflected dominant embedded beliefs about the scope of what was considered traumatic. In this iteration, the originating event was described as an event that "is outside the range of usual human experience and that would be markedly distressing to almost anyone."[23] What kind of event, however, should be *expected* to evoke significant symptoms of distress in almost everyone, and what are the parameters for an event to be considered outside of the realm of "usual human experience?" Long-term physical and emotional child abuse might fit the bill, as would the experience of being interned in a concentration camp, or witnessing combat atrocities. But what about a single instance of rape or long-term workplace sexual harassment? Recall that in the decades prior to the release of the third *DSM*, women's rights advocates were raising awareness about the pervasiveness of sexual harm. In 1979—the year prior to the *DSM*'s release—law professor Catharine MacKinnon published *Sexual Harassment of Working Women*, which catapulted the term "sexual harassment" into the vocabulary of the American public. Yet if awareness was growing about the nature and scope of rape, this particular iteration of the etiological criteria seems to fail to account for the regularity with which it occurs and results in posttraumatic stress.

Indeed, leaders in the mental health community themselves recognized the need to revise this criterion after the *DSM-III* release, in part because it was difficult to assess what would be distressing to a wide variety of people. Experts like Judith Herman also questioned the assumption that trauma existed in some distant sphere that was distinct from daily life.[24] As she writes:

> Rape, battery, and other forms of sexual and domestic violence are so common a part of women's lives that they can hardly be described as outside the range of ordinary experience. And in view of the number of people killed in war over the past century, military trauma, too, must be considered part of human experience; only the fortunate find it unusual.[25]

Herman is correct that it's unrealistic to assume that sexual traumas are rare and unusual, something worth gaping at because of their exoticness, when it's estimated that a violation occurs once every 73 seconds in the United States.[26] It is neither exotic nor rare but as ordinary as a McDonald's on a turnpike, an assumed part of life in the United States that we don't question because we don't notice. Moreover, data show that rape is not only likely but more likely than other potentially traumatic events to cause a PTSD reaction, due to the stigma and isolation associated with the event.[27] In the wake of the *DSM-III* release, then, awareness began to be raised about who was being left out of the diagnostic criteria and who, in turn, was able to find their suffering identified, validated, and labeled by mental health experts. Put differently, experts like Herman—who were drawing attention to the regularity with which women in particular were subjected to sexual harm—were also destigmatizing it so that distress could be reconceptualized not as an abnormal reaction to an unproblematic event but as a legitimate reaction to an event that never should have occurred in the first place.

The psychiatrists who crafted the *DSM-IV* recognized the need to widen the scope of harm, responding to the question of what constituted a traumatic event with a bracket creep, meaning they expanded what might qualify as the event that caused a posttraumatic response. This version abandoned the assumption that traumatic events were rare, and, equally significantly, it also dropped the assumption that there was some inherent quality to the traumatic event that would be predictably traumatizing. The result was that the *DSM-IV*'s definition of the etiological agent was split into two components, one of which described the pragmatics of the event while the other described someone's reaction to it. As it reads:

1. The person experienced, witnessed, or was confronted with an event or events that involved actual or threatened death or serious injury, or a threat to the physical integrity of self or others.

2. The person's response involved intense fear, helplessness, or horror. Note: In children, this may be expressed instead by disorganized or agitated behavior.[28]

These criteria assert that posttraumatic stress is evoked by a combination of both the practicalities of the event *and* the way the person processes it, meaning that whatever causes an event to be processed as a trauma isn't solely embedded in the event itself but rather has, at least partially, to do with the individual's experience of it. This was progress. Individuals who were raped could potentially locate their experience in these criteria, especially if their experience aligned with the dominant rape script and involved physical violence.

Nonetheless, this attempt at codifying the originating event for PTSD remained imperfect. Closer examination of the *DSM-IV*'s Criterion A reveals a number of complexities, first among them that the most severe stressors don't always cause a posttraumatic stress reaction, although rates of PTSD remain higher for sexual violations than other potentially traumatic events.[29] In other words, not everyone who experiences a sexual violation will develop PTSD.[30] Moreover, the reasons why an individual may develop PTSD may correlate with the specifics of the event but are not limited to them, as data show that factors like resiliency[31] and disorganized attachment early in life[32] are also predictors of the likelihood that a potentially traumatic event will result in PTSD.

There was another consequence to the changes to the PTSD criteria—individuals who were raped could now be expected to find their experiences within the diagnosis, especially if their cases went to court. But not all did find themselves within it, which could result in challenges to their credibility. Lawyers, for instance, could question the truth of a victimized party if they didn't seem particularly traumatized after the event. This might particularly backfire in the case of those who experience a sexual violation with a partner and then go out with that partner again because they believe their experiences do not meet the threshold for harm. Individuals who are victimized in this way may also be more likely to brush aside symptoms of PTSD because they haven't labeled the event as a wrong.

The development of the *DSM-IV*'s criterion for the originating event thus had the unintended consequence of helping to craft what I refer to as a post-rape script that encapsulates how an authentic victim presents in the aftermath of harm and encapsulates what's considered to be an acceptable response: Individuals should be able to quickly name what occurred. Ideally, they will have gone to the police or the hospital, told a teacher, reported the event to a friend or parent. PTSD quickly follows, perhaps along with suicidal ideation, depression, addiction, an eating disorder.

Bonus points for tears.

The post-rape script can cause us to judge victimized individuals in the days, months, and years following their violations, just as it may result in negative judgment on those who did not seem to suffer enough. Suffering, we have decided, becomes a victim. Indeed, it becomes a gateway for our sympathy, perhaps because the visible pain of someone suffering others them from ourselves.

"At least," we think, "we have been spared that horror."

This post-rape script of posttraumatic stress—of suffering—can also limit someone's ability to name wrongdoing.[33] Consider, for example, the story of Amy, a college student who passed out while drunk and woke up to discover that a man she had been kissing "was masturbating in my mouth."[34] Amy told this story to Donna Freitas, a professor who researches sexual violations, and it was Freitas—not Amy—who seemed disturbed about the event. As she writes:

> I sat there, sick from the images Amy's story provoked, saddened by the way she breezed past the experience as if it was nothing. How could something that, to me, was a clear-cut case of sexual assault seem to Amy merely another hookup gone awry? Even more worrisome: How could she so easily shrug it off?[35]

I think I can answer the questions Freitas poses, because my reaction to my own rape was, initially at least, very much like Amy's. It didn't fit into the narrative of the post-rape script that we've corporately subscribed to as a culture. I didn't label the wrong at the time because it didn't match the rape script, and while I did experience psychological symptoms resonant with PTSD, they only emerged—or I only took notice of them—after a latency period. Initially, at least, there was nothing to name because there was no reaction to name.

My assumptions about that night only began to shift when my reaction began to more closely mirror the post-rape script, and it became harder to ignore the symptoms I was experiencing. But even this was a subtle shift that occurred over a long period of time. My first memory of psychological distress occurred approximately two months after the attack, when I sat down to take a final exam in class and found that I couldn't concentrate or make sense of the essay prompt, almost as if I'd lost the ability to read. Nothing like this had ever happened to me before, and I was thrown not just by the anxiety but by how alien the feeling was to anything I'd ever felt in the past. I walked up to the teaching assistant and asked to leave, blushing, explaining that I was sorry but that I felt lightheaded and couldn't seem to read any of the words on the test. She let me go without further questions, and I blamed my reaction on end of the semester stress, but the anxiety didn't dissipate after the semester ended. It only got worse, which confused me, because there were no more tests to take.

Shortly after that, I began to have nightmares about getting coerced into sexual activity against my will. They weren't like other nightmares I'd had before, which I could clearly locate as the stuff of cognitive creativity, fantasy, mystery. I would wake up suddenly from each of these nightmares sweating, sometimes screaming, gagging for breath as if I'd been strangled, and with the sensation that I was reliving something that I'd experienced but couldn't place. The closest thing I can relate it to is *lethologica*, also known as tip-of-the-tongue syndrome, only this was more of a tip-of-the-body syndrome, what I might call *lethesoma*.[36] The surreal thing was that I hadn't forgotten the attack or the feelings I had during it; I just couldn't seem to make the connection between the sensations I had then and the sensations I was experiencing in the dreams.

This sense of *lethesoma* became more intense with time, coupled with increasingly crippling anxiety and the resurgence of an eating disorder. I don't remember when the heightened startle response kicked in, but by the time that two years had passed, I found myself on the phone with one of my psychology professors, telling her that I was planning to drop out of graduate school because I couldn't concentrate, was chronically worried and distracted, was afraid to sleep alone in my apartment, and struggled to get to class because my startle response was so sensitive that I inadvertently swerved whenever another car passed me and it didn't feel safe to drive. I thought I had an anxiety disorder and asked for a referral to a therapist; my professor suggested that I begin seeing someone at the university's anxiety disorder clinic, which I did.

I provided that therapist with no etiological event, no affirmative answer to Criterion A1 for PTSD, and so, presumably because I answered "no" during the intake to the question of whether I was ever raped, the therapist diagnosed me with generalized anxiety disorder (GAD) and not with PTSD. To the best of my knowledge, she didn't change the diagnosis when I began to talk about the rape in our sessions; however, once I did speak about it, I looked to the *DSM-IV*'s definition of PTSD for some context and recognized that many of the symptoms of PTSD overlapped with the symptoms of GAD. While I didn't really care what my diagnosis was as long as my therapist was able to help, I remember thinking that perhaps I was an illegitimate victim because I had developed the wrong psychological disorder.

My own wrestling with my lack of a PTSD diagnosis made me curious about Criterion A1. I wondered about the specifics of what it meant to have one's "physical integrity" threatened—was the threshold strangulation or did blood need to be drawn or was being pushed against a wall enough? I wanted a scale, some kind of objective ranking system by which I could quantify what constituted harm, which was really a way of saying that I wanted some external validation of my internal reaction. I hadn't yet realized that the sources we see as authoritative, the embedded beliefs that we implicitly privilege, are fallible constructs, and so when I couldn't see myself within the diagnostic criteria, my reaction was to blame myself—and not the rape—for the distress.

My questions and insecurity show the power that normative sources can have on the interpretative process of someone who's experienced rape, especially if they're not naming the event as such.[37] However, it's also an example of how we look to diagnoses for validation. This, perhaps, becomes most relevant in a courtroom or even a Title IX proceeding where a victimized person is asked about the impact of the event, and then their credibility is judged based on how they respond. If they never received a PTSD diagnosis, then they could be criticized for not suffering enough or in the right way. After all, if rape is supposed to be that bad, then shouldn't they have posttraumatic stress? But to have a diagnosis, they have to be able to name the event, and that isn't always easy to do. Of course, a diagnosis isn't always validating for a victim: Even in cases where a person does have a diagnosis, their credibility can still be attacked based upon their emotions. If they respond with no emotion or with too much calmness, they're deemed cold or unrelatable, and jurors may think they're lying or out of touch with the severity of the event. In contrast, too many tears or too much struggle signals that the victimized party is histrionic and unreliable.

Unrelatable or unreliable—it's a fine line to walk.

In some ways, the way that PTSD has been used to validate "real victims" is not the fault of the mental health community, so much as it is the fault of those who use its knowledge without noting that the field—like all fields of knowledge—is both fallible and still in the process of discovering. No one field of knowledge has all the answers, though I fear that far too many among us disagree with me.[38] But in the case of mental health, failing to acknowledge its fallibility affects how and whether victims speak, affording those victims with experiences that led to a PTSD diagnosis greater credibility than those whose experiences did not involve one. The mental health community, therefore, has tremendous power over the grand narrative of sexual harm, which is ironic, given that this same community oftentimes seeks to hand narrative agency back to individuals during therapy.[39] It also shows how important it is for practitioners in the field to remind their clients—and themselves—that diagnoses are not only constructs but the product of a field still in the process of learning about rape.⁴⁰

This is why an inclusive PTSD definition matters so much. It symbolizes that mental health experts recognize that trauma is not quantifiable. It is based on impact. Recognizing that alone may provide validation for those who are suffering in isolation, who can't seem to find themselves within the diagnosis and therefore don't seek help. The power of this validation is something I've experienced. I recall a conversation with a psychology professor while I was in graduate school where I explained that I had symptoms of anxiety but certainly didn't have posttraumatic stress, and this was, to me, a sign that I hadn't been raped.

"But you startle easily?" she said.

"Yes," I said.

"You dissociate?"

"Yes."

"You avoid places associated with the event?"

"I do."

"And you have flashbacks?"

"No. I only relive everything in my sleep. I don't think it happens as much when I'm awake." I went on to describe what was happening in the dreams, how I responded, how I woke up.

"Those are flashbacks," she said.

"But it's in my sleep," I said. "That doesn't count."

"It counts," she said. "Trauma doesn't have 9–5 hours. It operates round the clock."

At the time this conversation occurred, I was struggling to accept that any harm occurred, and I felt that I was losing my mind because I was experiencing psychological distress for no discernable reason. I had also taken the initiative to reach out to this professor, who was wise enough to recognize that it might be helpful to offer the external validation of an expert, of a disorder, of a symptom, because validation offered words and words offered a way to make sense of what seemed like the embodied version of a non sequitur. Having a name for what I was experiencing in the present eventually helped me feel more comfortable naming the Criterion A from my own past, a criterion that, shortly thereafter, would change again.

A couple of years after I read the *DSM-IV* PTSD definition, the manual underwent another significant revision that changed the criteria. This iteration eradicated Criterion A2—"The person's response involved intense fear, helplessness, or horror"—because the criterion was too subjective to evaluate. It also furthered the bracket creep seen in the *DSM-IV* so that individuals could be diagnosed with PTSD if they were exposed to a wider variety of events than those previously assumed to instantiate a posttraumatic stress response. It includes individuals who may have experienced harm, witnessed harm done to another, or learned of harm done to a friend or relative.[41] According to the *DSM-5*, the originating event now requires:

> Death, threatened death, actual or threatened serious injury, or actual or threatened sexual violence, in the following way(s):
>
> - Direct exposure
> - Witnessing the trauma
> - Learning that a relative or close friend was exposed to a trauma
> - Indirect exposure to aversive details of the trauma, usually in the course of professional duties (e.g., first responders, medics)

This latest bracket creep is certainly helpful to those with experiences of sexual violations, insofar as it creates more space for them to label harm using privileged psychological knowledge. No longer are originating events outside of human experience; no longer is the threat to physical integrity necessary. No longer does the mental health community see such events as exotic, and no longer is rape excluded. Put differently, when someone is suffering, having a framework for understanding it is helpful both for that individual and for their community. This latest definition provides a wider scope for naming, and it helps those who are suffering to realize that they are not having an abnormal response to an acceptable event but rather a normal response to an unacceptable event.

On the flipside, while the authors of the PTSD diagnosis recognized a need to further the bracket creep in order to more accurately represent the scope of what can cause a PTSD reaction, the continuing expansion leads to the question of whether Criterion A1 needs to be included in the PTSD definition at all. No other diagnosis in the *DSM* requires an originating event, including major depression, generalized anxiety disorder, and phobias, which all have significant symptomatic overlap with PTSD. Additionally, it runs the risk of continuing to be impacted by embedded beliefs about the nature and scope of harm that might be implicitly or explicitly motivated by sexism, racism, and other forms of intersectional systemic oppression.

Moreover, this criterion is always going to fail to represent the scope of what causes a posttraumatic stress reaction because there are so many ways that individuals experience and interpret a potentially traumatic event. Factors that affect overall wellness after it include not only the practicalities of it but also interpersonal support, internal resilience, systemic oppression, prior experiences, and neurobiology. The presence or absence of PTSD is contingent on all of these factors, making it impossible to predict based on Criterion A1 alone. Indeed, psychological studies reflect this, showing that complicated childbirth and the death of a farmer's animals can precipitate symptoms of PTSD, as can the belief that one has been abducted by aliens.[42] None of these are named as etiological events by Criterion A1. And if posttraumatic stress can emerge from an event that did not actually occur—unless one believes in alien abduction—then this raises profound problems for evaluating the credibility of victims based on the presence of PTSD symptoms because it lends credence to the possibility that it is possible to fabricate a story of harm and develop posttraumatic stress nonetheless. When one adds this to data that show that not everyone who experiences a sexual event that legally qualifies as rape acknowledges it or experiences PTSD symptoms as a result of it, then once again, one is left asking whether PTSD should be given so much authority to determine whether harm occurred. Indeed, we might ask whether the expectation that PTSD will develop in the aftermath of rape imposes a narrative of harm that tells people's stories for them, rather than giving them the narrative agency to construct the story themselves. It also neglects that trauma may be said to move both horizontally through time within the life of an individual and vertically across generations. In such cases of intergenerational trauma, the person seeking support did not directly experience the etiological event and may not even know what it is. Seeking therapeutic support for trauma symptoms, therefore, becomes epistemically and logistically complicated.

PTSD, in short, possesses enormous power in the imagination of the American public. On television shows about rape, rarely does a victimized character get portrayed without symptoms presenting. This is progress insofar as it validates and destigmatizes the suffering of many who have experienced a sexual violation. However, it also sets up the expectation that those who have been raped will necessarily become psychologically traumatized. The mental health community has therefore assisted significantly in raising awareness about the scope of sexual harm, even as it has at times adopted dominant embedded beliefs that kept those who survived a sexual violation from naming the wrong and validating their suffering.

Finally, one of the benefits of embedding an originating event in the PTSD diagnostic criteria is that it squarely locates the cause of suffering in it rather than in a potential character deficiency. This can be helpful in eliminating stigma against individuals who experience the disorder, but this is only the case if the disorder is actually diagnosed. Unfortunately, data show that implicit bias among counselors can result in diagnoses of oppositional defiant disorder (ODD) or conduct disorder (CD) in Black and Latinx youth rather than posttraumatic stress disorder, even when individuals meet the criteria for PTSD.[43] As a result, individuals from minoritized backgrounds may find that they face additional barriers to getting their psychological needs met, both because of the misdiagnoses and because these disorders do not have etiologies embedded within them, thereby making it easier—which is not the same as appropriate—to attribute fault for disruptive or unhealthy behaviors to global deficits in one's character. Implicit bias from dominant embedded beliefs in the United States, therefore, continues to impact the care that those who have experienced harm desperately need, such that it becomes continually necessary to evaluate the power that intersectional systemic oppression has in our ways of identifying the scope and impact of sexual harm on those who have been impacted by it.

Case in point: Black girls are more likely to be labeled as promiscuous or seen as unrapeable. If they have a history of sexual violations and act out in school, defiant with teachers and rude with other students, then they may be more likely to be diagnosed with ODD or CD, even though PTSD could also account for their irrational outbursts of anger. Moreover, because there is no originating event in ODD or CD, it may be more tempting for teachers to label Black girls as "bad" or "difficult" and to adopt an overall negative view of their character. A diagnosis of PTSD, in contrast, would help combat the stereotype that Black girls are unrapeable, reconceptualize the reason for irrational outbursts of anger by locating it in the originating event, and would provide more appropriate therapeutic support. This hypothetical example, therefore, suggests that implicit bias from dominant embedded beliefs in the United States continues to impact the care that those who have experienced sexual harm desperately need. It thus becomes necessary to continually evaluate the power that intersectional systemic oppression has in our ways of naming the effects of sexual harm in those who need psychological support.

How Journalists Tell Stories and the Ambiguous Case Against Aziz Ansari

As the #MeToo movement gained traction back in 2018, journalist Katie Way broke the story of an accusation of sexual assault against Aziz Ansari on the now defunct Babe.net site.[44] In the article, Way chronicled the night in which a young woman—identified only by the pseudonym of

"Grace"—describes going to dinner with Ansari, who, she says, paid for her meal, "did most of the talking," and made the executive decision of when to leave the restaurant and go to his apartment. After Ansari began kissing Grace in the apartment, she says she objected and asked to slow down. Grace then stated that Ansari performed oral sex on her and asked that she reciprocate the act, which she says she did:

> She [Grace] says Ansari began making a move on her that he repeated during their encounter. "The move he kept doing was taking his two fingers in a V-shape and putting them in my mouth, in my throat to wet his fingers, because the moment he'd stick his fingers in my throat he'd go straight for my vagina and try to finger me." Grace called the move "the claw." Ansari also physically pulled her hand towards his penis multiple times throughout the night, from the time he first kissed her on the countertop onward. "He probably moved my hand to his dick five to seven times," she said. "He really kept doing it after I moved it away."
>
> But the main thing was that he wouldn't let her move away from him. She compared the path they cut across his apartment to a football play. "It was 30 minutes of me getting up and moving and him following and sticking his fingers down my throat again. It was really repetitive. It felt like a fucking game."[45]

Grace says she attempted to physically and verbally signal her lack of interest, but reports that Ansari either didn't notice or didn't care. She describes eventually separating herself by going to the bathroom and splashing water on her face, and when she returned, she says she told Ansari that she didn't want to feel pressured to engage in sexual activity, at which point, he suggested they sit together on the couch. He took a seat. She sat on the floor, and then Grace reports that:

> Ansari instructed her to turn around. "He sat back and pointed to his penis and motioned for me to go down on him. And I did.

> I think I just felt really pressured. It was literally the most unexpected thing I thought would happen at that moment because I told him I was uncomfortable."
>
> Soon, he pulled her back up onto the couch. She would tell her friend via text later that night, "He [made out] with me again and says, 'Doesn't look like you hate me.'"⁴⁶

Grace says she again objected when Ansari pulled out a large mirror, had her bend over and imitated sex, and so he stopped the sexual interaction and sat with her on the couch to watch "Seinfeld."

Then he reportedly began to kiss her again.

Grace says she left the apartment shortly thereafter and texted Ansari the next day to explain that she was uncomfortable with the encounter. Ansari responded: "Clearly, I misread the moment and I'm truly sorry."⁴⁷

So what actually happened in this encounter? Easy to establish facts include that a high-profile, wealthy man took a woman to dinner. He bought her wine. Then things get murky from a journalistic perspective: Grace says Ansari sexually pursued her like a cat chasing a mouse, and then ensued a cycle where she either felt reticent or verbally objected until she left Ansari's apartment. The event is uncomfortable to read about, and yet, was there wrong done and if so, how did journalists label it? Within the article itself, journalist Katie Way made a determinative claim, referring to the event as a "sexual assault." Not every journalist agreed with her, however.

Inez Stepman, a senior commentator for the *Federalist* Tweeted that "If that Aziz Ansari story is rape than [*sic*] everyone who has been on the modern dating scene has been both victim and perpetrator. You all said you didn't want courtship, you wanted sexual liberation. Welcome."⁴⁸

Ashley Banfield, who was a news anchor for HLN at the time, spent over four minutes on air reading an open letter to Grace in which she said,

> You had a bad date.... Is that what victimized you to the point of seeking a public conviction and a career-ending sentence against

him [Ansari]? ... If you were sexually assaulted, you should go to the police right now. ... What you have done in my opinion is appalling. You went to the press.[49]

Bari Weiss, a writer for the *New York Times* simply said, "This Aziz Ansari story is deeply irresponsible journalism."[50]

What I'm curious about here is why this accusation became so divisive, an example of "deeply irresponsible journalism," when similar articles published at the time, such as those documenting the Harvey Weinstein allegations, did not.

Some members of the journalism community were quite transparent about their concerns. Caitlin Flanagan accused Katie Way of not giving Ansari enough time to respond to the accusation and of depicting the night so graphically that it amounted to pornography.[51] Others, like Inez Stepman, seemed to think the encounter simply wasn't bad enough to be wrong, especially when compared with the accusations being made at the same time about Harvey Weinstein. In contrast to the Weinstein claims—which were numerous, consistent, and levied by multiple women, many of whom were revered, wealthy, white household names who could provide documentation in the form of settlement claims—the charge against Ansari appeared hazy. As *New York Times* journalists Jodi Kantor and Megan Twohey write, "It was hard to tell whether his [Ansari's] behavior was just overeager and clueless or worse."[52]

Why was it that hard? Here's where I'd like to bring awareness to some principles that guide the journalists and their assessment of wrongdoing, principles that, in turn, impact public perception of the scope and nature of sexual harm.

The Role of Evidence

Journalists seek out evidence, much like the legal system does, in order to verify statements made by victims. Ideally, journalists want some form of data—a corroborating claim, a written document, a video, a photograph—that can be used to fact-check claims that a source makes. This is one reason why Kantor and Twohey, who broke the Harvey Weinstein story for the *New York Times*, expressed concerns about the Ansari article. They believed that Katie Way's research lacked integrity because the victimized person went unnamed and sources appeared uncorroborated, resulting in a story that they felt was one-sided and appeared to favor the victim's perspective while publicly condemning the accused without appropriate evidence.

The benefit to seeking corroborating evidence is that it seeks to protect people from being accused of virtually anything without warrant. Additional evidence provides additional reasons to support the claim, making it more robust, more compelling, keeping falsehoods from spreading, and preventing reputations from being ruined. Indeed, many journalists specifically seek out corroborating evidence under the assumption that truth is somehow related to the presence of data.

But there are some problems with applying this epistemology to sexual violations. First, it's a little reductive to believe that truth needs corroborating data to establish itself. But perhaps more importantly, most victims don't have the data available. This may be because sexual violations often take place in private, because they took place a long time ago, because the victimized person was a child, or because any evidence that was once extant was dumped in a trash can or disappeared with a witness's death. In other words, sometimes the evidence simply doesn't exist.

Another reason why this case is uncomfortable to discuss is that what Grace alleges Ansari did appears within the normal scope of male behavior, at least for some who read about it. "Normalized" and "harmless," however, have never been synonymous terms, something I've had to come to terms with in my own experience. I first voiced this incongruity in a letter that I wrote to a friend where I told her about my experience. Writing gave me a chance to edit, the certainty of controlling the words. What I told her was that this event was like an exclamation point tacked onto a sentence of manipulations. I recounted other events involving physical and psychological boundary violations that I couldn't quite recognize as wrong, though they left me feeling uncomfortable. I described the person who hurt me as an "animal," something I was only able to do because I had a fair amount of physical safety and temporal distance. I then went on to write, "At the time, I thought it was supposed to be erotic . . . but I think it was supposed to be erotic because it was frightening."[53]

My observation echoes the work of Catharine MacKinnon, who writes about the danger of categorizing sexual violations as random acts rather than acts that are embedded in gender norms that categorize men as aggressive and women as submissive. This binary justifies harm, especially harm of the type described in the alleged Ansari encounter, where the male pursues, the woman demurs, and it is all supposed to be part of the heterosexual dating script. I hadn't read MacKinnon yet, so I didn't have this framework available to help me make sense of what I was experiencing, but I eventually came to the conclusion that what I was led to believe was appropriate was actually the gateway to harm. Indeed, the normalization of violent sex scripts means that it may well be that those who perpetrate harm, especially those who identify as men, don't categorize their actions as harmful because they believe they were seducing their romantic partners or taking what is theirs by right of their gender.[54] In other words, Aziz Ansari may well be telling the truth when he responded to Grace's accusations by saying, "It was true that everything did seem okay to me, so when I heard that was not the case for her, I was surprised and concerned."[55]

Whose story to believe then—Ansari's or Grace's?

Or can we believe both?[56]

If assailants, especially those who fit into the male gender binary, are unable to categorize their own harmful behavior because it appears at face value to fit the dating script, then it conversely makes sense that victims may not categorize their experiences that way either. Insofar as we have collectively normalized this binary, it becomes difficult to pass negative judgment on any sexual encounter: The ones that look like Grace's are too close to normal to be wrong, and the ones that appear more obviously egregious become harder to adjudicate because violence is already intertwined with sex. Grace herself seems to recognize this when she reflects, "I was debating if this was an awkward sexual experience or sexual assault. And that's why I confronted so many of my friends and listened to what they had to say, because I wanted validation that it was actually bad."[57]

One could argue that this is the fallout of liberal feminism's impact on the feminist movement overall. The sexual revolution of the 1960s opened the possibility that women might be able to have the same sexual freedoms as men, but while it attempted to give women equal sexual rights, it failed to challenge the structures and beliefs behind those rights. It therefore became more permissible—though not equally permissible—for women to have sexual partners outside of marriage, and it made women more like men in this regard. It became more permissible—though again, not equally permissible—for women to engage in sex for entertainment rather than for procreation or the enactment of an emotional bond. In these ways, women were offered an opportunity to gain the rights of men, to become like men, to see sex the way men see sex. But the sexual revolution didn't revolutionize the structural gender norms that determine sexual scripts. For someone like Grace to label what she presumably experienced as a sexual violation, then, requires a countercultural epistemic shift or a willingness to name sexual encounters, even ones that adhere to sexual scripts, in countercultural ways. It requires a willingness to see sex from a non-dominant point of view, a willingness to see it from the point of view of vulnerability.

Gender norms and the sexual scripts that emerge from them, therefore, function as a powerful primer to the enactment of sexual harm, as Catharine MacKinnon explains in *Toward a Feminist Theory of the State*:

> Dominance eroticized defines the imperatives of its masculinity, submission eroticized defines its femininity. So many distinctive features of women's status as second class—the restriction and constraint and contortion, the servility and the display, the self-mutilation and requisite presentation of self as a beautiful thing, the enforced passivity, the humiliation—are made into the content of sex for women. Being a thing for sexual use is fundamental to it.

This approach identifies not just a sexuality that is shaped under conditions of gender inequality but reveals this sexuality itself to be the dynamic of the inequality of the sexes.[58]

MacKinnon's analysis does not, as is often believed, subsume sex into the category of rape, but it does suggest that there is a collective element to what appear to be individual actions. As long as the majority of those in the United States participate unquestioningly in the process of socializing gender along a binary that allows men to perceive themselves as sexual pursuers, then we also become complicit in fashioning women into what Ann Cahill has termed "pre-victims" of rape.[59] The same goes for how we talk about sexual violations: As long as we collectively speak of rape myths instead of speaking in ways that allow for the expression of the true scope of sexual harm, then we are all, to some degree, complicit in perpetuating a cultural *habitus*—or habit—of silence around it.[60]

Gender socialization and the entwinement of violence and sex also facilitate a unique brand of psychological torment that victimized individuals experience when the person who sexually violated them does so in a way that deviates from the acceptable script of harm. Because what they experienced doesn't align with their previous beliefs about the scope of violations, they may both observe the disjunct and not know how to reconcile it. But remember that they're only operating from the scripts available to them, the same scripts that are available to journalists who interpret their stories. This is relevant in regard to the Ansari accusation. What neither Way nor the journalists who critiqued her are doing is reading Grace's story in light of the gender socialization patterns that Grace and Ansari are operating within. This story would have looked quite different if Way and the other journalists had written about it with reference to the way that we construct gender and, by proxy, dating scripts. It might have also looked different if journalists acknowledged the normalization of violence in sex as opposed to operating from stereotypical understandings of sexual harm.

But this isn't what happened.

Likewise, journalists may assume individuals can both name and speak about a violation, which means that they are also dependent upon the ability of individuals—including victimized individuals and law enforcement officials—to identify that harm occurred. After all, journalists don't create stories out of thin air. They report on stories that exist but that may not be receiving public attention. However, they can only identify those stories if they are identifiable by others, which means that it might be difficult for journalists to report on forms of rape that deviate too far from dominant scripts, either because those who are victimized don't identify these events as harmful or because systems that could potentially corroborate the story fail to do so.

This all appears problematic because it is, and it is even more so when we recall that unacknowledged instances of sexual violations are frequent in some populations, such as on college campuses, where a victimized person might not categorize the event as a form of violation and, in turn, might not communicate the violation to others, including journalists. But college campuses aren't the only place where individuals struggle to speak. In other contexts, someone who survives a sexual violation may be financially dependent on the person who harmed them or fear estrangement from friends and family, fear charges of libel they cannot afford to fight, or the loss of their job or custody of their children. Those who experienced clergy sexual abuse may worry about ostracization from their faith communities. Child victims may fear that an accusation about a family member could result in that relative's incarceration or in the child's removal from the home, as Sujatha Baliga states when she explains why she did not tell anyone about her father's sexual abuse.[61] Members of minoritized communities—including Black, Latinx, and Native American individuals—may feel there is no one trustworthy to make a report to, given the way that the police have repeatedly failed them in the past. They may also be concerned about the wider social implications of their accusations, as Charlotte Pierce-Baker was. Pierce-Baker describes the tension she felt about identifying her assailant because publicly holding him accountable would simultaneously reinforce what Angela Davis terms "the myth of the Black rapist."[62] As she writes, "I felt responsible for upholding the image of the strong black man for our young son, *and* for the white world with whom I had contact. . . . I didn't want to confirm the white belief that all black men rape."[63]

Journalists, in short, are in a bind. If those who survive sexual harm cannot or will not speak, then they'll be unaware of their stories, and if victimized parties feel their story is too dangerous to tell or simply does not belong to pre-established categories like "rape" or "sexual abuse," then they may feel there is no point in turning to journalists anyway—if no one else believes them, why would a journalist? But perhaps most relevantly to the case study here, if victimized individuals see a story like the Aziz Ansari one being labeled "shoddy journalism" and an instance of "bad sex," and their story looks suspiciously like that, then it seems reasonable to assume that they would feel that what happened to them would be labeled likewise.

Now, in their defense, journalists often rely on experts—such as those in the legal community—to help frame a story of sexual wrongdoing. In other words, they're very much operating with a system of knowledge that frames sexual violations according to rape scripts; they're not creating it in isolation. They're merely reiterating what they're hearing from other corners of culture. Still, I can't help but wonder what might happen if journalists operated from a different epistemology, one that stopped relying upon rape and post-rape scripts that pit the story of the victimized and accused parties against one another in order to see which party is telling "the truth." We see these post-rape scripts used in the courtroom, where the defense and the prosecution thrust their most eloquent witnesses onto the stand in order to convince judge and jury that there is one truth that is absolute, binary, that proves beyond a reasonable doubt whether the accused's version of truth is the real one. Journalists also appear to operate from this post-rape script, searching for a singular truth that could be ascribed to one party or the other—to Ansari or to "Grace." The story they may seek to tell is an attempt at a metastory that overshadows the actual stories narrated by the various affected parties. What would it look like, then, if journalists didn't tend to idolize evidence or objective truth but instead allowed the narratives of those parties involved in an instance of harm to guide how their story got told? This would require that journalists shed some of the epistemic assumptions that they inherited from the legal community.

It would also require that they listen differently, and listening differently may be exactly what is needed not just for journalists but for all those who want to truly understand the reality and scope of sexual harm.

CHAPTER 5

On Setting and Story

IN *JUST SEX?*, Nicola Gavey raises this provocative question: "Can a woman be raped and not know it?"[1]

I was such a woman. In spite of an experience that would legally meet the current definition of "rape," I didn't label the event that way for several years and, in turn, didn't speak about it as a violation because I didn't speak about it at all. One reason for my silence was because of how culturally embedded beliefs used words to frame sexual violations, but that was not the only reason. Perhaps an equally powerful reason was that the words available through the setting of my life—embedded beliefs and relationships that held substantial sway in my private world but not in the culture at large—were equally unable to address what I was experiencing.

This is why it's important to explore how words can function in settings as a way to maintain the victimized party's silence and perpetuate their lack of acknowledgment. Two settings that operated this way in my early life will serve as a case study for this argument. It is possible to transcend or subvert these settings in ways that can cause individuals to question their power and, in turn, allow them to move through an interpretative journey that might result in acknowledgment of sexual harm—an outcome and journey that can be of epistemic value, or value that relates to our ways of knowing and constructing knowledge. It gives someone who has experienced a sexual violation epistemic credibility as well as a unique type of "know-how," to invoke Linda Martín Alcoff's term, that can be of use in the quest to better understand what sexual harm is and how the collective enacts it upon individual bodies.[2]

Foregrounding the process of interpretation is important to any investigation about the role that speech plays in rape. Listeners often don't consider the complicated reasons why a person who experiences a sexual violation might change the label they apply to the experience, even though they might simultaneously accept that perspective might shift in regard to their culpability, sense of shame, or the meaning they grant the event in the overall context of their lives. Changing how one feels about the event is one thing. Changing how one labels it is quite another. Examining the role of interpretation and its impact on labeling, therefore, helps listeners understand what they are listening to when they hear someone who has been raped speak, and it provides a counternarrative to embedded beliefs that penalize people who reframe or rename their experiences as vindictive, attention seeking, or "crying rape." It also challenges the assumption that sexual harm is easy to identify, even for the person experiencing it.

Recognizing that interpretation and labeling can shift is especially consequential in the legal arena, where defense attorneys can question victim credibility by challenging both the contents of their memories and their interpretation of them, so that the gaps and variations that victims name in their answers become an effective way to undermine their credibility. And yet, as Nicola Gavey and Mary Koss have recognized, those who have been victimized do not acknowledge events that meet the criteria of "rape" due to the impact of embedded beliefs that frame sexual violations according to myths and stereotypes. In other words, when victims recognize harm in spite of embedded beliefs that are designed to keep them silent, they demonstrate epistemic fortitude and subjectivity. Interpretation over time can, therefore, enhance rather than diminish credibility because the process affords the opportunity for understanding, which is what so many individuals who have experienced sexual violations want. A process of interpretation that involves epistemic transformation can also facilitate epistemic liberation, where liberation is not understood as happiness or delight but rather as freedom to recognize and rage against false ideologies.[3]

I recognize that a primary danger in this chapter is that it runs the risk of leaving the reader with the sense that the rape was beneficial, on the whole, because it facilitates an interpretative process that ultimately reveals previously unknown truths or that leads to wisdom that makes the experience worthwhile overall. This is not my point, nor is it a claim I would ever make. The learning is not worth the price, at the very least because anything learned could be obtained through other means, through books and teachers, through re-visioned socially embedded beliefs and practices. When I consider my own experiences, I see that what happened could have been avoided entirely had I *and* the violating party *and* the embedded beliefs that we participated in been rooted in healthier epistemologies and practices. But that was not the case. So while I am not proposing that a person needs to have experiences of sexual harm in order to gain beneficial knowledge, I do mean to say that the process of interpretation can impact not only what someone who experienced a sexual violation says but also how they say it. This process affords them unique and valuable epistemic credibility that allows them to use their voice as a prophetic one, by which I mean a voice that speaks truth, even if the truth is not one that others want to hear.

Prophets, after all, are usually unwelcome in their hometowns.

Setting as Infiltrating Interpretations

Many years after I was raped, I returned to the journals I kept at that time to try to get a better sense of what had happened. I expected to find some kind of validation in them, some kind of evidence that I was aware of the wrongdoing. I expected to see something of my current perspective in writings from the self that I was in the past.

I didn't find it.

I never wrote about what happened that night, though I did write about what I recall as being the earlier part of that evening—how my roommate lent me a pair of white sneakers with four leaf clovers on them, how I had eaten in a Mexican restaurant. I thought those details were worth recording, but I don't know why I stopped the story there.

Perhaps I didn't feel safe writing about how conflicted I felt.

Perhaps I didn't want to trust the page with a written record of intimacy.

I think the most likely reason is because it simply didn't seem important, because it struck me as normal.

In other entries, I did record several instances of what Linda Martín Alcoff calls "less than optimal sexual behavior,"[4] but these too are confounding to read in retrospect because I didn't describe them with concern. Instead, I seemed to think that I was writing about events that were not only morally blameless but also signs of normalcy. In one early entry, I described how this person asked me several times if I wanted alcohol, and I responded that I would prefer orange juice. They then snuck shots of liquor into my drink while out of sight, which I didn't realize until I took a sip. In the journal, I interpreted this as a compliment, despite the fact that I was underage at the time and that what I'd requested was ignored. In a later entry, I recounted another event, where I stated, "This person grabs me into this erotic kind of hug. And I wouldn't let them kiss me, in fact I started crying, saying, 'What do you want from me?'"[5] I ended that entry not with any concern that I was being grabbed and forced into sexual activities I wanted no part in but by writing, "I was *so glad* that they weren't just being flirty, that they do care so much."[6]

I had returned to these journals hoping to find some form of solidarity with my younger self, but what I discovered was that I hardly recognized her because I wasn't "her" anymore. Time had passed. I no longer had a relationship with the person who enacted the harm, which, in turn, meant they no longer played an active role in the narrative of my life. Indeed, I had co-written many valuable new chapters since then: I had married and birthed children, started a career, moved to a new place, and made new friends. The relationships that most impact my story now are ones I chose and ones that have been beautiful, loving, and good. What I saw before me, in other words, was evidence of how the self is, as Susan Brison explains, "fundamentally relational—capable of being undone by violence, but also of being remade in connection with others."[7]

Still, I felt embarrassed by this evidence I had of the existence of this younger self, by her assumptions, by her trust, by her flowery way of writing and her curious mixture of confidence, hope, and insecurity. She made more sense, however, when I began to think about what I will call her "setting," a set of embedded beliefs composed of the relationships she navigated, the norms that guided her social context, the requirements that needed to be met to stay in it. Each of us has a setting that emerges through our cultural context, relationships, time period, social norms, geographical location, socioeconomic dynamics, and racial and gender constructions. Early formational experiences often function as what I refer to as foundational settings, by which I mean the settings through which other settings emerge and get constructed. Settings shape the choices a person can make and how a person interprets those choices. As a young woman, my former self was no different. She was doing what we all do—trying to survive in a system predicated on specific rules of engagement that she could shape and resist only to a certain degree.

Understanding the setting that a person inhabits and the relationships that are formative in the process of self-construction becomes crucial to understanding both her interpretation of a given sexual violation as well as how and why her interpretation might change over time. But it's reductive to myopically focus only on the setting that existed at the time the harm occurred, because we're cumulative creatures. Our interpretations emerge through the accumulation of our settings, not only in relation to the current configuration of our lives. To that end, as Tricia Rose recognizes, one cannot understand the significance of sexual harm without reference to a more holistic understanding of that person's setting. In her compilation of interviews about Black women's sexual experiences, she writes:

> It is impossible to understand a woman's coming-of-age experiences without having a sense of the larger contexts that shape them, such as family dynamics, expectations surrounding gender and sexuality, economic and educational circumstances, religion, race, color, and weight. If a woman tells the story of losing her

virginity, then aspects of her life such as how she was raised, how expectations were communicated, and perhaps what her religious beliefs were become crucial to any understanding. Using simplistic categories may also encourage women who are looking for a way to express difficult experiences to grasp at the most socially acceptable label for their experience, thus collapsing complex and important aspects of their sexuality into this master narrative. It could be the case that a "single mother" might also be a "rape victim"—and she was also likely at some point a "virgin." How do we tell a story that moves across so many labels, as all of our lives do? And, most important, how can we—given the histories of manipulation, fragmentation, and denial of space for black women's own sexual stories—in good conscience subject black women's sexual narratives to these fragmenting strategies?[8]

Rose recognizes how the seemingly individual interpretation of a singular sexual experience is collective from the start, a process in which the individual brings to bear the input of the wider community that shapes her epistemological outlook. How a single person processes a given sexual violation, therefore, has to be understood with reference to the overall setting of the person's life and how their community shaped it.

Any fiction writer could tell you that settings matter because they set the parameters for what characters believe, what they perceive to be real and possible, and consequently, how they act. Likewise, scholars have recognized for quite some time that social constructions inherited through micro- and dominant discourses play powerful roles in our real-life settings. These function as what Carrie Doehring refers to as "embedded beliefs," beliefs that we inherit from the values of culture at large and assume to be true without even knowing we're making an assumption.[9] The setting a person inhabits—especially the foundational settings of our early lives—therefore tend to enable the formation of embedded beliefs. The process of interpretation has the capacity to allow people who have experienced violations to become more cognizant of the role that setting and embedded

On Setting and Story 141

beliefs play in their epistemological frameworks. They may also engage in a difficult evaluation of those beliefs, choosing to abandon some of them for deliberative, or consciously chosen, ones. In what follows, I consider the role of two settings in my early life, how they affected my initial interpretation of what I experienced, and how I subverted them in ways that caused me to change how I named the violation. These function as something of a case study to show how settings operate. My hope is that they will encourage readers to consider the settings of their own lives and how they impact their process of interpretation.

Foundational Setting One

Once upon a time, a mother in the Italian city of Naples watched her husband die. The year was 1898, or thereabouts. The mother, whose name has been lost to history, had three children, the youngest of whom was a toddler, and as she took a deep breath and assessed the financial and social state of things, she realized that she could support two of the children on her own, but not the third. So she took the youngest, who went by the name of Rosa, and clothed her in her finest white dress, and held her hand as they walked her down the cobbled streets of their neighborhood, whispering words of hope in her ear. Then the mother left Rosa on the doorstep of a nearby convent, with the expectation that she would be raised and kept safe there. Rosa never saw her mother again.

It did not take Rosa long to fall in love with the convent. There she learned to read, to write, and to sing, educational opportunities she wouldn't have had at home. She structured her days around the stability of the Daily Office prayers: Matins, Lauds, Prime, Terce, Sext, None, Vespers, Compline. Every day, hymns sung. Every day, a cloister to explore. Every day, candles lit for worship.

The words did not abandon her like her parents had.

Rosa grew close with the other girls whose lives had been entrusted to the care of the convent, and she dreamed of being a nun. She yearned to spend her life in prayer, dedicating herself to nurturing other young girls whose parents could not afford to raise them. Then one day, a man named

Francesco arrived on a horse with a dream of his own, a dream for which he needed a wife. He picked Rosa out of a lineup of the convent girls because she was the most beautiful, and he rode her home on the horse while he walked beside her. They married quickly, and, a few months later, they boarded a boat to the United States.

Rosa was already pregnant with her first child at the time.

She was sixteen years old.

She would birth eight more children, all of whom lived to adulthood.

She never became a nun.

Rosa is my great grandmother on my mother's side, a woman with whom I've always felt a particular kinship, though we've never met. I've wondered, at times, whether my predilection for religion descended through her blood to mine, whether I inherited the dreams she couldn't fulfill, whether I'm subconsciously telling her story through my own.

The setting of my childhood was quietly shaped by Rosa's memory. My grandma told me stories about Rosa that framed her life as mythical, the stuff of fairy tales. Rosa and Francesco had a magical relationship. He was her knight in shining armor, rescuing her from a life of solitude and whisking her off to the freedom and opportunity offered by a new country. I do not know how this story came about—was it the one Rosa told during bedtime stories? The one Francesco told? The one that my grandma and her siblings created for themselves? Later in life, Rosa confessed to my grandmother that she'd already birthed seven children before she learned how they were made. The nuns didn't teach her that in the convent, she said.

"Rosa refused to learn English," my mother once told me. "Most of the time, she sat in a rocking chair, watching us while she said the rosary. The only memories I have of her talking were the times when one of her nine children said they were pregnant and were planning to name the child 'Rose' or 'Rosie.' Then she would drop the rosary and announce that no one should be named after her because she had a hard luck name."

At least six of my relatives are named after Rosa, including my mother, whose middle name is a derivative of hers.

I inherited a number of embedded beliefs about language and sexual violations from Rosa's legacy that impacted my early interpretation of what happened to me. I assumed a certain amount of coercion was natural in a sexual relationship between men and women, and I absorbed this not just from the way that my family constructed Rosa's story but from the wider culture that gave my relatives a dominant embedded belief into which to situate it. Cinderella, Aurora, Snow White, and Belle are not so different from my great grandmother. Move those characters from a castle to a convent, and you could easily replace one protagonist with another.

There is so much I will never know for certain about my great grandma. Had Rosa ever really wanted to be a mother? To be an American? As an adult, I cannot help but wonder who Rosa would have been if she had been able to choose her own path, a path that was shaped both by women's inability to earn an income (perhaps her mother would not have given her to the convent if she had more financial freedom) and by global economics (perhaps Francesco would have stayed in Italy if the capitalistic hope of America didn't hold such allure). Would she have wanted to be a nun if economics and gender hadn't collided to make it impossible for her mother to raise her? Would she have wanted nine children? A life in the United States? Did she refuse to learn English as an act of resistance, or was she simply an introvert? Most importantly, what is the story she might have written, and who are the people she might have chosen as co-writers? Perhaps her life would look remarkably similar, and perhaps it would look radically different. I'll never know. But what I do know with certainty is that I exist because she existed. I am here because of a complex intertwine of religious, economic, and gender-based power that caused Rosa's abandonment, marriage, and motherhood, that brought my grandma and subsequently my mother into being. If Rosa's life was one of great loss and suffering, then is my existence worth the price she paid?

Long before I asked any of these questions, the quiet assumption I held about Rosa's life was that it was a great blessing, and for all I know, it was. But that's precisely the point—I *don't* know. On this point, Rosa herself is entirely silent. She left no words behind—no books, no journals, and then there was the grave, which magnified the muteness of her mortal life and exposed her story to all manner of editors. The only handwriting of hers that I have is a signature on a copy of her naturalization certificate, the piece of paper that stifled whatever remained of her former self and ensured she would never return to that convent in Naples. Perhaps she was lucky that Francesco rescued her and whisked her across the ocean to a new life that included both the United States and motherhood. Perhaps she wasn't. The point is that I assumed Rosa's life was a fairytale come true, and perhaps I assumed it because it fits perfectly another story that Americans like to tell—one in which men rescue women from themselves (see virtually every Disney movie prior to *Frozen*).

Rosa was far from the only one of my family members whose identity suffered the effects of linguistic redefinition. The silence was systemic and can be understood as a direct consequence of the vulnerabilities my Italian family experienced when they immigrated.[10] They arrived in the United States during the peak of anti-Italian rhetoric, forcing them to quickly assimilate into Anglo culture to survive.[11] Almost every member of Rosa's family changed their name, in a kind of linguistic code switch. Her husband Francesco became "Frank," and their first daughter, Magdalena, went by "Madeleine." Octavious was "Babe." Elena slipped into "Helen." Ciara—born during the 1918 flu—got renamed "Dolly" after Rosa got infected and the baby was entrusted to an Anglo nanny who renamed her because she looked just like the prized porcelain toys given to wealthy children. Of the nine siblings that my great grandma birthed, only a scant few went by the names on their birth certificates.

Rosa never changed her name, as she would have if she'd become a nun.

Meanwhile, her Italian American offspring used their names, their identities, as a way to cover, knowing the power of the dominant culture and how language and identity fit within it.[12] They understood that one needed to speak the dominant language, to find a way to be identified within it, and so sometimes these name changes were made deliberately by the family to facilitate the process of assimilation.[13] Other times, though, they were made without their consent. My mother, for instance, recently found her original birth certificate and gasped when she saw that her name was initially not listed as Marguerite.

"Some nurse changed my name to Margaret," she exclaimed. Behind the original, she found a second birth certificate, marked three months later, that corrected the spelling error, but to some extent, it never really mattered because she didn't go by either moniker.

To her friends and family, she's always been "Peggy."

Foundational Setting Two

Each of us is born into a family of origin. We may adore those individuals or we may sever ties with them, but either way, we usually discover that they are insufficient in and of themselves to be our only set of relationships, and so we complement or supplant them with a family of our choosing.

The cathedral girls' choir I sang in was my first experience of a family of choice. As an only child, I yearned for siblings from an early age, not so much because I wanted playmates as because I wanted companions with shared memories. I delighted in the close friendships that I developed over the ten years that I sang in the choir. We were a tight knit group of about twenty-five, ranging in age from eight to eighteen, united by our love of music and by the way that the choir gave a rhythm to our childhood. We shared an experience of time as simultaneously moving forward and being cyclical. We grew older with every school year, progressing into larger sized church robes when we performed, yet at the same time as we grew, we repeated Christianity's musical seasons of Pentecost, Advent, Christmas, Epiphany, Lent, and Easter. We experienced stability in the beloved hymns and anthems that repeated from year to year, embraced the challenge of sightreading new ones, always immersed in holy language that felt mystical, warm, and glorious. The choir was home for me, and it introduced me to hope and love and to the sense that there existed something beyond myself that I could never see but that I felt most poignantly in the company of other singers. We were also taught that, as children, we had the capacity to create beauty and hope and peace because we were Christmas joy for families and comfort for a grieving widower. This gave us a sense of a responsibility, a belief that when we sang together, it had gravitas and import, that our shared calling mattered.

Every girl admitted to the choir worked hard to excel, which meant that we not only wanted to be excellent singers, but we wanted to be excellent together because of the way our bodies experienced choral singing. We knew how transcendent singing as a group could be: It's not common for human beings to coordinate their breathing with others, sometimes breathing together and other times consciously making the choice to exhale longer so that someone else can be spared the space to inhale. Rarely do they physically harmonize with someone else or permit their bodies to vibrate with other people's, which makes singing both remarkable and countercultural because of the way that it allows for safe yet extraordinarily intimate experiences with the bodies of others.

Singing in a group is also a gateway drug for transcendent experiences because the way that the body is shared in vocal song isn't replicable. Playing in an orchestra provides similar access to embodied harmonization, but it's mediated through instruments. Speaking words is usually an interchange with a more limited vocal range. Singing together differs from both of these because it provides unmediated access to another person's breath and body as well as to creating sounds and sensations that go beyond oneself in ways that can feel primal and revelatory.

Like all gateway drugs, it is addictive.

Both I and the other girls I sang with allowed the choir to shape the formational setting of our childhood in profound ways. Girls who joined the choir committed to rigor and discipline in the pursuit of choral excellence. During services, we paired up and walked in a straight line to our seats, each couple equally spaced from the others. Our dress was dictated for us—we wore uniforms when we performed and were relegated to white bows or brown ponytail holders for our hair; earrings had to be studs; shoes had to have rubber soles and were required to be white in the summer months and black after Labor Day. We even hung our church robes in a certain way—with the cassock always under the surplice—and many of us, myself included, regimented our diets, cutting out foods like dairy products that can clog the vocal cords. I have no memories of spending Christmas Eve at home as a child because I spent that holiday and the days leading up to it with my choir family, which suited me just fine because the choir felt so safe, its expectations high but crystal clear.

Singing in the choir also meant committing to let our choirmaster shape our voices and identity. We gathered together at minimum three days a week and often four or six, training our voices to sing the same way, with a tone that was clear and crisp and clean. Our choirmaster taught us to sing only with our head voice, the willowy part of the voice that primarily resonates in the sinus cavities of the face, so as to avoid the richness and depth of the chest voice. This kept us from using a vibrato, which allowed us to both sound like angels—or children, depending on your perspective—and blend together more easily, so that our individual voices melded into this singular thing called the "choir." Disappearing into the group was exhilarating, a high that kept us all engaged as we became creatures who sang from the chin up, not the neck down.

Through the choir, I not only received a free musical education. I also discovered how the self could be amplified in community if one felt secure enough to share one's voice with others. Alone, all any of us could do was sing a solo. Together, we could harmonize to create a musical experience that was impossible to manufacture on our own, one in which each of our voices played a unique role, even if they were never individually discernable. We each knew that we contributed something important and unique to the group, that we were still a self even as our identities were very much made by and within the choir, because despite the many ways that we were made to conform, we each retained the singular timbre produced by our body's vocal cords, lungs, and resonant spaces. The group would not have been the same without any one of us. This is an oddly delicate balance—sing too loudly, and all a listener will hear is you, your individuality, your ego. Sing too quietly, and you disappear as a voice, as a self.

At its best, this is what I saw the choir doing, but I also saw how history impacted our lives in ways that posed challenges to us. Our choir emerged from something called the "English choral tradition" which was prominent in the Church of England and became part of many Episcopal churches in the United States. Historically, the kind of choir I participated in would have admitted only boys and men, and even in the cathedral where I sang, the boys' choir was decades old before someone got around to establishing one for girls, which became the first of its kind in the United States.[14]

The lack of gender parity between the choirs didn't occur in isolation. Like many Christian denominations, the Episcopal Church inherited a long history in which men were afforded leadership roles but women were not, the most notable of which was ordination. A number of Christian denominations continue to explicitly limit women's leadership positions, though the Episcopal Church first ordained women in the 1970s. Still, my childhood experiences of church were colored by this history. I did not see a woman functioning as an ordained leader until well into my teenage years, which set up the implicit assumption that women were incapable of this kind of role, their exclusion a sign that they were somehow inferior to men or not as close to God. But perhaps more relevant to me on a daily basis was the gendered hierarchy I witnessed in the world of church music, because the English choral tradition, historically at least, presumed a gender binary and, within that binary, it presumed that boys—not girls—had ideal voices. Theirs was a way of singing that was both innocent and pure. Moreover, it was transitory, destined to be deepened by puberty, the biological process that pivots a boy into a man or, one might say, that changes an asexual being to a sexual one.[15] As young girls, we were exposed to a tradition that said it was preferable to sing like the boys at King's College in Cambridge or St. Paul's Cathedral in London, because those were the normed, prized, and privileged voices. Historically, they were believed to harken to angels and could create a type of disembodied beauty that we could only ever imitate, a sound that was dispassionate while never being heartless. That, tacitly at least, we were expected to conform to the voice of a boy was a veiled direction to eradicate any sign of our gender. The most successful among us excelled at constructing our voices so that they sounded like what we were told a boy sounded like. Judith Butler might say that we performed a gender that was not ours through the way we used our bodies to produce sound.[16]

At times, this led to a competitive spirit between us and the boys. Yet I was also aware that our time in the choir was limited in a way that the boys' experience was not. Whereas the boys could undergo their vocal change and sing in the men's choir, we had no equivalent because there was no women's choir awaiting us. When we graduated from high school, we graduated from the choir, simple as that. Indeed, when women in the cathedral raised the option of creating a women's choir, my memory is that members of the girls' choir—myself included—were among its strongest opponents because, as far as we were aware, women weren't part of the English choral tradition, with its intense focus on the pure, angelic voices of boys.[17] For as much as we girls were one step removed from the boys by virtue of our gender, women were one further step removed by virtue of puberty. The maturity of their vocal chords meant that they sang with vibratos, with a timbre that made it more difficult for them to blend together, to erase their identities, to disappear into the group.[18] Women, one might even go so far as to say, were not vocally pure.[19]

Interestingly, one of the reasons that boys' voices were so prized in the choir was because they were the ones who were seen to have the transitory role. Destined for their voices to deepen, the timbre of their childhood was portrayed as evanescent and precious because of its liminality. Yet, in reality, it was the girls who had the most transitory identity, who were valued for the way their voices could imitate the voice of a boy, until they grew too old, and then they were given a handshake and forced to turn in both their folders and their identity as choristers. To the best of my memory, this went unspoken, perhaps even unthought. And why think about it? It was simply part of the way things were.

I think it is fair to say that the girls in the choir were not ignorant of how gender functioned—we were in a church run entirely by men, after all. I think it is also fair to say that we were aware of the many benefits of being in the choir, ranging from musical opportunities to friendships to the sheer joy of singing and the glimpses of a loving God many of us received in the process. We worked with a smart, dedicated choirmaster who expected and brought out the best in us, and we knew the value of that. The pros far outweighed the cons.

Still, the choir as an institution instilled in me a complicated set of embedded beliefs about gender and myself as a gendered body. None of that learning emerged from one individual. Instead, it was embedded in the system of cathedral choral singing that I inherited by my sheer immersion in it. Our training revolved around the implicit, unspoken assumption that there was an essential difference between a girl's voice and a boy's voice and that the former was somehow lesser than the latter. A girl's voice could never be as polished or as shimmery, and so the best we could do would be to imitate an identity that was not ours rather than embody our own. Hearkening to Simone de Beauvoir's famous quotation, I might say that the story of gender I absorbed from the embedded beliefs of the choir was that one is not born but rather becomes the voice of a boy.

The choir also instilled complicated views of the female body. In vocal training, there is a term called "body," but it doesn't mean the physical body from which the voice is produced. It means how rich and nuanced vocal production is. In our choir, we were taught to sing with very little body in the voice because we relied primarily on the ethereality of the head voice rather than the more resonant and robust chest voice. We were taught to minimize our vocal body—our unique vocal personality—so that we could blend in with each other. At its best, this allowed us to harmonize. At its worst, it became a danger because it permitted us to erase ourselves. I would argue that, at a subtle level, these vocal practices also reinforced the historic dualism that associates men with the mind and women with the body because of how we tried to eradicate body from our voices in order to imitate the voice of a boy.[20]

Perhaps most problematically, the way I learned to fragment my voice caused me to judge others who used their voices differently. It made me, for a time, into a vocal bigot. This became most obvious when I got to college and was hired to sing in a professional adult choir that was also rooted in the English choral tradition (in and of itself violating the assumption that women were incapable of singing in such ways). Continuing to sing without a vibrato as an adult was never a struggle for me because of the vocal training I'd received. In fact, I would have told you at the time that I had a well-trained voice, and I did—I did have "a" trained voice. But I'd never developed "my voice," never trained in a way that encouraged me to develop vocal body or personality. Indeed, I remember around this time that a voice teacher whose studio I'd desperately wanted to get into said this to me: "Who are you?"

"I'm Danielle."

"Yes, I know your name, but who *are* you? As a singer?"

"I don't understand," I said.

"Can't you sing with some passion?" she said. "Something that's yours?"

I raised an eyebrow. "I have no idea how to do that."

"I can tell," she said. "You sing like a disembodied angel."

I had become adept at the art of vocal imitation, and not only that, I had come to prize it. In so doing, I had lost something of my own voice, of my own self. I could sing to blend, but I had no idea how to sing to stand out. I had become an expert at being in community, but I had failed miserably at becoming a *self* in one. The identity that I had worked so hard to construct had turned me into a vocal chameleon, into someone who could imitate but who could never let her guard down enough to be authentic, individual. I wasn't ashamed of this. I prized it, and that affected how I judged the other singers around me, not to mention how I lived out other parts of my life. In this same college choir, I watched in rehearsals as other women who were paradigmatic professionals struggled to suppress their vibrato and constrain the natural fullness of their voice. I'm sorry to say that I looked down on them for it, privately chastising them for their inability to sing with the purity I'd come to prize, never questioning the assumption that perhaps there was more to the voice than what I believed.

It would be convenient to use what I've written as evidence that organized religion hurts people. And while it does, such a reading would be a far stretch from what I want the takeaway to be. No organization is perfect, and in so many ways, my choir was a product of its time. For any and all of its imperfections, I remain profoundly grateful for it. It formed me as a musician and gave me my earliest experiences of belonging. After I was raped, I initially ran from this identity, but then I returned to it, called upon it to help me re-establish a sense of self and a sense of community. Indeed, I do not think it would be trite to say that being able to sing at a time when I didn't feel able to speak saved my life.

Moreover, the choir provided my earliest and most profound experiences of faith, and these experiences by and large had a positive impact. Psychologist Ken Pargament writes that religions that teach people of a loving God can result in positive religious coping mechanisms. In other words, when trouble strikes, people's faith can either be an asset or a liability. This makes sense to me. If one believes that God is primarily punitive instead of primarily loving, then suffering becomes a sign of personal fault. If one believes that God is loving, then a person is less likely to interpret that same harm as a sign of personal fault. Instead, they are more likely to feel some kind of spiritual solidarity or support, perhaps from both God and their faith community. I am aware that for any and all flaws, the Episcopal Church excels at teaching of a loving God. That's the faith I absorbed from years of singing in the choir, from close to a decade of singing its theology until its beliefs were embedded in my heart. So when I was raped, the idea that God was punishing me never crossed my mind. The question of "Why me?" never arose.

But the desire to sing did.

The Process of Interpretation

I did not cognitively name my experience with rape due to the way that dominant embedded beliefs and setting intersected in my life in ways that caused me to identify "rape" as an event that aligned with dominant scripts. I eventually began to question my own categorization of the event for two reasons. First, my physical and psychological state deteriorated. Second, my setting shifted and, correspondingly, so did the role that my embedded beliefs played. Some of the choices I made during this time were liberating and some that were in the service of liberation were actually damaging, but in their own way, each allowed me to begin to question some of the assumptions I held about voice, naming, gender, and sex that were not serving a positive purpose in my life. During this time, I graduated from college, moved, and while I stayed in school to get another degree, a combination of loans and jobs gave me financial independence and freedom I had not known before. I stopped singing professionally for a time and traded my rigid musical upbringing for rebellious vocal practices that were antithetical to how I'd been trained in the choir. I used my chest voice. I bought every Britney Spears album on the market and began to sing with a vocal fry, which produces a harsh, gritty sound that many musicians believe damages the vocal cords, but I didn't care. It was the absolute antithesis of the angelic way I'd been taught to sing, and I wanted to feel the roughness associated with the sound. More productively, I also began studying with a new voice teacher who encouraged me to develop a vibrato, learn jazz music, and practice vocal improvisation, all of which were musical practices that expanded how I was able to use my voice and, in turn, how I understood myself. Several years after I began working with her, I returned to the world of professional choral singing. I rejoined the professional choir that I had quit suddenly and on a whim during college, and I was hired as both a singer and consultant to help start a brand new girls' choir that was modeled in the English choral tradition in which I had been raised. The director, Walden Moore, welcomed me with open arms, and he invited my feedback for how to create not just a musically rich experience for girls but also one that created healthy community among them. Singing with that group gave me a chance to return to the music that had meant so much to me as a child and to reclaim what I loved about it while also being able to help it grow and change.

Around this time, I also began studying feminism more intentionally, especially the work of feminist theologians and philosophers who think about the role that patriarchal structures play in society and who pay considerable attention to how these structures have embedded themselves in our beliefs and norms in ways that are often insidious because we do not question their acceptability. Feminist scholars like Catharine MacKinnon, Andrea Dworkin, and Susan Brison profoundly shifted my understanding of gender and sexual violations; Serene Jones, Sallie McFague, Phyllis Trible, Rosemary Radford Ruether, and Catherine Keller reshaped how I understood theology as well as women's identities and roles in organized religion; Katie Geneva Cannon, Emilie Townes, and Delores Williams forever changed how I thought about the intersection of race and gender, as well as how I thought about the purpose of suffering.

These scholars modeled what the best scholars do—they can change both how human beings see the world *and* how they live in it. They helped me to live a better, healthier life, a life for which I am profoundly grateful. They gave me courage. They helped me to construct a self that made sense. They also encouraged me to reconsider the embedded beliefs about gender, race, and class that I'd been raised with as a child, to see my family history and myself a new way. Thanks to the wisdom they shared, I began to recognize the role that words, narrative, and speech played in how I constructed my own identity and experiences, and I began to recognize that the reason I had not named my own violation as such was because various structures—including linguistic structures—had not given me the cognitive framework to do so.

Relatedly, the experience of being in graduate school offered a new setting and a fresh opportunity for me to question my embedded beliefs and to develop deliberative or consciously chosen ones in their place. Many people experience graduate school as a stressful time exacerbated by the competition that students either tacitly or overtly practice with one another. This was not my experience, in part because the graduate program in which I was enrolled taught students not just how to think differently but also how to speak and act differently in the world. I attribute this to the role that fields like practical and pastoral theology played in the program. Pastoral theology is an interdisciplinary field, profoundly shaped by the social sciences, especially psychology. Pastoral theologians are often interested in the ways that narrative shapes human interpretations of faith and their own experiences of suffering. Also relevant here is that pastoral theologians care about how witnesses receive the speech of others, in other words, how they listen. Scholars in the field are particularly skilled at listening in ways that enhance the agency of the speaker, and it is typical for them to utilize active listening practices including asking open-ended questions and leaving silence in conversations. I would argue that the speech practices espoused by experts in this field remain countercultural because they're grounded in giving careseekers epistemic credibility while witnesses listen from a place of epistemic humility.[21] The kind of trust embedded in the way that my fellow students listened, even in casual conversation, was markedly different from the way I'd experienced speech before, and, without knowing it, they made me feel safe enough to begin to explore some of the assumptions I had about speech, words, and the events that had taken place in my own life.

The ability to finally say, "I was raped," helped me to make sense of my state of mind, my behaviors, and my reactions, but it didn't solve all my problems. Indeed, in the short term, it resulted in further questioning. I felt responsible for what had happened and shame for not being able to stop it, especially given the lack of physical violence. Why, I kept wondering, had I accepted this behavior as normal? Why hadn't I walked outside of my own bedroom and grabbed my roommate—who was quietly working on homework—and told her what happened or told him to leave? These questions were torturous. They became an *idée fixe*, a preoccupation I just could not resolve. Moreover, what felt more powerful than the blame was the confusion that arose from being unable to identify in the moment what seemed so obvious in the aftermath. It did not occur to me that setting and embedded beliefs could play such a profound role in how a person categorized and interpreted an event.

Eventually, naming was helpful in the same way that a doctor's diagnosis is: The bad news isn't what anyone wants to hear, but at least the diagnosis gives a linguistic locus against which one can rail and respond. In the same way, the process of moving through the trauma was painful, filled with anger, fear, anxiety, lack of safety. But twenty years later, I also believe that the act of naming and the processing that emerged from it gave me a chance to see the world and see my place in it differently. As my sense of self and assumptions about the world shattered, a new self emerged, constructed within a community of trusted friends from whom I never needed to remain silent. New wisdom and ways of knowing emerged as well, and while I do not believe that suffering justifies the learning—indeed, there are many ways to learn what I learned that do not involve directly experiencing harm—it is hard to deny that I nonetheless did learn much that mattered about everything from vulnerability to the body's wisdom to generosity to systemic oppression. That learning, along with the relationships I formed, was so impactful that with time, I no longer came to think of myself as the same person.

Some scholars in psychology—notably Richard Tedeschi and Lawrence Calhoun—might characterize what I'm describing as posttraumatic growth. In contrast to resilience (the ability to "bounce back" from a negative event), posttraumatic growth often involves difficulty with resilience or an inability to bounce back after a trauma that results in a struggle and resolves in growth in relation to five dimensions: overall appreciation of life, relationships, future possibilities, personal strength, and spiritual transformation.[22] But what's not identified explicitly in these five categories is epistemic transformation—by which I mean a transformation in how one knows and interprets the world around them. And yet, that transformation does happen, and it affects not only how one knows their own life but also how they know their society and its structures. It affects how one understands the nature of sexual harm as well as the nature of justice. In other words, it makes it hard to stay silent any longer.

Acknowledging the extent to which unjust and unnecessary sufferings exist in the world because of unjust structures galvanizes people like me—people who have experienced the product of these structures—to change them and to help those who have been harmed by them. That epistemic transformation can also be empathic and embodied, giving someone who has survived harm a greater embodied understanding of what this kind of suffering looks like that can be used in the service of compassion and kindness. This changed worldview and changed sense of one's identity perhaps more closely mirrors what philosopher Linda Martín Alcoff refers to as "know-how" or embodied knowledge that can precipitate altruism, empathy, and activism.[23]

Indeed, I would say that there is a certain kind of epistemic freedom that accompanies these realizations that causes me to disagree with Susan Brison, who writes about her own rape, "It has been hard for me, as a philosopher, to learn the lesson that knowledge isn't always desirable, that the truth doesn't always set you free. Sometimes, it fills you with incapacitating terror and, then, uncontrollable rage."[24] Brison's reflections make sense if we conceive of freedom as something like salvation or joy. But freedom can also be epistemological, as when one is liberated from a false ideology. This form of freedom isn't the same as the exhilaration experienced when one earns a driver's license or can afford to move out of their parents' house and into their first apartment. There is nothing jubilant about seeing how systems of oppression affect the lives of women, children, and those whose gender doesn't conform to the dominant binaries. There's nothing ecstatic about seeing how institutions like schools and churches and businesses and governments routinely protect those who abuse at the expense of those whose lives have been shattered by victimization. But the ability to see and to name is, nonetheless, a form of epistemic freedom that allows one to identify the role that dominant embedded beliefs and the individual settings of our lives play in the construction and ongoing perpetuation of suffering. Once we've done that, then we can finally act in resistance.

The way that we've used dominant embedded beliefs and settings to cover our eyes has allowed far too many who live in the United States to avoid acknowledging how these systems have functioned as a kind of cultural misorientation, transmitted between generations in destructive, insidious ways. The way to move forward from this toxic cycle is first to name and then to respond in whatever way we are called to in order to make sure that the structures that normalize and permit the perpetuation of rape become so abhorrent to us as a culture that we dismantle them. This is a tall order and a countercultural one, but I believe it is possible, and in the final chapters of this book, I want to propose a vision for doing so.

CHAPTER 6

On Listening Well

THE PRIOR CHAPTERS together illustrated how specific words and embedded beliefs thwart the narrative agency of those who have lived through a sexual violation, making it difficult for them to speak about their experience of harm. These frameworks also function as epistemic idols—idols of how and what we know—that inappropriately monopolize how we collectively define the contours of rape, depriving those who most need language of meaningful ways to conceptualize their experiences, and leaving them to categorize intimate and violating memories against external parameters.

The way that society requires those who have lived through a rape to go through this process essentially amounts to a form of epistemic rape in which those who were once deprived of narrative agency are once again asked to subsume their story into the story of another. Only this time, it is not the story of the violating party that dominates. This time, what dominates are the culturally embedded stories about rape that misogyny, patriarchy, racism, and classism write. Those who recognize the impact of these stories on their lives may feel as if they continue to be on the defense, resisting the epistemic attack long after the physical one ends.[1]

Individuals who are wise to the power exerted through the words and stories we tell about rape often feel that they need to justify their pain against preset standards in order to procure the belief of others, which is not so much a luxury as a necessity of recovery. They know that they need supportive witnesses in order to restore the safety and agency that the person who raped them took. They also understand, if only implicitly, that listeners evaluate their claims against these dominant embedded beliefs.

Not only do those who have been victimized face obstacles to speaking, but just as significantly, listeners face obstacles to hearing.

My goal in this chapter is to propose that listening performs in a specific way in response to speech and, at its best, can co-construct the self of both the victimized person and the listener. However, listeners can also do the reverse, damaging the self of the victimized party and themselves through their response. To consider how and why listening performs well, I will consider the power held by listeners. I will then offer a vision for how witnesses can constructively listen and respond to those who need to be heard. My hope is that this framework, rooted in a hermeneutic of humility, might create space to both disrupt dominant embedded beliefs and also hand narrative agency back to those who desperately need it.

On the Credibility of the Speaker

Before we consider the way that listeners hear narratives—however fractured—about sexual violations, it's worth considering the credibility they tend to give to the individuals who speak them. Which victims are reliable narrators? Collectively, who do we believe is telling the truth? The short answer is that victimized individuals face multiple barriers when it comes to their credibility, barriers that are rooted in a variety of factors. For some listeners, hearing about traumatic experiences viscerally causes them to turn away. Unable to acknowledge the extent to which suffering pervades the world, it is easier for them to deny its existence.

But there are also historical reasons why victim speech lacks credibility. In many cultures, women were historically understood to be property—first the property of their fathers and then the property of their husbands. As such, their sexual violation was justifiable because they were seen as essentially objects to be used and not subjects with agency. They thus could not lie about something that could not happen.

Within the historic context of the United States specifically, Black women slaves were likewise considered property, thereby justifying their violation, but the case of white women was more convoluted. As scholars like Angela Sims have argued, white women were known to make false claims about Black men raping them which, in turn, resulted in lynchings. Sometimes white men encouraged their wives to make such claims. Sometimes, as Sims documents, white women chose to do so of their own volition. By way of example, Sims interviewed a woman named Katherine Louise Clark Fletcher, who recalls a lynching she remembers happening when she was a girl. The lynching occurred because a white woman accused two boys of raping her while she was walking home from the movie theater. As Fletcher explains:

> She wasn't raped; she just said that she was attacked. She was late getting home. But when she tells where this attack took place, she said a shortcut through an alley. But the alley was really out of the way for her to have been there. It was generally accepted in the black community that she was just making up a story because she was late getting home.[2]

According to Fletcher, shortly after the white woman made the accusation, two Black boys—both dropouts—were arrested and put in jail without an investigation. The next day, community members gathered in protest, demanding the boys be released to them. The sheriff eventually released one of the boys, who was then stabbed, chained to a car, dragged down the street, hung to a tree, and set on fire.[3] Stories like this one show the way in which the concept of "rape" could be used to justify the lynching of Black men and, thereby, maintain a white supremacist status quo. Indeed, the public nature of lynching was intended to very clearly display who had power and who did not.

False accusations made by white women gave them power in a culture in which they had relatively little in relation to white men. Contrary to their husbands or even their sons—against whom they had little authority—white women could exert power over Black men, because the accusations could lead to their lynching. This gave white women more influence and freedom than white male supremacist culture otherwise afforded them. By way of example, consider this instance, recounted to Sims by a man named Junius Nottingham Sr. Here Nottingham recounts that:

> There was a deacon in my church, Deacon Harrison Byrd. And, as a boy—and he said his mother would take in laundry for the white woman down the road. And when she would finish, he would have to take the laundry down in a wagon. He would take it down, and he said—but every time he would take it down, the woman would make him get in the bed with her. And, he said, he told her—"I can't do this." And she told him, "If you don't, I'm going to tell them you raped me." So he said, he had to do it. He said—but one day he went into town, and he heard the white men talking, how they were going to hang him up, because somehow or another, they must have gotten wind of what was going on. And he said he was so afraid, he came home, he told his mother, he said, "I'm leaving." He said he left [North Carolina] that day, came to Philadelphia. He never went back home.[4]

In this story, the white woman exploited the stereotype that Black men rape in order to rape the Black man, coercing him into having sex by employing the threat of lynching. Power plays like this afforded white women a degree of power they did not have over their white male husbands, but they also undermined their credibility. Indeed, because it was well known that white women benefited from lying about Black men sexually violating them, it correspondingly meant that their veracity was questionable when they told the truth. If white women lied about Black men, it was reasonable to assume they lied about white men. Therefore, the conclusion was simple: No matter who white women were accusing, it wasn't true.

The history that white women lie about sexual violations is but one narrative that we've inherited as a culture about who is telling the truth when it comes to claims of sexual harm. But who we see as an unreliable narrator of sexual harm extends far beyond white women. Indeed, problems related to victim credibility are only exacerbated further when we consider other individuals who might make a claim. Assumptions about men's strength and virility become strikes against them when they claim to have been sexually violated. Black, Asian, and Latinx women are stereotyped to have insatiable sex drives. Children are said to have active imaginations or are considered easily impressionable so that they too become unreliable narrators when they make an accusation. And the list goes on. Stereotypes about groups, therefore, collide with historic contexts in which some white women did lie about being sexually violated in order to cohere into a narrative that can be summarized thus:

> Don't believe people who claim to be victims. They're not telling the truth.

On the Power of the Listener

Here is where the theory of performativity intersects with power and listening. Performativity is a theory originally developed by the philosopher J.L. Austin, who states that when we speak words, they often don't just express thoughts. They can also enact some kind of change. If they successfully enact the change, they "perform." If they do not, then they "misfire." Power is part of every spoken interaction between a speaker and a listener. Indeed, the power attributed to speaker or listener is one reason why words perform or misfire, as Austin recognizes.[5] Take Austin's paradigmatic example of two individuals seeking to get married and the minister who declares them husband and wife. The three parties present for that encounter—minister and future spouses—all tacitly agree that the minister has a specific kind of power in this interaction, namely the power to formally alter the nature of the relationship that exists between the soon-to-be married couple, so that when the minister speaks that well-worn "I declare you" sentence, it manifests a new identity and relationship between the couple.

This is what happens when everyone agrees on their respective roles and the significance of what is being said. But the statement can fail to perform if that agreement doesn't occur.[6] For instance, Austin suggests that at a wedding, language performs effectively to manifest the marriage when both members of the couple say, "I do." However, these two words could be said in many other contexts without resulting in a marriage (for example, if two children are asked if they want ice cream and both say, "I do"). The words "I do," in other words, only perform in a way that enacts the marriage as long as someone asks the question, "Do you take so-and-so to be your spouse?"[7]

As a result, in the case of a wedding, it is not just the individuals who answer the question *but also* the person who asks it and listens to the answer who can cause the language to fail to perform. And yet, at times, one only becomes the listener because one has spoken a question. So, in the case of a marriage, the minister comes to occupy the role of "listener" precisely because they asked whether the couple cares to be married. Their own speech, therefore, performs in ways that affect their own role and responsibilities as a listener. So what happens in the seemingly very simple interchange between the couple and the minister is quite complicated, from a performative point of view. The minister asks a question, and by so doing, linguistically performs themselves into the role of listener. The couple then answer the question, which only performs if the minister listens to the answer. Then—assuming the couple says, "I do"—the minister can pronounce them married, speaking in a way that changes the nature of their relationship. However, that speech only changes the nature of their relationship if the couple *and* their wider community listens *and* believes the words of the minister.

Here's how I propose this works in relation to sexual violations. In the United States, we often assume that speech performs when a person discloses a rape to a listener, meaning that it is the victimized speaker—and not the listener—who is believed to have performative power in the conversation. Why? Because we assume that the victimized party can do something performative, dangerously transformative, when making an accusation: The harmed party can speak the identity of a person into being by making an accusation. Their words are the ones that have the power to make an ordinary person into a "perpetrator." And listeners know that being labeled as a "perpetrator," being known as a "perpetrator," being Google-able as a "perpetrator," is to become essentially inhuman, vile, treacherous, worthy of punishment, unworthy of dignity.

Worse, though, would be to carry an association between one's name and "perpetrator" when one did nothing wrong.

The word "perpetrator" is therefore a perilous word, a word that performs in a way that causes others to negatively perceive the identity of the one who bears the title. The fear of how this word performs, coupled with the assumption that a victimized person might wield it with ill intent, causes listeners to doubt victims and their speech. Better to demote their authority and their words. Better to protect the one who really has something to lose—the one who might be labeled as a "perpetrator."

The power that we assume is afforded to victim speech becomes particularly visible when accusations hit the media and the public at large has a chance to function as witnesses who evaluate victim speech. Consider, for example, the comments Chanel Miller read in one of the early articles about her violation by Brock Turner:

> He was only nineteen! She hooked up with a freshman? Doesn't that make her the predator? Haven't you ever heard of gang rape in India. There are women out there suffering real abuse and you want to call this assault....
>
> This is the real mystery: This was a top athlete, a highly intelligent, good-looking boy! One might think he'd find a lot of girls who wanted to hook up with him! Instead, he ruins his life by doing this? It's hard to credit.[8]

For another prominent example, consider Donald Trump's reaction to the accusations made against Brett Kavanaugh, who was still a Supreme Court nominee at the time: "It's a very scary time for young men in America, where you can be guilty of something you may not be guilty of."

Here we see the anonymous commenters and the former president remarking on how speech performs in the life of the accused. They start from the premise that the one making the accusation is not speaking truthfully. They also assume that the one making the accusation has linguistic power such that their statements perform negatively in the life of the accused. Trump adds an additional layer to the concern when he equates public opinion with a court of law in which one is innocent until proven guilty.[9] His concern is that victim speech performs so powerfully that it prematurely marks the accused as "guilty," and this, to Trump's mind, is inexcusable because it violates a fundamental tenet of personhood in the United States, that one's personhood is innocent until a preponderance of evidence deems it otherwise. Trump and those who think like him believe that victim speech alone ought to lack the power to provide that evidence, and the problem is that it has been given too much authority by the public, too much of an opportunity to perform in ways that become dangerous for the accused.

The way that Trump and others who share his way of thinking assess victim speech has always seemed reductive to me, perhaps because psychological studies show that those who have experienced a violation often go to great lengths to minimize the harm or to defend the person who harmed them.[10] Victims know how taboo it is to be called a "perpetrator"; they recognize the damage that can be done if someone is labeled a "sex offender" or sent to prison or put on a registry. Many do not see that as accountability but rather see it causing more conflict, stress, and pain.[11] Moreover, those who experience rape recognize that there is usually little to be gained by making an accusation and easily identifiable losses, given the ways that they might well be vilified by listeners who include not only their friends, family, and co-workers but also internet trolls, students on their college campus, the media, prosecutors, trusted spiritual leaders, or, in the case of Brett Kavanaugh cited above, prominent politicians. I do not think, therefore, that the speech of those with embodied experiences of sexual violations always performs the way some believe that it does, in a way that has so much power that it de facto inflicts damage on the identity of the accused.[12] At least in some cases, it can perform vulnerability instead of power.

That vulnerability may be most likely to manifest when intersectionality is not at play; however, in cases where it is at play, vulnerability may take more of a backseat. Consider, for instance, the case of Carolyn Bryant, a white woman who accused Emmett Till—a fourteen-year-old Black boy—of making inappropriate sexual advances toward her. Shortly thereafter, Bryant's husband and his half-brother abducted and violently murdered Till, dumping his body into the Tallahatchie River; a jury found the two white men not guilty of murder. Bryant's statement that some kind of sexual violation occurred shows how white power can trump gender's vulnerability, especially if one is making an accusation against someone who is not only of a different race but also poor or suffering from a disability. My suggestion that an accusation always performs vulnerability, in other words, needs to be taken with not just a grain of salt but a spoonful of it. Nonetheless, there remains enough stigma against individuals who make claims of sexual violations that it often does perform in ways that enhance their vulnerability, and so I'd like to explore how that vulnerability functions in what follows.

Vulnerability as Performative in the Speech of Harmed Parties

Vulnerability, by definition, involves a person's ability to inhabit emotionally uncomfortable, even emotionally risky terrain.[13] Many humans go to great lengths to avoid encounters that make them feel vulnerable, either because they believe that vulnerability is a sign of weakness or because, as an emotion, vulnerability feels unsafe.[14] Individuals who speak about rape, then, don't perform power with the disclosure so much as they perform vulnerability, because they are sharing difficult emotions as well as intimate details about their body and a time during which they lacked control.[15] The words that signal their own vulnerability then perform in a way that invites listeners to encounter vulnerability, which may, in turn, make listeners uncomfortable because they perceive vulnerability as signaling weakness or because they're uncomfortable with strong emotions.[16]

Here's a concrete example of what I mean: Imagine that one friend hears another friend say the words "I was raped." The story may elicit strong emotions like anger, fear, or sadness in the listener that make her feel vulnerable because the presence of those emotions themselves can often feel unsafe or overwhelming.[17] The speaker's body may also communicate vulnerability, if, for instance, he cries or displays other strong emotions. In response, the listener may want to escape the situation as quickly as possible in order to remove their own sense of vulnerability, which is another way of saying that they are trying to escape their own discomfort with what the person who experienced the sexual violation said and feels and what the situation is causing them to feel in response. So the listening friend may try to escape vulnerability in one of several ways. They might deflect or change the topic to something that feels safer to them. They might say something like, "Gosh, that sounds pretty awkward. Didn't something like that happen to that actress—what's her name?—Gwyneth Paltrow? You know, she was in that show called *The Politician*, I think. Did you see it? I thought the acting was solid but the plot was bizarre."

Even if the listener doesn't shut down the conversation entirely, she may try to control the story or emotions of the victimized party as a way to control her own emotional safety. This might take the form of platitudes or gaslighting or emotional manipulation, which can leave the victimized friend doubting his own interpretation of events or feeling discredited. In this scenario, the listening friend might say something like, "At least you're growing stronger from this experience," "This is all part of God's plan," or "It's probably best to think about this as little as possible and try to move on."[18]

In each of these sample responses, the listening friend is able to acknowledge the violation occurred but isn't able to engage with vulnerability enough to continue the conversation. Instead, the listener controls the victimized friend's narrative by telling him what to do and feel in the aftermath of the rape, which shuts down both vulnerability and the possibility of empathy. At the very least, though, the listening friend acknowledges that harm occurred, showing that she can be vulnerable enough to recognize the reality of pain and suffering. A more intense denial of vulnerability would occur if the listening friend cannot do that. This might happen when the listener interprets the speaker's vulnerability as so socially unacceptable, weak, or uncomfortable that it is more comfortable not to acknowledge it. Denial might also occur if the disclosure causes the listener to question her assumptions about the scope and reality of sexual harm when she is not ready to do so. This might happen if the victimized party accuses a mutual acquaintance or someone close to the listener. It might also occur if the listening friend believes that rape occurs elsewhere, certainly not in the safe neighborhood where they live, and that it only happens to people who deserve it. Rape doesn't happen to people who follow the right rules, who do not drink to excess or walk alone at night or wear revealing clothing. The listener, in other words, believes that there are self-protective measures, and recognizing that these have limits, that one cannot control one's own victimization, may be a vulnerability too great to bear.[19] This may cause the listener to feel so unsafe that they need to escape the conversation by shutting it down entirely. Examples of this kind of reaction would include responses like, "That doesn't sound like what rape really is," "You've always been an attention seeker," or "When people like you make an accusation, then it takes away from the people who really did experience something bad."

The Burden of Shame and the Need for Social Belonging

Shame plays a profound role in the lives of many individuals with a firsthand experience of rape. It can cause them to feel responsible for the harm and may also make them afraid to talk to others about it.[20] Isolation becomes a consequence of shame. It becomes a burden, depriving those who are already struggling of the social belonging that is a necessary component of any healthy life.[21] This leads to distress, to feelings that one is alone or unlovable, and it can even lead to the inability to achieve basic needs like clothes, food, shelter, or an education. This desire for social belonging, therefore, stems not just from a reaction to the violation at hand but also from a need common to all human beings. So people try to find ways to transcend the isolation. Speaking about the violation offers one possibility because it provides a chance for the harmed party to be acknowledged, to be known, to be accepted by a group while also maintaining an individual sense of self.

Human beings who disclose a violation often attempt to perform this need for social belonging, even if they don't explicitly state it as such. Yet, the extent to which their words change something or do something in relation to this need is not up to them alone. It requires help from listeners. The disclosure thus gives power to the listener, who has the ability to either extend social belonging or to deny it, and that makes the person who spoke vulnerably more vulnerable during the conversation because they are the one who made a request that the listener now has the power to grant.

The listener's power in regard to effecting social belonging can also be amplified depending on their relationship to the victimized individual. Examples of this include when the person listening has more power by virtue of professional identity, authority, or expertise. So when a person discloses to a teacher, a parent, a police officer, a boss, a human resources representative, a Title IX coordinator, a faith leader, or a popular person in their social circle, then there is a greater risk that the listener can respond in a way that significantly thwarts social belonging. The teacher might start treating the victimized person differently from other students in class or penalize their grade. Police officers, human resources representatives, or Title IX coordinators may refuse to pursue the allegation. The popular friend may start bullying the victimized party or convince others in their social circle to distance themselves. A parent who discredits their child's accusation may leave the child feeling as if they aren't loved by a primary caretaker. Faith leaders who fail to acknowledge the harm may leave someone who experienced a rape feeling spiritually disenchanted or with the feeling that God hates them, as if even the Divine has denied them social belonging. In short, the need for social belonging places the victimized party in a substantially less powerful position in relation to the listener because it is the listener who has the power to bring to reality the victim's need for social belonging. It is the listener who has the power to manifest a necessary component of the more vulnerable party's wellbeing.

To summarize this first part of the chapter: There exists a widespread assumption in the United States that those who have been raped possess exceptional linguistic power because of how a disclosure can perform to transform the identity of an ordinary individual into the identity of a perpetrator. However, this assessment fails to account for the ways that those who experience rape are at a linguistic disadvantage. Recognizing the role that vulnerability and social belonging play in the life of a victimized party and in their speech illustrates that performativity does take place, but it occurs in a way that actually affords listeners greater power than it affords speakers. In other words, disclosing a violation gives listeners power by virtue of their evaluative role—they are the ones with the power to respond to vulnerability in ways that can either harm or enhance the self of the person who dared to show it. They are the ones who can enable or thwart social belonging. In short, when a person is brave enough to make a disclosure, then her speech performs in a way that removes power from her and grants it to the listener. In light of this reality, I'd like to spend the remainder of this chapter providing a framework for listening that privileges the victimized party's epistemic capabilities while also taking the listener's power into account. This framework is composed of several best practices for listening to those who have survived a rape, which I will describe below. From a wide lens, what binds these practices together is a hermeneutic of humility rooted in the recognition that our ability to hear the speech of the violated is de facto tainted by dominant embedded beliefs that cause us to fail at the task of giving those who need linguistic freedom the ability to speak freely and, in turn, to truly regain narrative agency. To combat the power of these embedded beliefs, listeners can practice humility by placing the needs of the most vulnerable first, utilizing active and layered listening, and employing narrative trust.[22]

Placing the Needs of the Most Vulnerable First

A cornerstone of fields like practical and pastoral theology is that the needs of the most vulnerable come first.[23] This core tenet derives from the belief that while all human beings have essential dignity, someone who is struggling or seeking help is in a more vulnerable position than someone who is not. In the case of someone who is making a rape disclosure or requesting help, this means that they are in a less powerful position than the listener is.

My suggestion, therefore, is that those who listen to the testimony of those who've survived a rape do so with the recognition that they are in a relative position of power. So, if the person has trusted the listener enough to tell the story, then they hopefully assume that the listener has some degree of trustworthiness, and the listener's response can either confirm that trustworthiness or abuse it. In other words, the opinion of the listener matters, which gives them power that they can wield to either help or harm. This is why it's important for the listener to be mindful of their relative power. The person who experienced the sexual violation is the one speaking about a moment of embodied vulnerability, who discloses an event that causes pain and that places them on the defensive because of the way that their testimony can be received not with belief but with suspicion. The listener's understanding of the power they possess during a disclosure conversation can, therefore, change the entire tenor of it.[24]

The way that listeners speak can, in and of itself, be one way that they practice putting the needs of the most vulnerable first. Here's an example: There is a significant difference between saying, "Why were you drinking?" and "It sounds like the presence of alcohol in your system means you don't remember much about what happened. Tell me more about how that's affected you." One request is accusative and presumes negative judgment, while the other creates space for someone to tell the story of what happened in their words and on their terms. Likewise, there's a difference between saying, "I don't understand how it's possible to be raped without physical coercion" and saying, "If I'm understanding your experience right, you felt violated when he verbally coerced you into having sex." In the former statement, the listener presumes that their own definition—a definition that reflects dominant embedded beliefs—ought to define how the victimized person reacts to the event.[25] This diminishes the person's narrative agency and selfhood. In the latter response, the listener turns narrative agency over to the victimized party instead, thereby helping to strengthen their sense of self. Listeners, therefore, speak performatively in ways that either diminish or enhance the victimized party's perception of their own narrative agency and selfhood.[26]

Active Listening

Someone who actively listens places the needs of the person who experienced the violation first by putting aside their own interpretative judgments and focusing on not just what the speaker communicates verbally but also on how the speaker is using their other senses to communicate. An active listener notices, for instance, if the speaker's shoulders are hunched or if they're sitting straight, if they're sitting on their hands, if they stutter over a certain word, or if they're unable to make eye contact.[27] Likewise, this kind of listener focuses entirely on what is being said and then leaves a moment of silence to prepare their answer instead of getting distracted from the speaker's words by crafting their own brilliant follow-up. The listener may reflect back the essence of what the victimized party said, ask an open-ended question to create space for the victim to further process, let them speak without interruption, and withhold their own judgment in order to understand what is being said from the victim's perspective. Active listeners also refrain from doing most of the talking because the story is not theirs to tell and the interpretation is not theirs to make.[28] Their job, rather, is to try to help survivors by creating space—perhaps by asking open-ended questions or allowing comfortable silence within a conversation—so that the victimized party has a safe place to interpret their own experiences on their own terms, which, as prior chapters have shown, is often countercultural.

Relatedly, active listening involves listening for the language that those who survived a violation choose to use in the conversation. Such individuals choose specific words for a reason, perhaps because one term resonates most with their experience or because none of them seem to resonate at all or because they're not ready to label the event as a form of wrongdoing. Some may only feel comfortable with the term "sexual assault." Some may only feel comfortable with the term "rape." Some may use terms like "sexual abuse" and "rape" interchangeably. Some may refrain from using labels entirely, instead choosing to say something like, "I was touched inappropriately and against my will" or "I don't know what to call it." Linguistic ambiguity or confusion about the violation may also signal that the person is struggling with how to label the experience, perhaps because their story doesn't align with the scripts provided for them. In such cases, they may feel as if wrong occurred but not know how to name it. Listening carefully to how the person tells the story and describes the violation, therefore, becomes an important way to signal that they are being understood. Indeed, it may be worthwhile to ask about their choice of language.[29] It also becomes equally as important to listen for what is *not* said in addition to what gets spoken. As Emma Justes recognizes,

> Words do not say it all. Beneath, beyond, between, within, and around the words that are spoken lie pools of deep meaning. . . . One who truly listens must be able to tune into, to be aware of, to be willing to approach, acknowledge, and sometimes inquire about the meanings of that which is communicated but unspoken.[30]

Active listeners ultimately pay such close attention to the speaker's narrative, choice of words, and those things that go unspoken as a way of practicing empathy. Here I define empathy as the ability to "feel in" rather than to "feel with." In other words, to orient oneself toward the speaker with the desire to feel as they felt, rather than how the listener hypothesizes they might have felt had they experienced the same event.[31] Empathy, therefore, functions as an act of solidarity and a form of resistance that seeks a way to dismantle the isolation that victimized individuals often experience both during and after a violation. Empathy also helps create a sense of social belonging because of how the practice creates a space for understanding and acceptance. Here's an example of what I mean: I recall one profound instance of active listening in my own life when, after I told a friend what had happened to me, she sat in silence with her legs over the arm of a chair. I initially thought she was being so quiet because she didn't believe me or thought I was overreacting. But then after a few moments, she said that she was trying to imagine what the experience must have been like for me. I remember being profoundly moved that someone had tried to put themselves in my place when doing so, I believed, would expose them to suffering and violence. That anyone would do that for another person seemed remarkable to me.

Today I believe that imagination is an essential tool for the kind of active listening that yields to empathy. Our imaginations, at their best, are brave and creative and willing to go to the spaces from which logic and order and judgment try to steer us away.[32] They allow us to encounter vulnerability with less resistance and to create a kind of social belonging that helps us believe in what could be rather than what is. A person who listens with imagination, then, listens with an openness and non-defensiveness that ultimately helps another person to regain trust and agency.

Layered Listening

Active listening that uses imagination to foster empathy is not always easy to practice. It exists along a continuum on which fusion lies at one end and disengagement at the other.[33] In fusion, listeners hear the event and identify so intensely that it becomes difficult to distinguish the speaker's experience from their own, while in disengagement, listeners distance themselves so much from the speaker that they can become overly hostile or judgmental. Both of these stances rob the speaker of subjectivity and subsume the speaker's subjectivity into the listener's, and listeners are as likely to adopt one of these stances as they are to engage in the kind of active listening that facilitates empathy.[34]

This is where layered listening becomes important. Layered listening involves both the practices of active listening as well as an awareness of the listener's relation to, and reaction to, the topic. This is not to say that the listener elaborates on these topics during the conversations—in a professional relationship like a counseling or spiritual care conversation, this would violate professional best standards because it would redirect the conversation from meeting the needs of the care seeker to meeting the needs of the listener. What layered listening does involve is the ability of the listener to be internally aware of their own reaction to the speaker, how they are engaging with the speaker, and whether they are fusing or disengaging during the course of the conversation in order to process their own emotional needs or avoid vulnerability. They need to be aware of their own triggers and biases, of their own boundaries and emotional limits, of how they speak and how they are heard by others.[35] They also need to develop an awareness of their own sociocultural location and awareness of those that differ from theirs or, at the very least, a stance of humility about their lack of knowledge, because culture plays such an important role in how a person interprets and names a rape.[36] The experience of a child who was raped at a Catholic school in Ireland involves different cultural dynamics than the experience of a teenager who was raped on her way home from school in Mumbai or a middle-aged white heiress who was raped by a husband's friend after a dinner party at her summer house in Newport, Rhode Island. Though these events may involve some similarities, the way a person names and processes it might differ because of the role that culture—including spiritual culture—plays. Likewise, Stephanie Crumpton has written about the ways that the systemic oppression of Black women affects the way they name, interpret, and integrate sexual violations into their lives in ways that might not affect a person of a different race in the same way,[37] as has Phillis Isabella Sheppard, who summarizes that "[t]he self cannot be excised from the social milieu, and moreover, this social context gives rise to a gendered cultural, sexual and racial/ethnic self."[38] Layered listening, therefore, requires an awareness of one's own social context and the role constructions play in it as well as the role that these forces have played in the life of the one who is speaking.

Relatedly, recognizing one's own cultural limitations also involves recognition of one's biases, which may impact not only how a listener hears what someone says but also how the person speaking perceives a listener. Those who lived through a sexual violation may sense that a listener has limited understanding or, worse, limited respect for their ways of being and knowing. They may wisely or inappropriately project judgment onto the listener because they perceive that the listener will be unable to understand the significance of rape in their lives.[39]

Listening from Narrative Trust

Practically, then, listeners might put the needs of the most vulnerable first by recognizing the role that dominant embedded beliefs play and the ways that they function like a bully on a symbolic playground who is attempting to silence the more vulnerable party. This is why narrative trust becomes transformative. It requires listeners not only to accept the reality of harm but also to accept that harm might not adhere to accepted contours, such that the listener is being asked to extend their own understanding of what harm is.[40] This is not a natural position for listeners to adopt, because their own interpretative lenses have been colored by dominant culture's embedded beliefs, which usually encourage distrust of survivor speech under the assumption that those who claim to have been raped are likely individuals who need attention or who are histrionic and manufacture stories to exact revenge or receive a settlement. Practicing narrative trust, therefore, is often not the default orientation of listeners. Even in the wake of the #MeToo movement, it remains a countercultural act of resistance. And that is precisely why it is needed, because we listen differently when we start from a place of trusting the speaker—offering epistemic credibility to the speaker—than we would otherwise.[41]

Narrative trust also requires a willingness to listen when individuals who speak about sexual violations do so using their own language instead of using terms that feel comfortable to the listener. Those with personal experiences of harm may be much more comfortable speaking through artistic media like painting, sculpture, and song that remove the burden placed on speech and replace it with other forms of communication that might be more adept at relating the power of the event. They may prefer to never use words like "rape" at all or it may be the only thing they can say. By way of example, I will never forget a graduate school professor who exempted me from a final paper for our theology of trauma class and allowed me to make a musical recording instead. I wanted to describe the spiritual trauma of rape, but I didn't want to speak about myself; I didn't really want the project to *be* about myself so much as I wanted it to be about the topic. So I turned to another way of communicating that had always felt natural to me: song. I recorded myself singing, a cappella, a medieval chant version of Psalm 22, "My God, my God, why have you forsaken me?" Then three singers I often worked with joined me and we recorded a four-part a cappella version of Psalm 121, "I lift up my eyes to the hills." What I meant to communicate through the music was the way that trauma isolates individuals while recovery reconnects them, and while I could have written that down (as I am now), music felt like a more multidimensional, enfleshed way to communicate because it allowed me to utilize the pitch and timbre of my own voice and to incorporate the voices of others.[42]

In addition to giving those who have been sexually violated the freedom to speak in ways that feel most authentic to them, I'd like to propose one more practice essential to narrative trust. Perhaps most impactfully, narrative trust requires a willingness to change on the part of the listener. Hearing the words and story of someone who survived sexual harm often challenges the listener's own embedded beliefs about safety and autonomy, about how pervasive systemic injustices like racism and sexism are. When listeners employ narrative trust, they open themselves up to the epistemic transformation that this kind of testimony demands. Their own way of being in the world, therefore, changes in ways that not only support those who need it but that also prevents future sexual violations because of how hearing the story changes *them*. Listeners may think and talk about rape differently in ways that change how others perceive it. They may become more active in advocacy efforts. They may raise their children differently than they would have otherwise. In all these ways, listeners change and the communities they are a part of change in ways that raise awareness and become part of a movement to resist and transform the structures that perpetuate and normalize rape.

* * *

I have framed the practice of listening as a primarily individual exercise. But listening is also a collective one. We, as a culture, listen when high-profile individuals like Bill Cosby or Donald Trump are accused of rape. We hear the stories of the person making the accusation and the person on the receiving end of it, and in so doing, we act as judge and jury, oftentimes normalizing the latter and vilifying the former because this is what our embedded beliefs about rape have primed us to do. We also listen collectively within the boundaries of the institutions in which we participate. Faith communities often find themselves divided when a leader is accused of rape.[43] Leaders at educational institutions have all too often sought to cover up student accusations about campus rape in order to protect their reputation or their economic bottom line.[44] The investigation of allegations made by gymnasts against Larry Nassar showed the way in which USA Gymnastics sought to cover up or discredit the testimony of those who experienced the violations. In all of these cases, institutions had a chance to place the needs of the most vulnerable first, to engage in active listening and layered listening, and to employ narrative trust. In all of these situations, they failed.

One might say that institutions are complex, that the stakes are high for them. But that defense fails to account for the power that institutions have in relation to a lone person or group making an accusation. Their resources can be vast, and, oftentimes, their credibility seems to be infallible. The power of institutional response can, in turn, be devastating for victimized individuals, who are often penalized for their attempts to speak, their reputations privately or publicly smeared. It can seem as if they have no power in relation to the institution. These examples signify the need for the more powerful party to concede some of their power as a way to make things right. It also signals the need for community accountability in addition to accountability from the one who inflicted the sexual violation. I thus turn in the final chapter to restorative justice as a resource that allows victimized parties to speak while also creating space for meaningful individual and collective accountability.

CHAPTER 7

On Restorative Justice

IN THE SPRING of 2014, a high school senior who'd been admitted to Harvard invited a freshman girl to a rooftop at St. Paul's School, an elite New Hampshire boarding school. The senior, Owen Labrie, was participating in the "Senior Salute," a school tradition that involved graduating boys inviting younger girls to engage in sexual activity with them. Prior to the night on the rooftop, Labrie wrote the name of the girl in capital letters, along with the names of others that he planned to "slay," and he shared the list with his male friends, presumably for some kind of accountability or moral support. Afterward, Labrie told his friends that he and the freshman had sex, while the girl visited a campus nurse and stated that Labrie had raped her. Harvard rescinded Labrie's admission. The state brought charges against him. A trial ensued. A judge convicted Labrie of misdemeanor sexual assault and endangering a child's welfare, and meted out a penalty of a year in prison and a lifetime on the sex offender registry. His sentence was initially suspended while he appealed the decision, but the court rescinded that after he violated curfew on several occasions, including one where he ran into a journalist on the Boston subway and told her that he'd been visiting his girlfriend of three years at Harvard.[1] He subsequently served six months of his sentence, before being released early for good behavior.

Meanwhile, two years after the violation occurred, the girl publicly identified herself as Chessy Prout in a *Today Show* interview, created a Twitter hashtag to support other harmed parties, advocated for changes at the national level in conjunction with New Hampshire Congresswoman Annie Kuster, and wrote a book about her experience.[2] Her family also brought a lawsuit against St. Paul's, which was settled out of court, and the State of New Hampshire launched an investigation into multiple allegations of sexual violations that had occurred over a period of decades at St. Paul's.

I was working as a boarding school chaplain at the time Labrie's case was in the limelight, and the time I spent around teenagers humanized the many individuals in this story. It also left me curious about what meaningful accountability would have looked like for Owen Labrie and whose job was it to make that decision. Was it Chessy Prout's job? The school's? The government's? A combination of all of the above?

It also appeared that the larger system of St. Paul's, which enabled his choices, wasn't being held accountable. I say this because the leadership at St. Paul's had a long history of receiving accusations from students who had been sexually violated on campus. They also had a long history of discarding them, even vilifying those who brought the claims forward.[3] If this was true, then the root of the problem for Owen Labrie wasn't that he emerged from the womb as some kind of monster whose sole purpose in life was to cross off the names of girls on a list after he coerced them into intercourse. Cultural norms and expectations, at least to some extent or other, played a role. This meant that Labrie needed to take responsibility for what he'd done *and* the wider culture needed to take responsibility as well.

The recognition that singular acts of sexual wrongdoing are not undertaken in a vacuum changes who needs to be held accountable for violations as well as what accountability looks like. So, in a situation like the one at St. Paul's, an acknowledgment of the role that the larger system played meant that Labrie wasn't the only one who needed to be accountable. The culture that enabled the harm needed to be held accountable too, as members of that culture had established the setting, even if he had carried out the plot. For instance, perhaps Labrie might not have harmed Prout if the school had been more proactive at clamping down on the "slaying" lists and simultaneously been more proactive about teaching appropriate sexual conduct or reacting more visibly to other victimized individuals who brought claims forward during the previous decades. Likewise, perhaps Labrie might have thought twice had he not grown up marinating in the toxic masculinity that we've normed as normal masculinity in the United States. Put differently, Labrie didn't act in a vacuum; misogynistic rape culture impacted both his and Prout's lives for the worse. As a result, while Labrie needed to undertake meaningful accountability to make things right for Prout, the wider culture—including the school—needed to make amends as well.[4]

What happened to Chessy Prout is but one example of an infinite number in which we fail to take a systemic approach to eradicating sexual harm. This story happened in a privileged setting, in one of the wealthiest high schools in the United States. Many do not. But regardless of privilege, the issue remains the same. We don't seek accountability often enough for victims. And when we do, we think it's enough to punish the person who directly perpetrated the harm. But it's not. So if we're willing to admit that sexual violations that appear to be individual and isolated are actually systemic and interconnected, then systemic accountability is needed.

Now here's the rub: The justice system in the United States isn't equipped to provide the kind of systemic accountability that I'm suggesting needs to happen. It punishes the person who inflicted the sexual harm for a crime against the State, instead of seeking meaningful accountability from all the constituent parties who enabled wrongdoing. What I'd like to propose in this final chapter, then, is that we need a different way to enact justice that restores narrative agency to victimized parties while also creating meaningful accountability not just for those who inflict sexual violations but for the larger system from which those individuals emerged. In this way, justice doesn't simply limit itself to the punishment of one person but rather becomes an act that allows for the transformation of society at large. I propose that the criminal justice system, as it currently exists, is ill-equipped to provide this kind of accountability because of its individualistic, punitive, and racist structure. As an alternative to this system, I propose that we turn to restorative justice as a more constructive way to address the needs of those who have been raped—including their linguistic and narrative needs—and that we work on reforming the criminal justice system and reserving it for situations where restorative justice is not an option.

The Silence of the Criminal Justice System

The criminal justice system silences participants in ways that harm those who survived sexual violations, those who perpetrated them, and their wider communities. This section will address how those ritualized forms of silencing ultimately affect the way that individuals in the United States at large conceptualize and speak about their experiences. To that end, I'll be discussing four issues, namely: the problems emerging from the criminal justice system's individualistic focus; how the system fails to privilege the narrative agency of those who experience sexual violations; the racial bias within the system; and the reasons why punitive measures are often ill-equipped to deal with the problem at hand.

Individual Accountability

The criminal justice system in the United States predicates itself on the assumption that it's appropriate to hold individual human beings accountable for individual actions, such that when one person rapes another person, then the one who enacted the harm can be punished by the State for their actions. In this way, the criminal justice system presents a high ontology of human beings, insofar as it claims that grownups in particular—excepting in cases of relevant forms of mental illness—*can* know how to make choices that do not violate the law and therefore *ought* to act according to it. This vision of adult identity assumes two things: First, it assumes that adults have the cognitive and psychological capacity to know what the laws are, and second, it assumes that they have the capacity to live according to them.

The trouble with these constructions concerning human nature is that they deny our inherent relationality as well as the way that relationships can prime individuals to perpetrate harm. In other words, they neglect that individual human bodies require relationships to survive. The dominant embedded beliefs in the United States only perpetuate this misconception: Since its founding as a nation, the United States has overvalued individualism and conflated it with masculinity, resulting in beliefs and practices that twist, gaslight, and negatively construct those who live relationally. Children need relationships with caregivers in order to survive, but rather than implement systemic support for that relational need, the United States government offers no maternity leave, subsidized childcare, social-emotional learning in schools, adequate psychological support, or appropriate compensation for public school educators. Likewise, adults also require relationality to survive, but this, too, all too often gets overlooked by those with power in the United States. Most adults in the United States require the assistance of others to harvest their food, fix damage to their homes, educate their children, diagnose and treat their medical ailments, or provide a sense of social belonging, not to mention the intimate ways that we all need the earth to provide resources for our basic food, clothing, and shelter needs.[5] However, neoliberal capitalism rewards those who succeed seemingly—and "seemingly" is the key word here—independently and penalizes those who need assistance by limiting social service supports and then punishing those who desperately need them to have their basic needs met.[6] (In theological terms, individualism might be considered a form of systemic or collective misorientation that epistemically misses the mark, causing people to misunderstand the motivations for wrongdoing. In other words, it misses the mark in terms of how and what we know to be true.)

This cultural misorientation, or misguided emphasis upon the individual, extends to the prison system.[7] Writing specifically about how individualism performs in the criminal justice system in the United States, Danielle Sered explains that:

> Incarceration is also limited as a tool because it treats violence as a problem of "dangerous" individuals and not as a problem of social context and history. Most violence is not just a matter of individual pathology—it is created. Poverty drives violence. Inequity drives violence. Lack of opportunity drives violence. Shame and isolation drives violence. And like so many conditions known all too well to public health officials, violence itself drives violence.[8]

We survive, in other words, not because we are self-sufficient individuals but because we are individually embodied selves who are formed and sustained through our relationships with others. So, when the criminal justice system undertakes accountability as if it were a singular enterprise—as if individuals decide to enact wrongdoing in isolation from the other relationships in their lives—then it silences an honest representation of ourselves and leads to false ideologies about our identity as autonomous rather than relational.[9]

There is, in other words, something reductive about the criminal justice system's suggestion that those who commit wrongdoing make their decisions apart from other formative influences, and that reduction both silences an important part of who we are as humans and reinforces a false idol of self-sufficiency that overattributes autonomy. It also allows violating systems of knowledge to maintain their power, constructing individuals and their choices as if they were made apart from dominant embedded beliefs and ideologies that prime humans to make choices colored by misogyny, toxic masculinity, racism, homophobia, wealth inequality, and distorted language.

Here's how this cashes out practically: Recognizing the role that systems of knowledge and relationships play in an individual's actions reframes who and what is culpable for the harm done to Chessy Prout. Yes, Owen Labrie undertook the concrete violation and needs to be held accountable for that, but one might make the argument that his actions were also enabled by other boys in his class who normed and reinforced the idea, and by the adults at St. Paul's who tacitly endorsed it by leaving the Senior Salute unaddressed. Those adults saw the Senior Salute the way they did because of the overarching acceptance of misogyny and sexual violations in the dominant culture of the United States. All of these embedded beliefs and the people who advanced them laid an insidious foundation upon which the wrongdoing occurred. In other words, given the dominant culture of St. Paul's in which Owen Labrie was immersed and in which he came of age, it is worth asking how much he was exposed to other narratives about women and sex that might have impacted his actions. This does not let him off the hook, but it does extend the scope of who needs to be held accountable.

Narrative Agency of the Harmed Party

I proposed in earlier chapters of this book that the harm done in instances of rape is fundamentally—if not exclusively—narrative. Those who inflict the violation do so in a way that interrupts someone else's story, inserting undesired characters, stalling the plot or inserting twists that cause someone to believe that they no longer have any control over it, that they will be always stuck within the scene of the violation and never move on from conflict to resolution. The criminal justice system does little to empower those who experience such harm as narrative selves, beginning with the story it tells about sexual violations. According to the penal codes in the United States, any act of sexual harm that is brought to the attention of the criminal justice system is not codified as a crime undertaken against the person who experienced the harm but rather as a crime against the State, so in Chessy Prout's case, for example, the court proceeding was labeled as "*State of New Hampshire v. Owen Labrie*" and not "*Chessy Prout v. Owen Labrie.*"[10]

Because of that framework, the story of the harmed party and the needs that arise from that story are not the primary locus of concern. Rather, what is being addressed by the State is the violation of a policy that was designed to establish a universal—or universal within a given jurisdiction—delineation of right and wrong action. Title IX procedures on college campuses function much the same way. What is being addressed within them is not primarily whether a person experienced a sexual act as violating but rather whether there was a violation of the university's policy on appropriate sexual conduct.[11] In this way, both the criminal justice system and the Title IX system consider the epistemic contributions of those who were victimized to be secondary to the epistemic credibility of laws and policies designed by other humans who usually inhabit places of power that reflect the dominant embedded beliefs of the United States.[12] Put more succinctly: Laws and policies are only as victim-centered as the beliefs that inform them.

While the criminal justice system at large is primarily disinterested at best and oppositional at worst to the stories of those who experience harm, this same dynamic also appears in more subtle ways in the courtroom. By way of example, linguist Susan Ehrlich documents how those who experience a sexual violation also experience linguistic and epistemic violations within the courtroom, describing trials in which judges and lawyers allow defendants to employ what Ehrlich calls a "grammar of non-agency." Here defendants speak about the sexual acts in the passive voice, which psycholinguistics has shown leads listeners to believe that the offending party inflicted less harm.[13] See, for instance, the testimony of one person that Ehrlich analyzes who was brought to trial in a Canadian court. This individual uses an agentless passive voice to describe the events of the evening:

> MA [the defendant]: At that point we laid back down on the bed again and, as before, *our pants were unbuttoned* and we began to touch each other.
> SC [questioning lawyer]: Are her pants on at this point?

MA: I think they were not totally off but *they were pushed down* such that I was able to move freely.¹⁴

Nuanced linguistic choices like these—even if subconsciously adopted by defendants and subconsciously acquiesced to by lawyers—ultimately affect the way that juries construct the narrative of events. Indeed, the fact that these linguistic choices go unacknowledged by lawyers and judges signals that the court is, to some extent, complicit in the desire to privilege narrative constructions that challenge the veracity of those who are already on the receiving end of the sexual harm. Ehrlich notes that a similar linguistic dynamic occurs in university proceedings.¹⁵

If the above proposal seems like a stretch, that a judge or lawyer wouldn't be that aware of such subtle grammatical constructions, then consider this additional data point from Ehrlich, who writes that those who cross-examine victimized parties routinely make choices that do the "ideological work" of gaslighting and casting doubt on their narratives.¹⁶ In one university tribunal setting, Ehrlich writes of a cross-examiner who said, "*What might have been your option? I see an option. It may not have occurred to you but I simply want to explore that option with you.* Uhm did it occur to you that you could lock the door so that they may not uh return to your room?"¹⁷

In another university court setting, Ehrlich writes that the cross-examiner said to the victimized party:

> So I guess my my [sic] question to you is uh you had a choice at this point even though you say in your your [sic] oral testimony that you didn't have a choice. Everybody has a choice . . . and your choice was that you could have asked him to leave. So I'm wondering why you didn't ask him to leave? We all have free will. Let me rephrase the question or put another question to you in the absence of an answer to that one. Why did you let uh what you say happened happen?¹⁸

In both of the examples above, the cross-examiner made deliberate and explicit linguistic choices that negatively framed the agency of the victimized party, implying that they misunderstood the situation, that there was a choice all along, that they were responsible for the harm that occurred. Linguistically, then, the decisions that the cross-examiners made in these settings were not reflecting the way that the people describing the harm narrated the event so much as they were attempting to discredit their narratives by distorting them, twisting them into stories in which those individuals had enhanced agency. It is as if the victimized party handed the story of that night to the cross-examiner who red lined the draft and said, "No. It would make a more satisfying story if you wrote it *my* way."

Here is where the power to construct the story becomes the power to inflict a narrative rape in which the court robs the victimized person of narrative agency by recasting the plot and its significance in ways that are easier for others to hear, that align with embedded beliefs about innocence and guilt. This reframe also suggests that the court believes that someone who experiences a sexual violation should reasonably be able to function as what Ehrlich calls a "rational, autonomous, and freely-choosing individual," such that the assumptions that lawyers make about the story of a victim's identity may fail to align with their own self-construction, thereby again denying them narrative agency.[19] The overall effect of these linguistic choices is that they reinforce the embedded commitment that the United States has to autonomy while denying how systemic oppression can constrain the choices an individual has at any given moment. Ultimately, this enables the power of embedded beliefs and unshackles those who perpetrate crimes, freeing them to return from their temporary shame to public redemption and liberation while the oft unnamed victimized party retreats further into anonymity, just as her story retreats from the public story told by history. In short, the way that the criminal justice system operates, both at a large scale and at the level of nuanced linguistic choices, signals that the system routinely deprives those who experience sexual violations of narrative agency, failing to place their stories front and center and failing to directly address their needs, leaving them retraumatized, discredited, isolated, and silenced.[20]

Racial Bias in the System

Back in 1968, in Selma, Alabama, a woman who would later become a leading anthropologist by the name of Nancy Scheper-Hughes was working alone at the SNCC (Student Nonviolent Coordinating Committee) Freedom House, where she lived with colleagues who were civil rights activists, when a Black man she refers to as "James X" entered the home and attempted to rape her. After police discovered the incident—Scheper-Hughes does not know how—she was called in to a courtroom to identify the man who threw her on a bed, ripped her clothes off, and asphyxiated her. One of the things Scheper-Hughes knew from her work in the civil rights movement was that the criminal justice system was not kind to Black men, and so she refused to identify James X in the courtroom when a judge made the request. Neither he nor Scheper-Hughes cared to speak. When Scheper-Hughes was pressed, she answered only the question of whether she knew James X. This was her reply, as she reflected in a 2016 essay about the event and its aftermath: "'I never met the S.O.B. in my life', thus adhering to the civil rights workers' code of keeping our dirty laundry to ourselves while expressing contempt for the segregationist court."[21]

Nancy Scheper-Hughes received no justice for the harm done to her, unwilling to compound the harm she experienced with the harm she saw the criminal justice system inflicting upon Black human beings. Indeed, she is far from alone in recognizing how the criminal justice system is biased against members of the Black community. Antiracist scholars have drawn attention to how the prison system in the United States developed in the aftermath of Jim Crow in ways designed to promote the incarceration of Black bodies, thereby continuing the practice of legally controlling and subordinating them in the service of white supremacy and privilege.[22] The so-called "war on drugs" that increased penalization for drug use played a pivotal role in the cultural landscape of the United States in the

1970s and 1980s, as did media suggesting that violent criminals and child abductors were both imminent threats to the American public and likely to be Black. This collective gaslighting on the part of the government caused the American public to support policies designed to bloat prisons with Black bodies.

Today, one in three Black men are incarcerated in their lifetime, some for violent crimes and some for non-violent crimes.[23] Many are imprisoned for crimes they did not commit at all, a byproduct of the prominence given to plea bargains as a way to avoid costly and lengthy trials, to ease the burden on judges and prosecutors and overworked public defenders, and theoretically relieving arrested individuals of the possibility of a lengthy sentence if conviction of all charges occurred. Of course, the problem with plea bargains is that they leave individuals with a record so that when they're arrested again, the penalties become more severe, which is especially problematic if law enforcement disproportionately targets one's race.

The incarceration of those who are not white leaves lasting effects on the individual as well as the community—the person incarcerated might well experience trauma while in prison. Upon release, they might find it difficult to get an education because many schools don't admit those who have a record or may deny financial aid or scholarships. They might have difficulty finding employment because of background checks done during the hiring process. They might lose their voting rights. Children might be unable to see their parents on a regular basis once they're imprisoned and may experience shame concerning the incarceration. The community at large might feel hopeless or disempowered by the high rate of incarceration, leading to increased mental health challenges and drug use.[24] All of these experiences signal that incarceration is not doing the work of restoring people to wholeness, assuming, in fact, that they did commit a crime. Instead, it's robbing them of opportunity, hope, and healing. Danielle Sered describes this as the "myth of the monster," meaning that those with power in the United States who seek to maintain racially oppressive systems have instilled an embedded belief that those who inflict harm are both Black *and* monster-not-human, such that it becomes appropriate to treat them as different, as other, as unworthy of compassion or a chance at rehabilitation.[25] These practices, in short, maintain the power of white supremacy while simultaneously silencing innate dignity through practices of subjugation designed to intimate that Black and/or incarcerated bodies are somehow of less worth than other bodies, somehow less than human.

Punishment as Ineffective Silencing

Punishment is a cornerstone of the criminal justice system. When someone does something wrong, the response of the court is to dole out some kind of punitive measure—such as a prison term—to procure accountability. More severe wrongdoings receive more severe sentences, as a kind of temporally based version of Hammurabi's Code in which the pulling of an eye is replaced by a cell and the watching eyes of the prison guard. The problem with these punitive responses is that research shows they're ineffective, as Danielle Sered recognizes when she writes that "If incarceration worked to stop violence, we would have eradicated it by now—because no nation has used incarceration more."[26] Indeed, the United States has the highest rate of incarceration in the world, housing 25% of the world's prison inmates, despite being only 5% of the global population. Hence, if punishment were effective, then the United States ought to have radically declining rates of violence of all kinds which, in turn, would correspond with declining rates of incarceration. Yet the United States Sentencing Commission found that 63.8% of violent offenders committed another violent crime within twenty-four months of their release.[27] Approximately 40% of non-violent offenders did likewise.[28]

Punishment, in other words, simply isn't working. It might instill shame, fear, and infantilize through the regimented schedule of prison life, but it doesn't create space for the person who enacted wrong to discover what motivated their choices or why they might want to make different choices in the future. Instead, it silences the possibility of the violating party's active accountability, growth, and rehabilitation so that, in many ways, the criminal justice system does the same thing to victimized individuals that it does to those who sexually violate, inflicting further harm and dehumanization rather than enacting forms of justice that, in turn, lead to healing, wholeness, and the prevention of future wrongdoing.[29] The lack of privacy and social control within prisons can lead inmates to become infantilized, agentless, rather than moral agents capable of taking responsibility for their actions, and the physical violations they might experience at the hands of prison guards and fellow prisoners can instantiate further trauma.[30] Incarceration also exposes inmates to sexual violations at the hands of both prison guards and fellow inmates who have more power within the system, so that ironically those who entered the system without a history of rape may emerge with one.[31] But perhaps most importantly, punitive measures are far more likely to inflict shame rather than cultivate vulnerability, making a wrongdoer defensive in ways that prevent them from softening their heart enough to take responsibility for the wrong done.[32] The prison system thus appears to be more effective at silencing the humanity of inmates than it is at creating opportunities for meaningful accountability, which only compounds shame and dehumanization rather than ameliorating them. This benefits neither the people who directly experience rape nor those who perpetrate harm; the former deserve not only the assurance of physical safety from the person who violated them but also the assurance that further harm isn't enacted as a consequence of their coming forward. Likewise, those who inflict harm deserve an opportunity to make amends, to reform, and to learn to live less destructively.

Finally, there seems to be another insidious reason why the prison system in its current form maintains its monopoly on defining the terms of justice, one that appears behind closed doors in many American homes and that goes uncritiqued by many American adults: the punishment of children. Most American adults punish their children as a matter of course. If Sally hits her brother Sam, then Sally's parents send her to her room, give her a timeout, take away candy for a week. They may invoke corporal forms of punishment, like spanking.[33] They might march her over to Sam and have her recite the memorized script of an apology—"Sorry Sam. I won't do it again"—in the hope that the words will transmute into a new morality. Schools also use this approach: If Sam bullies Jamie on the playground, then the principal suspends Sam in a kind of junior version of the prison system where time apart equates to compensation for the wrong done. Police officers have handcuffed children as young as five, providing an obvious example of how child discipline has become conflated with the criminal justice system.[34] Punishment has become the Ethics 101 course for children in the United States, teaching them from a young age that it is the only way to make amends for wrongdoing, even though child psychologists have increasingly presented evidence that critiques the practice, finding the same results that we find in the criminal justice system: punishment is an ineffective means of changing behavior or hearts.[35] In other words, revoking access to candy doesn't teach Sally to be kind to her brother, and Sam's suspension doesn't convince him that he shouldn't have bullied Mike as much as it gives him a chance to catch up on the latest YouTube videos. But both Sally and Sam have learned that it's appropriate to punish someone who errs, so when they grow up and their children engage in misconduct, they will invoke the same forms of restitution: time-outs, forced apologies, spanking, and suspensions. They've also internalized that punishment is the correct way to manifest accountability, and without other alternative models at their disposal, punishment becomes a kind of epistemic idol, the only way of knowing that is relevant to restitution. What's been silenced through the practice of norming punishment from an early age in children, therefore, is the knowledge and experience and healing that other forms of accountability bring about, of which restorative justice is one.

What Is Restorative Justice?

Thordis Elva was a sixteen-year-old high school student in Iceland back in 1996 when she was raped by an eighteen-year-old Australian exchange student named Tom Stranger, who was also her boyfriend at the time. For almost a decade, she said nothing about the attack to anyone, mindful of the prejudice that might exist against her in Iceland and aware that 70% of those who brought forward a claim of rape in the country failed to achieve a conviction. So while she looked as if she was thriving—becoming valedictorian of the college she attended in the United States and later turning the private feelings she voiced in her writings into successful plays—she admits that she was coping through overachievement as she internally battled doubt and fear.[36] But when she received an invitation to go to Australia for a playwrighting conference, she decided to send Stranger an email, asking if he was willing to meet. He wrote back saying that he would be unable to do so because he lived on the opposite side of the continent. This released a new form of rage that emboldened her to speak, and so she wrote a letter to Stranger detailing the violation and asking for some kind of accountability.[37] Experts in the field of sexual harm support writing these kinds of letters as a way to craft a narrative of the event and receive some kind of closure, but they usually suggest locking them in a drawer or destroying them after, as sharing them with the person who hurt them might raise both legal and safety concerns. Thordis Elva, however, violated the script of what the ideal victim is supposed to do with her story—process it privately, keep it close—when she sent the letter back to Stranger. And then Stranger violated the script of the ideal perpetrator when he wrote back and took responsibility for his actions.[38] This initial exchange began a multi-year correspondence that culminated in an in-person meeting in South Africa, with both the virtual and in-person communication being painful at times but also allowing Thordis to ask questions and receive answers directly from Stranger that she felt were invaluable to her recovery, while Stranger found healing in accepting responsibility and following Thordis's lead in making things right. Later, the two wrote a book together and gave a joint TED talk about the value of speaking their way to recovery and restoration.

Now, not all harmed individuals want to directly engage with people who hurt them, and for justifiable reasons. Some may feel that they are physically unsafe. Some may feel that they've given the person who raped them enough of their attention and mental energy. Some may have a conviction that this person's rehabilitation is not their responsibility.

Others, however, dream of an apology or they have questions about the attack that only the person who enacted the harm can answer. In these cases, the linguistic constraints of the court system are of no help because it is lawyers—not victimized parties—who pose questions to defendants, and lawyers who discourage wrongdoers from admitting their guilt in order to avoid lengthy prison sentences. In Thordis Elva's case, though, there was no trial, as she sensed that her experience deviated enough from rape scripts that there was little hope of a court response, which, in turn, initially made her feel as if there were no alternative options for accountability.

That is, until she sent Stranger the letter and began what might be described as an informal restorative justice process.

Restorative justice is a philosophy that proposes the primary goal of justice is to make things right for those who experienced wrongdoing. It encompasses a number of practices, including circle processes, conferencing, and victim–offender mediations. All of these occur with the help of at least one facilitator who assesses whether participants are a good match for the procedures, prepares them for the processes via one-on-one conversations that occur prior to any larger group meetings, and leads larger group sessions.

Restorative justice has a long tradition of use and historically has been normed in a number of indigenous cultures as a way to effectively meet the needs of victimized parties and create effective forms of accountability for those who enacted harm.[39] Over the past few decades, it has also gained prominence in western cultures, becoming the default system of accountability for minors in New Zealand, a more central part of the criminal justice system in Canada, a more integral part of the disciplinary system in primary education in the United States, and is increasingly used as an alternative to the criminal justice system in several states, most notably Colorado, Vermont, California, Minnesota, Montana, and Texas.

While restorative justice procedures have been effectively used to respond to wrongdoing ranging from school bullying to murder,[40] there has been greater reluctance to employ them in cases where sexual wrongdoing occurred, primarily because, ironically, the relational emphasis of restorative justice that is normally perceived to be its strength is seen as a weakness. Opponents argue that those who survived a rape may not want to sit face-to-face with the person who harmed them because they worry about being triggered or fear for their physical safety.[41] Others cite the high recidivism rates among sex offenders as a sign that they are beyond rehabilitation and therefore would not benefit from a restorative process.[42] This was exactly the kind of argument presented by Amira Elwakil, a British-Egyptian feminist, who petitioned the Women of the World festival along with over 2,000 other feminists and academics, to bar Tom Stranger from appearing at a conference with Thordis Elva, as they believed that someone who committed rape shouldn't be given a chance to publicly share their narrative—even receive applause from the audience—because it would normalize sexual harm and take space away from the necessity of hearing the stories of the violated.[43]

The responses of such feminists and activists make sense, given that those who rape and those who have been raped are epistemically and linguistically not on a level playing field, and their stories are apt to be received differently because of the way others construct or make assumptions about their identities. However, restorative justice advocates counter that constraining the speech of those who sexually violate does not benefit victimized individuals because when conditions and systems are set up in ways that allow violating parties to take responsibility for their actions, then speech performs in a way that responds directly to the needs created by the sexual violation. In other words, when a person says, "Yes, I did this. I apologize. Now what do I need to do to make this right?" then that person is treating the violated individual as a subject, thereby returning agency by both taking responsibility *and* asking how they can be supportive in helping the victimized party to rewrite the shattered narrative of the self.[44] This is exactly the opposite of what happened in the violation.[45]

Nonetheless, some individuals who've been sexually violated simply do not want this kind of direct interaction, even if the person who raped them was willing to take responsibility, leading to the question of whether restorative justice is limited to rare cases like Thordis Elva's, where the victimized party feels safe enough or brave enough to reach out to the person who enacted the harm and seek direct, active accountability. To address this concern, Alissa Ackerman and Jill Levenson suggest that vicarious restorative justice procedures can effectively address the needs of all parties alike while avoiding direct contact. In these processes, a surrogate can represent either the victimized or offending party. A surrogate who represents the victimized party, for instance, might read a statement written by the actual victimized party or share their own personal experience of rape to give the person who inflicted the harm an opportunity to hear the impact of their actions. If a surrogate offending party is involved in a process, then they may do likewise, explaining either through their direct experience of wrongdoing or through reference to a statement from the person who inflicted the violation. Such a statement might include an explanation of what motivated the harm, and would likely also take direct responsibility for it and express an openness to undertaking acts of accountability that feel meaningful to the person who experienced the rape.[46] In this way, the story of the violation changes both for those who were the recipients of it and those who inflicted it, because the restorative process adds a new embodied memory that involves both the pain of the past alongside the accountability of the present.

The Benefits of Restorative Justice for Those Who Experienced a Sexual Violation

The restorative system differs from the criminal justice system in several ideological and practical ways that benefit those who bring forward a sexual violation claim. Foremost, the restorative system isn't based in pre-established legal codes, which means that the victimized party's credibility isn't evaluated against external definitions of harm. Instead, restorative processes start from a place of empathy in which listeners try to understand how the victimized party understood the nature of the wrongdoing and then, in turn, lets that person explain what needs to be done to make things right. This means that victim speech operates very differently in a restorative setting than in a retributive one.[47] In a criminal justice procedure, victimized parties are always on the defensive: they are the ones responding to a lawyer's questions, not the ones asking the questions. A lawyer examining or cross-examining them can reframe their speech, strike their words from the record, or contest their statements on the basis of an argumentative tone or message.[48] District attorneys or personal lawyers prep individuals who made accusations for their time on the stand so that they are armed not with the words that are authentic to their experience but with the words that are most likely to convince a judge or jury of their credibility and the defendant's guilt. That judge and jury, meanwhile, establish the credibility of the person who experienced the sexual violation against legal words and codes that may not express their understanding of why the harm was actually harmful or may not represent the harm at all, in cases where the rape violated the scripts embedded in the law.

None of this happens in restorative justice because there are no lawyers constraining the speech of those who were violated, no laws against which to evaluate their claims. Instead, restorative justice gives the victimized party an opportunity to speak freely, without limits on their tone or time, and to define the contours of harm in terms that relate to their particular body's experience of it. The speech of victimized parties, therefore, performs differently in restorative justice than in the courtroom because the epistemic freedom granted through restorative justice allows those individuals to speak in a way that gives them agency over what words to use, when to use them, and how to use them. The victimized party also has an opportunity to reclaim agency because the perpetrating party (or surrogate), facilitator, and wider community agree to these parameters of speech, listening in a way that affirms and co-constructs the self of the person who experienced sexual harm, rather than attempting to annihilate it. In this way, the speech that occurs in a restorative space has a chance to directly counteract the harm done to the self during the sexual violation, validating the victimized party's body, agency, and desire rather than attempting to destroy it, and opening possibilities for that person to imagine and create a narrative of the self in community that contrasts with the experience of rape.

Finally, the way that listeners receive the words, story, and embodied testimony of someone who experienced rape is different than in the courtroom, where the goal is to establish credibility and to evaluate how convincing and truthful their statements seem to be. Listeners do not have to assess credibility against pre-established laws that do not emerge from, or take into account, the nuanced forms of sexual harm or the multiple ways that human beings may respond to it. In short, those who listen, in a restorative setting, to a person who was raped are neither judge nor jury, intent on assessing their credibility as a knower, but rather participate with a presumption of belief and with the primary goal of supporting and returning agency to the harmed party. This, in turn, removes the linguistic constraints imposed by the courtroom for those who were raped, freeing them to speak in ways that are meaningful for them—rather than in ways intended to impress a jury—and to use terms like "rape" in ways that they define rather than in ways that align with the court's definition. Listeners thus give those who were raped space to tell the story of harm in a way that resonates with their experience, instead of requiring that the legal story of harm narrate the experience for them. This difference, in turn, gives those in need of it a chance to reclaim agency and to engage in a process of co-constructing the self after the violation within the confines of a supportive community.

Benefits for Those Who Inflict Sexual Violations

Those who experience a sexual violation often have questions about the harm that only someone who inflicted the harm can answer: Why did this person choose them? Did they think this was appropriate behavior? Do they even think about what they did? The linguistic constraints of the courtroom prevent them from both asking and expecting honest answers to these kinds of questions, as it may not be in the best interest of the offending party to answer honestly, especially if answering honestly means risking increased punitive measures against them. This can leave the violating party feeling as if those who inflicted the violation have no remorse and are unwilling to take accountability—which may be true—though it is also likely that they're being coached by their lawyer to speak in ways that don't reflect what they might say if given the chance to speak freely. Removing the linguistic constraints of the courtroom as well as its prescribed ways of punishing thus benefits those who have been raped, who may receive more of the honest answers that they need, while also freeing those who enacted harm to speak more honestly, authentically, and openly about the harm they've done.

Second, a restorative justice space is primarily one that is intent on meaningful forms of accountability that align with the victimized party's needs because it focuses on making things right for the person experiencing the harm.[49] This attempt to reframe what justice means benefits all parties because it removes the solely punitive emphasis that may cause those who rape to get defensive when it comes to taking responsibility. It also means that when the person who enacted wrong does make amends, they will know that they're doing so in a significant way that makes a difference.

But perhaps most importantly, restorative justice challenges those who inflict sexual violations to transform their own understanding of what rape is and the harm it causes so that they can change how they live as sexual selves.[50] In this way, restorative justice is a far more challenging form of justice to engage in than retributive justice, because it requires active participation on the part of offending parties. Restorative justice requires that they be open to hearing the pain they've caused, to reflect on why they caused it, to engage empathically, to reconsider their actions, and to take concrete steps to change so that they will act differently in the world going forward.[51] This contrasts with the retributive system, in which those who inflict sexual harm sit quietly next to their lawyers while others speak about their actions, before a judge or jury doles out punishment—if punishment is given at all—that will lead them to sit in a jail cell. This is not a process that promotes active accountability but rather a process that thwarts it from the first moment the offending party's lawyer tells the one who perpetrated not to answer a question. The restorative space, in contrast, encourages agency by encouraging those who enacted wrong to absorb how the story of the person who survived the harm changes their own, and to voluntarily agree to incorporate that story into their life in a way that transforms how they exist in the world in the future. These acts, hopefully, will be steps toward restoring wholeness in the person who enacted wrong.

However, just as a person who was raped cannot reconstruct the self without external support, neither can the person who raped take accountability and experience their own healing without help from others. This is where the wider community's role in restorative justice comes in.

Recall that this book began with the assertion that behind every person who enacts a sexual violation is a society that upholds values that make the harm possible in the first place. This may be hard to see in a country as diverse as the United States, but it is easier to identify when one looks at sexual harms that take place in a closed system, like St. Paul's School. Consider this: Chessy Prout was not the only girl to make an accusation that sexual harm occurred at St. Paul's. Numerous individuals brought claims forward in the decades prior to Prout's allegations, many of which only received attention after her case gained notoriety. Since the State of New Hampshire began its investigation into the Prout case in 2014, news stories have chronicled the toxic culture at St. Paul's.[52] Those stories described how rape culture permeated campus life, tacitly encouraging males—both students and teachers—to pursue female students. That same culture seeped into the school's administration and board, which, assuming reports are to be believed, turned a blind eye toward traditions like the Senior Salute, to language like "slaying," to past allegations. It also appears to have primed leaders to silence anyone who did come forward with a claim and sealed the stories of their rapes off in confidential settlements destined to become the stuff of cobwebbed, clandestine lore, spoken of in whispers, and, eventually, not spoken of at all. So, while St. Paul's cast aside reports of rape on campus, traditions like the Senior Salute that Labrie participated in by and large appear to have gone unquestioned in what essentially amounted to a closed system of relationships and knowledge. All of that made St. Paul's into an environment that both prevented those who experienced sexual violations from exercising narrative agency while enabling boys like Labrie to enact sexual harm. It also constructed an embedded belief that there was only one story about rape at St. Paul's, and that was that it didn't happen because the men and boys at the school were intelligent, elite, and classy. They were the teachers and future leaders of the country, nay, of the world, and so certainly—*certainly*—they could not be that thing called a "rapist" because they did not look like or act like rapists.

One might propose that the culture at St. Paul's represents a microcosm of the embedded beliefs that privilege the powerful, and, insofar as they are a metaphor for power, one sees these embedded beliefs reflected in the wider culture of power in the United States. It is a kind of power that silences the victimized. It maintains the status quo for those who rape. It maintains misogyny and racism because those who possess power tend to benefit from its beliefs and practices, one of which is rape. It is, therefore, incumbent upon the wider community, but especially those members of the community who hold and maintain power, to be self-reflective about their own complicity in harm and to allow humility to be the ally of self-reflection. Only then can these members of the wider community help to actively manifest opportunities for meaningful accountability both out of a desire to prevent future wrongdoing and out of an awareness that their actions and beliefs create the conditions that allow sexual violations to occur.

The larger community that was involved in and impacted by any violation, therefore, needs to be accountable for its role and to do so by taking the lead from those who experienced the harm about what that accountability means and looks like. Restorative justice is well-equipped to help the community do this, through listening circles that allow the community to hear from those who experienced sexual harm and to seek meaningful opportunities for accountability. As a result, the community hears firsthand what restitution means both ideologically and practically, without making assumptions or shutting down direct lines of communication, as might be done in a courtroom.

Restorative justice processes, therefore, prevent the community from jumping to assumptions about what someone who was raped needs to reclaim a sense of self—body, agency, and desire—or to regain a sense of narrative social belonging. This is something that those who experienced sexual harm both need and request. St. Paul's, for instance, did eventually offer Prout a settlement in the aftermath of the harm she endured, but Prout—like Lacy Crawford, another person who experienced a sexual violation at St. Paul's—was also interested in changing the culture and leadership practices at the school in ways that would dissipate the power of misogyny. Victims like Prout hoped the school would issue apologies or take responsibility for the role leadership and culture played in their assaults, but these statements were either not issued at all, issued far too late, or perceived as disingenuous. The State of New Hampshire tried to create some kind of accountability by requiring the school to hire a compliance officer. But victimized parties felt a new sense of hopelessness when the officer resigned and issued a statement in which he cited aggressive behavior from school administrators who tried to thwart his work, creating an "intolerable working environment."[53]

In many ways, the failures at St. Paul's symbolize the kinds of problems that occur when communities try to respond to rape: They may not take responsibility at all, their response may be perceived as self-interested or insincere, or they may try to enact accountability in a way that seems appropriate to them but is not what the victimized party ultimately wants. These responses serve neither the person harmed nor the larger goal of transforming the culture around rape. So, to counteract these kinds of problems, it becomes even more important for the larger community to hear directly from those who experienced the violation about what accountability means to them, and to listen in the ways described in the previous chapter as a first step toward restoring collective agency. Then, it becomes incumbent on the community to follow through with the agreed-upon requests so that the community doesn't become a site of secondary rape—a site in which the person's body, agency, desire, and narrative again feel violated—but rather a site in which self and narrative are restored.

Restorative justice is equipped to engage in this kind of community accountability in a way that the court system is not. Representatives from the wider community can participate in circle processes in order to hear directly from those who experienced a violation about the harm done and what is needed to make things right. Moreover, when community members hear directly from someone with personal experience about what rape looks like and what its ramifications are, their collective understanding about the violation grows beyond the confines of rape scripts to a more holistic conception. In this way, a community that is willing to hear and trust the words of someone who knows sexual harm firsthand helps to dismantle the embedded beliefs ingrained in larger society. These embedded beliefs include myths that have functioned as idols in determining the scope and reality of rape, including the myth of stranger rapist, the Black male rapist, and the pure white victim. They also include embedded beliefs about racism, sexism, homophobia, and transphobia that perpetuate the idea that rape is either justified or exotic and rare rather than common and insidious. Insofar as the larger community changes its beliefs, speech, and practices around rape as a result of participating in restorative justice, then, there is a chance that the process might not only create a means of accountability for those who experienced the wrongdoing directly but also prevent future harm. Restorative circle practices can also be used to more broadly discuss issues related to topics like gender and power so that participants can learn about how these ideas are constructed, the impact they have, and how they can be practiced differently. Indeed, these preventative conversations are important ways of educating others about what rape can look like and why it occurs. That education can, in turn, transform the ways we live our lives as embodied stories in the world, because just as it takes a village to rape someone, so it will take a village to stop rape from occurring again.[54]

A Note of Caution

While restorative justice has much to contribute to both responding to and preventing rape, it is not appropriate for all instances of sexual harm. For instance, some victimized parties may not want to engage in the process, either because they don't feel safe or because they believe that prison time is the best possible response both for accountability and to make sure that the offending party does not continue to engage in harmful behavior. In addition, the person who perpetrated the harm may be a poor candidate for a restorative process. This might be because they refuse to take accountability, because they find it difficult to engage in introspection or self-examination, or because they are unwilling to engage with the victimized party. In both cases, restorative justice should not be employed if it will cause more harm than good because in any response to sexual harm, one of the goals is to restore agency to those whose agency was removed via the offense. If a restorative process functions in such a way that a survivor is forced to engage with their assailant or the assailant disrupts the process, then the eradication of agency is only made worse. To prevent this from happening, it is important that a skilled facilitator assess whether the process is going to be a good fit for both the victimized party and the offending party through individual conversations prior to any formal process occurring. Indeed, these pre-conversations are essential to assessing whether a restorative justice process should be used. They are also helpful for giving facilitators the data they need to prepare participants and conduct a process well.

Finally, one of the reasons that participants, especially those who enact harm, may struggle to engage in restorative processes is because the dominant embedded beliefs in society have become so permeated by epistemologies that privilege intersectional oppression that it is beyond their ability to engage with other ways of knowing and being in the world. Put into simpler terms: They think they're right because society tells them they're right. Likewise, the communities they are part of may be similarly enmeshed in these ways of knowing. To the extent that individuals are unable to engage in the processes, it can also signal the stranglehold that these ways of knowing have on so many of us. Nonetheless, some will be able to see differently. Some will be open to challenging these assumptions. Some will want to take accountability, and with each changed heart and mind, a larger community forms that can both prevent and make things right in cases of sexual violations.

* * *

The philosopher Ann Cahill has argued that the reality of rape fashions women into pre-victims whose bodies are inscribed with the understanding that rape is a possibility for them.[55] This is true, yet I would add that the way that embedded beliefs in the United States function to perpetuate beliefs and practices that enable and normalize rape means that society at large has become what I would call a pre-accomplice. In other words, we are primed not to question embedded beliefs about what qualifies as a "real rape," not to question the role of physical violence, the prior relationship between "assailant" and "victim," and the role that race, gender, and sexuality play in our construction of harm. As a result, we become complicit in perpetuating the continued normalization of sexual violations that do not fit into our embedded beliefs, to the detriment of acknowledgment and accountability. We, therefore, need processes like restorative justice that take a grassroots, holistic, and spacious approach to responding to rape in ways that both meet the needs of those whose lives have been directly affected by rape and also prevent future harm. This requires not just active engagement from the one who directly inflicted the sexual violation but also active engagement from the community that played either a passive or active role in allowing it to occur. Restorative justice, therefore, is equipped not just to dismantle the criminal justice system's individual, punitive methods of redress that are, by and large, ineffective at solving the problem of rape. It also creates space for victimized individuals to regain agency through speech and for both the person who directly inflicted the harm and the wider community to create meaningful accountability through listening and action, which is essential not just to addressing a rape that already occurred but also to preventing sexual violations in the future.

CONCLUSION

YEARS AGO, I sat on an airplane reading a copy of Susan Brison's *Aftermath*. The book was relatively new at the time, assigned to me by a professor named Serene Jones, who was teaching a course on theology and trauma, and I had brought it with me while on the way to a friend's wedding. In it, Brison describes a physically violent rape and attempted murder that she experienced while on a walk, in broad daylight, in France, and she uses that event to generate questions about the way that trauma impacts one's sense of self and, in turn, requires its remaking in community.

I read the entirety of Brison's book on that flight, underlining important phrases, making notes in the margin to summarize a salient point or ask a question or pose a challenge. I had never encountered an academic book that seemed to speak so directly to me, that captured the crisis of knowing that I was facing. But equally as importantly, Brison's book offered solidarity; I discovered an epistemic companion. Here was someone who was asking the same questions I was trying to ask but felt unable to vocalize, someone who had wrestled as I had, and who had found ways to talk about something that I felt was beyond the confines of speech. Thanks to her words, the profound loneliness I felt lifted for the first time.

One image from that book has always stuck with me, perhaps because of the hope embedded within it. Toward the end of the first chapter, Brison writes that several years after the trauma:

> I no longer cringe when I see a woman jogging alone on a country road where I live, although I may still have a slight urge to rush out and protect her, to tell her to come inside where she'll be safe. But

I catch myself, like a mother learning to let go, and cheer her on, thinking, may she always be so carefree, so at home in her world. She has every right to be.[1]

Nearly two decades later, I still reflect on this image, wonder who this hypothetical woman was, imagine her running along a road lined with tall trees and no sidewalks, never once looking over her shoulder, never once sensing fear. I smile when I think of her arriving back at home, wiping her forehead with a towel, and when her partner asks how the jog was, she says, "Beautiful," and then they proceed to scramble eggs and fry some bacon, unaware of what could have been. The vision Brison offers is a reflection of what I and so many others desperately want this world to provide—a right to safety, to joy, to health, to freedom. This woman deserves to savor the simple pleasure of running on a paved surface, surrounded by the songs of birds, immersed in the sound of her own deep breathing and pounding heart, symbols of her pulsing life. Indeed, every human being deserves this kind of simple bliss, regardless of their race, gender, economic status, citizenship, religion, or body's abilities.

Yet I'm keenly aware that the rights Brison imagines are increasingly under threat in the United States, that many people are more vulnerable under the law now than they were at the time of Brison's writing twenty years ago. Of course, the #MeToo movement did raise significant awareness about the pervasiveness of sexual violations in the United States. Many survivors felt emboldened, able to come forward and tell their stories because there is strength in numbers, and that act of collective storytelling opened hearts and minds, fostered solidarity, and helped to change laws. Still, it's far from enough. Critics have noted that the #MeToo movement had significant problems, even at its height. Notably, it undermined Tarana Burke's original intent for the movement to help Brown and Black women, instead centering attention on the violations that white women experienced, particularly those who spoke from places of economic and social power. As Anita Hill reflects:

Public enchantment with a depiction of a harassment victim as a glamorous starlet, in part based on the rape myth of the perfect victim, did a disservice to those who were featured in the initial #MeToo stories as well as many others, such as service workers. . . . It's a shame that the narrow representation of sexual assault and harassment coming out of the #MeToo movement left out Burke's intended survivors as well as lesbian, gay, trans, queer, and bisexual people's broad range of experiences. Statistics show that LGBTQ+ individuals are at higher risk of violations than straight and cisgender women.[2]

In addition to the critiques Hill levies at the #MeToo movement, Miranda Pilipchuk notes that the movement sensationalized those who did disclose. This is problematic, as some survivors either do not want to or cannot disclose for practical reasons that range from the possibility that one may lose one's job to the possibility that one may have one's child taken away. There are many valid reasons not to disclose, just as there are many compelling reasons to do the opposite. However, the #MeToo movement's implicit approval of those who spoke of their own experiences publicly tacitly created a moral hierarchy between those who do disclose and those who do not. Pilipchuk, rightly, suggests that back in 2018, it might have been more worthwhile to focus on survivor healing rather than the glamorization of disclosure.[3]

Finally, while #MeToo has led to the passage of a number of laws intended to, for instance, prevent harassment in the workplace, the vast majority of perpetrators still walk free, just as the misogyny and racism that enable sexual harm still remain pervasive and, at times, glamorized.[4] It is notable that voters in the United States overlooked allegations against then-nominee Donald Trump, as well as statements such as the one from the *Access Hollywood* tape in which Trump bragged that as a famous man, he could "grab 'em by the pussy" and do as he pleased.[5] Speech performs here to assert power in fundamentally destructive ways, and it must be called out for what it is: It is speech that rapes, violating the bodies, agency, and desires of some listeners while emboldening others to perpetrate further harm.

Of course, it's important to note that Trump isn't the only president in recent history with allegations of inappropriate sexual conduct leveled against him. As Anita Hill observes, three of the past five presidents—Joe Biden, Donald Trump, and Bill Clinton—have been accused of inappropriate sexual conduct.[6] Among the current justices on the United States Supreme Court, two—Clarence Thomas and Brett Kavanaugh—have had significant allegations leveled against them by multiple women, and in neither case were all the women who made accusations allowed to testify about their experiences to the Senate Judiciary Committee.[7] But perhaps, one might argue, it doesn't matter that these accusations were heard. After all, as Susan Collins noted at the time of Kavanaugh's confirmation, the Senate Judiciary Committee is not a court of law, not intended to be a place where guilt or innocence is determined. It is, however, a place where we deserve a chance to speak in truth, to share stories that are important for the public to hear as a way of embodying our fundamental rights. All too often, however, those with power do not agree, as evidenced by the attempts they make to silence those who want to speak.

This silencing extends to the passage of laws themselves. Those with legal authority in the United States are systemically implementing damaging laws that take us backward instead of forward in the fight for justice, equality, and dignity, as evidenced by changes such as those made to restrict voting rights or changes to the nation's Title IX policy under Betsy DeVos, which sought to enhance the rights of accused perpetrators while limiting the rights of those who make accusations. Perhaps most notably, the Supreme Court's decision to overturn *Roe v. Wade* has ushered in an era where pregnant individuals are no longer safe in their own bodies, where privacy can no longer be assumed, where pregnancy, miscarriage, and abortion can be criminalized, where lawyers and not doctors are making medical decisions, and it all foreshadows a future erosion of rights for others who have minoritized identities.

It is, therefore, incumbent that we begin to recognize that this erosion of rights is, in and of itself, a form of rape, just as the inability to procure reproductive medicine is. As Judith Jarvis Thomson recognized decades ago, a pregnancy that occurs without one's consent is, in and of itself, a violation—a pregnancy that can't be terminated is likewise a violation, a failure to recognize that pregnant individuals are all too often faced with multiple life-altering choices of which abortion may be most ethical.[8] The failure to recognize this is not just a failure to value a pregnant person's moral agency but also a rape of their narrative agency.

Yet even as I harbor concerns about the rape of human beings, I also see the problem of rape extending far beyond the human realm. Approximately a week after the Supreme Court overturned *Roe v. Wade*, it issued another decision limiting the Environmental Protection Agency's ability to regulate greenhouse gas emissions. In so doing, the Court dealt a blow to activists and experts who are desperately trying to keep the earth from suffering the worst effects of an already dire climate crisis, a crisis brought on by humans' constant, unrelenting rape of its generativity.[9] These violations range from ripping tree roots to fracking the earth's crust, drilling the ocean floor, and poisoning the air with noxious gases. And while it might be anthropomorphic to impose language of "consent" or "narrative" onto constructions of the earth's identity and the harm done to it, it might nonetheless be worth risking that the earth does have a story, a story that predates each of us and that will surpass the mortal existence that any of us have. Human beings have, at many points, tried to tell this story and to impose meaning onto it, to construct how and to what extent we are justified in trying to rob the earth of its subjectivity. Indeed, the current ecological crisis might be seen as the outcome of years upon years of subjectivity violation such that—perhaps—the earth does possess a language of protest, a language of hurricanes and forest fires, of melting glaciers and dying coral reefs. As wildlife go extinct, as temperatures and oceans rise and once robust habitats become increasingly uninhabitable, humans bear the sole responsibility for violating the earth's body, agency, and desires at the most primal level.[10] We are, in other words, doing to the earth what we do to one another, and while we are all complicit in that violation, it falls to those with the most systemic power to make the most systemic change.

But all too often, those leaders are failing.

So just as we have to fight to change violating laws, we also have to change the mindsets that enable them. The originalist view that Supreme Court justices like Brett Kavanaugh, Clarence Thomas, and Amy Coney Barrett hold—a point of view that takes a narrow, literal view of the Constitution that essentially amounts to legal prooftexting—diabolically resembles and is enabled by literalist biblical interpretations. Both assume that they can, with certainty, read into the minds of the texts' authors. Both assume the texts have one and only one truth that can be discerned with certainty when read from the point of view of the original author in their original cultural context. Both assume that this point of view is not only relevant but the only way we should live our lives today. I see this as a categorical insult to the creativity of the writers, the nuanced spirit of both of these texts, and as a sign of hubris on the part of their contemporary interpreters. If Shakespeare can be read so many different ways over so many centuries, shouldn't the Constitution and the Bible have at least as many dimensions?

I see in both of these forms of reading a tremendous violation to the text's generativity, a form of literary rape. I am also deeply concerned that these ways of reading violate everything from the authors' creativity to the nuance of the text itself to human ingenuity. Most importantly, such readings inflict concrete harm because of the way that those in power use their way of reading the text to impact everything from policy to law to social discourses. That these leaders do not—or choose not to—acknowledge the harm that this form of reading does to children, people of color, those without financial means, those with differently abled bodies, women, and members of the LGBTQ+ community is prideful and in itself a form of sin. Moreover, the way that justices like Kavanaugh and Barrett read the Constitution as a thinly veiled justification for their own religious beliefs essentially functions as a simultaneous rape of both Christianity and the law. Dogma certainly lives loudly in them, as Senator Dianne

Feinstein said, but the dogma is a false ideology engineered to help those with power maintain it, instead of an authentic wrestling with the spirit of these important texts that treats them with all the care they deserve.[11] In other words, it is a dogma that those of us who care about ending sexual violations must resist.

In the wake of this increasingly dire attempt by those with power to eradicate the rights of so many in the United States, we need to transform how we live in the world and what we live for. Those of us in academia must find ways to speak differently, to communicate the wisdom of what we've learned through our research in ways that draw people in and empower them, instead of alienating them with words that only ever appear in our guilds and not in daily life. Those of us who are members of faith traditions that aren't represented by evangelical, conservative Christian ideologies need to become much more vocal about how our faith is being coopted by those who are twisting it for their own gain. Those with expertise in law, medicine, mental health, and other fields must likewise not only be experts but activists.

This is, in the end, not just large-scale legislative work but also grassroots work, one-on-one work that begins in our homes, our churches, our classrooms, and our offices. For just as it takes a village to rape a human being, it also takes a village to prevent it, and that change requires us to live differently than we have before. It calls us to act differently, and it calls us to think differently. And finally, it requires us to find ways of speaking differently in the service of ending rape once and for all.

ACKNOWLEDGMENTS

THIS BOOK EMERGED from a vulnerability that sought understanding. It is the culmination of years of seeking, of struggling with the loneliness that emerges when one cannot speak, of yearning for expression and clarity and community. In the early years after I was raped, I believed I would never be able to make sense of what happened. My trust in the world was shattered, and I did not expect to be able to trust other people again. I was wrong. With the help of friends and family and teachers and insights from other authors, I found voices that graced me with their steadiness, thoughtfulness, hospitality, kindness, and knowledge. The work I've done to survive and understand this part of my life remains the work of which I am most proud. And while any wisdom I gained was hard-earned, I did not discover it alone.

I wrote the majority of this book during the COVID-19 pandemic, and as the air became suspect and leaders across the United States struggled to contain the chaos, I, like many others, cloistered in my home. Determined to finish this book, I would wake long before dawn and sit alone with my computer at the kitchen table before my husband and children began to stir. When I needed more sustained time to write, I was lucky enough to be able to drive from our home in Austin, Texas, to a cozy guesthouse in Covington, Louisiana, where I escaped for days at a time. I am grateful to my husband, Eric, for taking care of our children during this time, as well as to Helen Curran and Cleosia Seay, Marian and Bruce Margotsen, and Bill and Sandy Miller, who all provided space and respite to write.

I am graced with wise colleagues at Emory University's Candler School of Theology who are generous with their time, encouragement, and support. I am particularly grateful to Jennifer Ayres and Liz Bounds, both of whom read the full manuscript and generously offered feedback. Geoff Goodman and Gabby Thomas read sections of the book and shared suggestions from their areas of expertise. Justin Fannon was an exemplary research assistant who assisted toward the end of the project. The Center for Faculty Development—directed by the incredible Allison Adams—provided a much-needed grant to help ensure the book's voice would be heard. The faculty at Seminary of the Southwest also provided support earlier in this project's journey, opening space for generative conversations. Claire Colombo, Awa Jangha, Marlon Johnson, Cheryl Kirk-Duggan, Cynthia Kittredge, Gena St. David, and Jane Patterson all shared guidance and insights, and Becky Watts provided invaluable research assistance early in the book's development. The Conant Grant I received supported the restorative justice facilitator training that I completed through the University of San Diego and also funded writing retreats and conversations with experts in the field, the most valuable of which was the time I spent with Becca Stevens and the women who survived sex trafficking and prostitution who are now members of the Thistle Farms community. Their willingness to welcome me into their lives and share their stories remains a gift.

A number of professional organizations supported the development of this work. *The Journal of Pastoral Theology* published my first article on this topic—"Absent a Word"—which became the seed article out of which the larger book project emerged. The Religion, Culture, and Psychology group at the American Academy of Religion graciously welcomed me to speak on the bracket creep in the *DSM*'s definition of trauma, and the comments from participants in that meeting impacted much of the material presented about the construction of the traumatic event. In addition, I am indebted to the faculty and students in the University of San Diego's Restorative Justice program. David Karp, Justine Darling, Camille Lizarríbar, Blaz Bush, Hyacinth Mason, Ksenia Sidorenko, Anita Sharif-Hyder, and L'Tomay Douglas became important conversation partners as I learned about the principles and practices of restorative justice. Alissa Ackerman-Acklin and

Neshama Carlebach were also transformative guides and soul friends who created space to talk about and practice restorative justice in relation to sexual harm in faith-based communities. I am indebted to members of the Society for Pastoral Theology who have been supportive beyond measure, especially to Carrie Doehring and Nancy Ramsay, who model what it means to be a leader in this guild. Mindy McGarrah Sharp and Leanna Fuller encouraged me to keep writing during our weekly writing group meetings, and Pam McCarroll's laughter, levity, and clarity created space on countless occasions to delve deeply into topics that matter to me in our field, just as Emmanuel Lartey and Greg Ellison remain generous, steady, and kind colleagues locally at Emory University.

Outside of my field, I am profoundly grateful to those scholars and colleagues who generously invested their time and wisdom as I developed this project. Blakey Vermeule and Masha Raskolnikov engaged in lively conversations about Chaucer and etymology. Barbara Brown Taylor was a gracious, grounded, and wise listener. Jennifer Scheper Hughes never failed to respond to my queries in record time. Stephanie Arel read the roughest, rawest early version of what I thought would be a journal article and encouraged me to turn it into a book. Kate Malin, Karen Silberman, and Kat Banakis also read early drafts and offered encouragement. Jean Wehner helped me remember how lifegiving writing can be. Lacy Crawford, Lenore Wright, and Donna Freitas provided detailed comments on the manuscript as a whole. The team at Fortress also worked tirelessly to make this book a reality. A particular thanks goes to Carey Newman, who handled the subject matter with great care and answered every question at a moment's notice.

I began asking the questions in this book back when I was a student, oftentimes in the offices of trusted professors. I wanted to understand so much and so intensely, and I have tremendous gratitude to these professors who were as willing to share what they knew. In Siobhán Garrigan's classroom, I learned about social construction, performativity, and the power of language both within and beyond theology.

Elie Wiesel emboldened me to voice suffering and hope with whatever artistic resources I could draw upon. Susan Nolen-Hoeksema and Kristi Lockhart taught me important psychological concepts related to gender and trauma. Serene Jones introduced me to the intersection of theology and trauma studies; Emilie Townes offered me my first opportunity to integrate it all in a thesis project on language, theology, and trauma; and Shelly Rambo offered me the opportunity to continue to develop my research as a doctoral student. Walden Moore, Rob Lehman, and members of their respective choirs helped me regain my trust in the world in the most profound of ways. The opportunity to sing with these individuals remains one of the greatest privileges of my life, as does the training I received from Robert Ludwig as a child. I also owe a tremendous debt to my classmates during those years, who, both in and out of the classroom, allowed me to bring my whole self to the academic project. Many who survive a sexual violation feel that no one believes them. Thanks to this group of peers, I never did.

Finally, I owe tremendous thanks to Marilyn McCord Adams, Susan Brison, Kristen Leslie, and Shannon Craigo-Snell, all of whom offered trust, hope, and solidarity over the course of more than two decades. They model the finest of both academia and friendship, and I have learned much from them over long walks, cappuccinos in college town coffee shops, and through their scholarship. Their friendship and collegiality have a beauty that defies language.

NOTES

INTRODUCTION

1. In reflecting upon the trial surrounding her rape and attempted murder, Susan Brison writes that her French lawyer stated that "a certain amount was typically awarded for '*un viol gentil*' ('a gentle rape') and a somewhat larger amount ... for '*un viol méchant*' ('a nasty rape')." That it is possible to draw a distinction between gentleness and nastiness due to the presence or absence of physical violence in any case of rape may say more about the power of rape myths in public discourse than it does about the nature of how the brain processes traumatic stress, just as it raises questions about the possibility of attempting to correlate internal suffering with external stimuli. Chapter 1 will explore this topic at greater length. See Susan J. Brison, *Aftermath: Violence and the Remaking of a Self* (Princeton, NJ: Princeton University Press, 2003), 91.
2. The Rape, Abuse, and Incest National Network, more commonly known as RAINN, states that in approximately 80% of adult cases, victimized parties know offending parties prior to the attack. That number rises to 93% in cases where the victimized party is a minor. See RAINN, "Perpetrators of sexual violence: statistics," www.rainn.org/statistics/perpetrators-sexual-violence.
3. Heather L. Littleton and Danny Axsom, "Rape and seduction scripts of university students: implications for rape attributions and unacknowledged rape," *Sex Roles* 49, no. 9 (November 1, 2003): 465–75, https://doi.org/10.1023/A:1025824505185.
4. Psychological studies document that a majority of women whose sexual experiences meet the definition of rape—whether that definition is a legal one or one set by researchers—do not acknowledge their experience using this term. In the general population, it is estimated that only 39.5% of women identify their experiences as rape. On college campuses, the rates are higher, with only 28% of women acknowledging experiences of rape in their lives. See L.C. Wilson and K.E. Miller, "Meta-analysis of the prevalence of unacknowledged rape," *Trauma, Violence, and Abuse* 17 (2016): 149–59; L.C. Wilson and A. Scarpa, "Unacknowledged rape: the influences of child sexual abuse and personality traits," *Journal of Child Sexual Abuse* 8 (2015): 975–90; C. Cleere and S.J. Lynn, "Acknowledged versus unacknowledged sexual assault among college women," *Journal of Interpersonal Violence* 28

(2013): 2593–611; M.S. Harned, "Women's labeling of unwanted sexual experiences with dating partners: a qualitative analysis," *Violence Against Women* 11 (2002): 3374–413). L.C. Wilson, K.E. Miller, E.K. Leheney, A.D. Ballman, and A. Scarpa, "Examining the psychological effect of rape acknowledgment: the interaction of acknowledgment status and ambivalent sexism," *Journal of Clinical Psychology* 37, no. 7 (2017): 864–78.

5   I am not making the assertion here that nothing more *could* be said about it. I maintain a more optimistic view of our ability to fully capture and express trauma than Cathy Caruth, who suggests that there is an element to traumatic experience that gets missed or that is beyond knowing in the direct experience of it. See Cathy Caruth, *Unclaimed Experience: Trauma, Narrative, and History* (Baltimore, MD: Johns Hopkins University Press, 1996).

6   The reader will note that I have chosen not to state the details of the sexual violation. This is a purposeful choice on my part. As I propose in what follows, I believe that there is an overemphasis upon the pragmatics of sexual trauma to determine its validity, creating arbitrary distinctions and a hierarchy of suffering based on a variety of factors that do not necessarily correlate with the reality of what suffering looks like on an individual level. Because of that, I refuse to offer the reader a narrative in which I give a detailed description of what this particular person did in order to obtain credibility as a victim. I believe those details are irrelevant. As an alternative to such a description, I will be focusing on the impact of the act.

7   For a groundbreaking work on performativity in language, see John L. Austin, *How To Do Things With Words* (London: Oxford University Press, 1976).

8   Ludwig Wittgenstein, *Tractatus Logico-Philosophicus* (London: Kegan Paul, Trench, Trubner, & Co., Ltd, 1922).

9   For more on the intersection of language and power from a Foucauldian perspective, see Linda Martín Alcoff, *Rape and Resistance* (Cambridge, UK: Polity, 2018).

10 The term "embedded beliefs" signifies inherited, often culturally dominant beliefs about a given concept. While Carrie Doehring generally uses the term primarily to refer to spiritual beliefs, I use it more broadly and as a deliberate alternative to Foucauldian language such as "dominant discourses," which I find problematic to invoke, given Foucault's own involvement in both enacting and promoting sexual practices that harm others. For a more expansive definition and consideration of the term "embedded beliefs," see Carrie Doehring, *The Practice of Pastoral Care, Revised and Expanded Edition: A Postmodern Approach* (Louisville, KY: Westminster John Knox Press, 2015), 18–25.

11 For a more detailed analysis of how the body processes trauma, see Bessel A. van der Kolk, *The Body Keeps the Score: Brain, Mind, and Body in the Healing of Trauma* (New York: Penguin Books, 2015).

12 Here I am reminded of Stephen Grosz, who writes, "When we cannot find a way of telling our story, our story tells us—we dream these stories, we develop symptoms,

we find ourselves acting in ways we don't understand." Stephen Grosz, *The Examined Life: How We Lose and Find Ourselves* (New York: W.W. Norton, 2013), 10.

13 See "Rape: on coercion and consent," in Catharine A. MacKinnon, *Toward a Feminist Theory of the State*, (Cambridge, MA: Harvard University Press, 1991), 171–83.

14 Mary Koss coined the term "unacknowledged rape survivor" to describe the phenomenon of women failing to acknowledge their own experiences of rape. Rates of unacknowledged rape remain high, with studies stating that over 60% of women fail to acknowledge their experiences as rape. Studies of male survivors are rare, but the research that has been done suggests that rates are high among this population as well. Victims are most likely to leave rape unacknowledged when the assailant is known to the victimized party and when there are lower levels of physical force, in other words, when their experiences fail to correlate to rape stereotypes. See M.P. Koss, "The hidden rape victim: personality, attitudinal, and situational characteristics," *Psychology of Women Quarterly* 9 (1985): 193–212; M.P. Koss, "Hidden rape: sexual aggression and victimization in a national sample of students in higher education," in *Violence in Dating Relationships: Emerging Social Issues*, edited by M.A. Pirog-Good and J.E. Stets (New York: Praeger, 1989), 145–84; K.G. Weiss, "Male sexual victimization: examining men's experiences of rape and sexual assault," *Men and Masculinities* 12 (2010): 275–98; S.T. Shepela and L.L. Levesque, "Poisoned waters: sexual harassment and the college climate," *Sex Roles* 38 (1998): 589–611; B. Bondurant, "University women's acknowledgment of rape," *Violence Against Women* 7 (2001): 294–314; M.S. Harned, "Does it matter what you call it? The relationship between labeling unwanted sexual experiences and distress," *Journal of Consulting and Clinical Psychology* 72 (2004): 1090–99; D. McMullin, and J.W. White, "Long-term effects of labeling a rape experience," *Psychology of Women Quarterly* 30 (2006): 96–105.

15 For the record, the term "repressed memory" has by and large been dismissed by researchers. The remembered distance that some survivors experience in the aftermath of trauma may be better described as a type of dissociation in which the brain is trying to separate the survivor from the event as a protective mechanism. Either way, to say that I repressed the memory would not be accurate to my experience. My inability to speak about the trauma was not an issue of forgetting; it was an issue of linguistic labeling.

16 For more on how narrative is essential to recovery from a traumatic event, see Judith L. Herman, *Trauma and Recovery: The Aftermath of Violence—From Domestic Abuse to Political Terror* (New York: Basic Books, 2015).

17 Brison's understanding of how trauma works reflects longstanding best practices in the psychiatric community about how the brain can be rewired through speech, about how trauma be integrated into the narrative of a person's life. Brison, *Aftermath*, x.

18 As Susan Brison summarizes, "It may be that the every-dayness, the mind-numbing repetitiveness, the very banality of rape, is precisely what adds to its significance,

its weightiness, as something which should concern us all because it is a political event for which we are *all* responsible." Susan Brison, "Justice and Gender-Based Violence," *Revue Internationale de Philosophie* 67, no. 3 (2013): 268.

19 For a helpful defense of the term "sexual violation," see Alcoff, *Rape and Resistance*, 12–15.

20 For a helpful primer that summarizes what is at stake for feminists in the victim vs. survivor dichotomy, see Liz Kelly, Sheila Burton, and Linda Regan, "Beyond victim or survivor: sexual violence, identity and feminist theory and practice," in *Sexualizing the Social*, edited by Lisa Adkins and Vicki Merchant (New York: Palgrave Macmillan, 1996), 77–101. For an article that summarizes the historic contours of what is at stake broadly in feminism when thinking of women as victims or agents, see Elizabeth M. Schneider, "Feminism and the false dichotomy of victimization and agency," *New York Law School Law Review* 38 (1993): 387–99.

21 Howard Zehr, Allan McRae, Kay Pranis, and Lorraine Stutzman Amstutz, *The Big Book of Restorative Justice: Four Classic Justice & Peacebuilding Books in One Volume* (Good Books, 2015), 14–15; Alissa Ackerman and Jill Levenson, *Healing from Sexual Violence* (Brandon, VT: Safer Society Press, 2009).

22 Larry Nassar, for instance, was routinely described by gymnasts as one of the most welcoming people they interacted with, and many experienced him as being far kinder than their coaches were, and, indeed, his friendliness often made it difficult for adults and even for the gymnasts themselves to believe that the abuse was real.

23 Studies by George Bonanno document that a majority of individuals exposed to traumatic events demonstrate resiliency, although there are four trajectories their PTSD symptoms may follow: chronic, delayed, recovery, and resilience. Bonanno's studies, including one metastudy that considered 54 other PTSD studies, have consistently documented that resiliency—not posttraumatic stress—occurs in a majority of individuals exposed to a traumatic event. George A. Bonanno, Sandro Galea, Angela Bucciarelli, and David Vlahov, "Psychological resilience after disaster: New York City in the aftermath of the September 11th terrorist attack," *Psychological Science*, 17, no. 3 (March 2006): 181–86, https://doi.org/10.1111/j.1467-9280.2006.01682.x; Isaac R. Galatzer-Levy, Sandy H. Huang, and George A. Bonanno, "Trajectories of resilience and dysfunction following potential trauma: a review and statistical evaluation," *Clinical Psychology Review* 63 (July 2018): 41–55, https://doi.org/10.1016/j.cpr.2018.05.008.

24 For a selection of important research in the psychological subfield of religious coping, see Kenneth I. Pargament, ed., *APA Handbook of Psychology, Religion, and Spirituality* (Washington, DC: American Psychological Association, 2013); Kenneth I. Pargament, *The Psychology of Religion and Coping: Theory, Research, Practice* (New York: The Guilford Press, 2001).

25 For more on the spiritual epistemic crisis that can emerge in the aftermath of sexual harm, see Shelly Rambo, *Spirit and Trauma: A Theology of Remaining* (Louisville, KY: Westminster John Knox Press, 2010).
26 "Religion in America: U.S. Religious Data, Demographics and Statistics," Pew Research Center's Religion & Public Life Project, accessed October 21, 2020, www.pewforum.org/religious-landscape-study/.
27 For a sampling of authors who have made disclosures in their pastoral theological work about traumatic experiences, see Carrie Doehring, "Searching for wholeness amidst traumatic grief: the role of spiritual practices that reveal compassion in embodied, relational, and transcendent ways," *Pastoral Psychology*, 68 (December, 2018): 241–59; Jeanne Stevenson-Moessner, *Overture to Practical Theology: The Music of Religious Inquiry* (Eugene, OR: Cascade Books, 2016); Nancy Ramsay, "Compassionate resistance: an ethic for pastoral care and counseling," *Journal of Pastoral Care* 52, no. 3 (Fall 1998): 217–26.
28 Mary P. Koss, "Hidden rape," 145–84. See also Mary Koss, "The hidden rape victim," 193–212. Barrie Bondurant, "University women's acknowledgment of rape," *Violence Against Women* 7 (2001): 294–314: doi.10.1177/8010122182451; Renee Botta and Suzanne Pingree, "Interpersonal communication and rape: women acknowledge their assaults," *Journal of Health Communication* 2 (1997): 197–212; doi:10.1080/108107397127752; Bonnie S. Fisher, Leah E. Daigle, Francis T. Cullen, and Michael G. Turner, "Acknowledging sexual victimization as rape: results from a national-level survey," *Justice Quarterly* 20 (2003): 535–74: doi:10/1080/07418820300095611; C.B. Hammon and K.S. Calhoun, "Labeling of abuse experiences and rates of victimization," *Psychology of Women Quarterly* 31 (2007): 371–80; doi:10.1111/j.1471-6402.2007.00386.x.

CHAPTER 1

1 Speaking about personal experiences of sexual harm can be challenging for many survivors, for reasons ranging from shame to fear to neurological effects on the brain wrought by posttraumatic stress. When the victimized person is from a minoritized population, speaking can be even more complicated. For an important womanist analysis of this issue from the perspective of pastoral theology, see Stephanie M. Crumpton, *A Womanist Pastoral Theology Against Intimate and Cultural Violence* (Palgrave Macmillan, 2014), 25–64.
2 I am indebted to conversations with Susan Brison and Kristen Leslie, both of whom helped me recognize the relevance of context to the understanding of words like "rape" and "sexual assault."
3 I take the term "snapshot" from Susan Brison, who utilizes it in relation to her own experience of testifying at the trial of the man who attempted to rape and murder her. She writes, "Our conventions of justice require that a witness be viewed as

presenting something as close to a snapshot as possible—a story unmediated and unchanging—from the perspective of a detached, objective observer." However, once the jury reached a verdict, Brison writes that

> I could finally let down my guard, get fuzzy about the particulars, leave at least some of the horror behind, consign it to wherever they'd taken and left my clothes, my shoes, my belt, the fingernail scrapings, the hairs, the swabs, the leaves, the twigs, the blood, the mud. Now I could, in a sense, forget what had happened to me. Now I could afford to think about it.

Brison's account explains the way that epistemological expectations affect the freedom and flexibility with which a person who survived sexual harm is asked to remember and, in turn, speak about her experience of harm. See Susan J. Brison, *Aftermath: Violence and the Remaking of a Self* (Princeton, NJ: Princeton University Press, 2003), 109, 108.
4   "State Law Database," RAINN, accessed October 2, 2019, https://apps.rainn.org/policy/index.cfm.
5   In 2014, the FBI removed the requirement of force from its definition. "Frequently Asked Questions about the Change in the UCR Definition of Rape," Federal Bureau of Investigations, https://ucr.fbi.gov/recent-program-updates/new-rape-definition-frequently-asked-questions (December 11, 2014).
6   RAINN—the Rape, Abuse, and Incest National Network—which is the largest anti-violence advocacy organization in the United States, states that 230 of every 1,000 sexual assaults are reported to police (this is, of course, assuming that victims acknowledge the crime occurred). Of those, forty-six result in an arrest, nine are referred to prosecutors, five receive felony convictions, and 4.6 will be incarcerated. Rates of reports, convictions, and incarcerations remain lower for sexual assaults than for robberies or assault and batteries. Please note that "sexual assault" is the term used on the RAINN website; RAINN does not specify the parameters of what constitutes sexual assault. See "The Criminal Justice System: Statistics," RAINN, accessed September 30, 2019, www.rainn.org/statistics/criminal-justice-system. For an examination of the low rates of prosecution and incarceration of offenders from the perspective of pastoral theology, see Kristen J. Leslie, *When Violence Is No Stranger: Pastoral Counseling with Survivors of Acquaintance Rape* (Minneapolis: Fortress Press, 2003), 20.
7   It is worth noting that researchers themselves use inconsistent definitions for words like "rape" and "sexual abuse" across their studies, which complicates any collective assessment of their findings. See Peterson, Voller, Polusny, and Murdoch, 2011. See Zoë D. Peterson, Emily K. Voller, Melissa A. Polusney, and Maureen Murdoch, "Prevalence and consequences of adult sexual assault in men: review of empirical findings and state of the literature," *Clinical Psychology Review* 31, no. 1 (February 2011): 1–24.

8   Laura C. Wilson and Katherine E. Miller, "Meta-analysis of the prevalence of unacknowledged rape," *Trauma, Violence, and Abuse* 17 (2016): 149–59, doi:10.1177/1524838015576391
9   Mary P. Koss, "Hidden rape: sexual aggression and victimization in a national sample of students in higher education," in *Violence in Dating Relationships: Emerging Social Issues* (New York: Praeger, 1989), 145–84. See also Mary Koss, "The hidden rape victim: personality, attitudinal, and situational characteristics," *Psychology of Women Quarterly* 9 (1985): 193–212, doi.10.1111/j.1471-6402.1985.tb00872.x
10 L.C. Wilson, K.E. Miller, E.K. Leheney, A.D. Ballman, and A. Scarpa, "Examining the psychological effect of rape acknowledgment: the interaction of acknowledgment status and ambivalent sexism," *Journal of Clinical Psychology* 37, no. 7 (2017): 864–78.
11 Karen G. Weiss, "Male sexual victimization: examining men's experiences of rape and sexual assault," *Men and Masculinities* 12 (2010): 286. Another research study suggests rates of acknowledgment may be lower among men because of stereotypes about masculinity that preclude victimization, including the idea that men have insatiable sex drives and would never turn down an opportunity to engage in sexual activity. That same study stated that the Department of Justice only changed its definition of rape in January of 2012 to include males as possible victims. Tiffany M. Artime, Ethan B. McCallum, and Zoë D. Peterson, "Men's acknowledgment of their sexual victimization experiences," *Psychology of Men and Masculinity* 15, no. 3 (2014): 313–23.
12 RaeAnn E. Anderson, Lesley A. Tarasoff, Nicole VanKim, and Corey Flanders, "Differences in rape acknowledgment and mental health outcomes across transgender, nonbinary, and cisgender bisexual youth," *Journal of Interpersonal Violence* 36, no. 13–14 (July 2021): NP7717–39, https://doi.org/10.1177/0886260519829763. Interestingly, the rate was highest among bisexual gender nonbinary men, whose acknowledgment was 79.9%.
13 Barrie Bondurant, "University women's acknowledgment of rape," *Violence Against Women* 7 (2001): 294–314: doi.10.1177/8010122182451; Renee Botta and Suzanne Pingree, "Interpersonal communication and rape: women acknowledge their assaults," *Journal of Health Communication* 2 (1997): 197–212: doi:10.1080/108107397127752; Bonnie S. Fisher, Leah E. Daigle, Francis T. Cullen, and Michael G. Turner, "Reporting sexual victimization to the police and others: results from a national-level study of college women," *Criminal Justice and Behavior* 30, no. 1 (February 1, 2003): 6–38: doi:10.1177/0093854802239161; Bonnie S. Fisher, Leah E. Daigle, Francis T. Cullen, and Michael G. Turner, "Acknowledging sexual victimization as rape: results from a national-level survey," *Justice Quarterly* 20 (2003): 535–74: doi:10/1080/07418820300095611; C.B. Hammon and K.S. Calhoun, "Labeling of abuse experiences and rates of victimization," *Psychology of Women Quarterly* 31 (2007): 371–80:

doi/10.1111/j.1471-6402.2007.00386.x; Heather Littleton, Danny Axsom, and Amie Grills-Taquechel, "Sexual assault victims' acknowledgment status and revictimization risk," *Psychology of Women Quarterly* 33 (2009): 34–42: doi.10.1111/j.1471-6402.2008.01472.x; Heather L. Littleton, Danny Axsom, Carmen Radecki Breitkopf, and Abbey Berenson, "Rape acknowledgment and postassault experiences: how acknowledgment status relates to disclosure, coping, worldview, and reactions received from others," *Violence and Victims* 21 (2006): 761–78; Heather Littleton, Carmen Radecki Breitkopf, and Abbey Berenson, "Beyond the campus: unacknowledged rape among low-income women," *Violence Against Women* 14 (2008): 269–86: doi.10.1177/1077801207313733; Heather Littleton, Deborah L. Rhatigan, and Danny Axsom, "Unacknowledged rape: how much do we know about the hidden rape victim?" *Journal of Aggression, Maltreatment and Trauma* 14 (2007): 57–74, doi:10.1300/J146v14n04_04.

14 For an expanded discussion of self-reflexivity, see Carrie Doehring, *The Practice of Pastoral Care, Revised and Expanded Edition: A Postmodern Approach* (Louisville, KY: Westminster John Knox Press, 2015), 167–8. See also Carrie Doehring and Allison Kestenbaum, "Interpersonal competencies for cultivating spiritual trust," in *Chaplaincy and Spiritual Care in the Twenty-First Century: An Introduction*, edited by Wendy Cadge and Shelly Rambo (Chapel Hill, NC: University of North Carolina Press, 2022), 134–55.

15 Brison, *Aftermath*, 4, 9. See also Susan J. Brison, "Surviving sexual violence," *Second Opinion* 2, no. 11 (1994).

16 For a helpful discussion of common myths and distortions about sexual violence, see Leslie, *When Violence Is No Stranger*, 14–22.

17 Brison, *Aftermath*, 10.

18 Herman, *Trauma and Recovery*, 2, 9.

19 Coleman urges readers to press against this instinct, stating that what is at stake is the act of "naming the sin in our midst and fighting against it." According to Coleman, then, the purpose of worship thus creates space for not only the praise of God but also the identification with and acknowledgment of corporate sin. Monica A. Coleman, *The Dinah Project: A Handbook for Congregational Response to Sexual Violence* (Eugene, OR: Wipf & Stock, 2010), 30.

20 For more on Monica Coleman's experience of rape and the ways in which various religious professionals responded to her disclosure, see Monica A. Coleman, *Bipolar Faith: A Black Woman's Journey with Depression and Faith* (Minneapolis: Fortress Press, 2016), 123–207.

21 Womanist biblical scholars have offered some of the most important and incisive analyses of these texts. See Renita Weems, *Battered Love (Overtures to Biblical Theology)* (Minneapolis: Augsburg Fortress Press, 1995); Wilda C. Gafney, *Womanist Midrash: A Reintroduction to the Women of the Torah and the Throne* (Louisville, KY: Westminster John Knox Press, 2017).

22 For an important analysis of this text and others that describe sexual violations in the Hebrew Bible, see Phyllis Trible, *Texts of Terror: Literary-Feminist Readings of Biblical Narratives* (Philadelphia: Fortress Press, 1984).
23 Susanne Scholz, *Sacred Witness: Rape in the Hebrew Bible* (Minneapolis: Fortress Press, 2010).
24 Schaberg includes a foreword in the twentieth anniversary edition of the book in which she describes the harassment and persecution she experienced at the hands of the press, the public, the Roman Catholic Church, and the Jesuit university where she taught following the book's publication. She felt that these interactions compounded the sexism she already experienced by virtue of her gender in the academy. As she describes the backlash from a misleading article in the *Detroit Free Press* about her work, she writes, "Even now this article, and the milk crates of letters and articles it generated, are more difficult for me to read than the cancer journal I kept during my year of chemo 14 years ago." See Jane Schaberg, *The Illegitimacy of Jesus: A Feminist Theological Interpretation of the Infancy Narratives*, expanded twentieth anniversary edition (London: Sheffield Phoenix Press Ltd, 2005), 3–15.
25 Sallie McFague, *Metaphorical Theology: Models of God in Religious Language* (Philadelphia: Fortress Press, 1982), 148.
26 Framing this challenge theologically, Kristen Leslie writes,

> Naming and being named are sacred activities in the Judeo-Christian tradition. To be named is to be known; to name is to claim power. Jacob wrestled with the messenger who had no name.... Naming the experience [of sexual victimization] is crucial to the healing process. This naming process is often a wrestling match, with the wrestling partners being self-blame and the question of consent. (Leslie, *When Violence Is No Stranger*, 105)

27 Tirana Burke began using the phrase "Me Too" in 2006; the term was subsequently adopted and became synonymous with the MeToo hashtag and greater awareness of it in 2017.
28 Jodi Kantor and Megan Twohey, *She Said: Breaking the Sexual Harassment Story That Helped Ignite a Movement* (New York: Random House, 2019), 84–5.
29 "State Law Database," RAINN, accessed September 30, 2019, https://apps.rainn.org/policy/compare.cfm.
30 "Sex Crimes: Definitions and Penalties, Utah," RAINN, https://apps.rainn.org/policy/policy-crime-definitions.cfm?state=utah&group=3&_ga=2.251739585.931815605.1569876124-1245578939.1547238087.
31 For an introduction to intersectionality as a tool for pastoral caregivers, see Nancy Ramsay, "Intersectionality: a model for addressing the complexity of oppression and privilege," *Pastoral Psychology* 63 (October, 2013): 453–69. For an important

introduction to intersectionality from outside of pastoral theology, see the work of Kimberlé Crenshaw, paradigmatically emblematized in "Mapping the margins: intersectionality, identity politics, and violence against women of color," *Stanford Law Review* 43 (1991): 1241–99.

32 Angela Y. Davis, *Women, Race, & Class* (New York: Vintage, 1983), 172–202. See also Leslie, *When Violence Is No Stranger*, 22–28.

33 While rape shield laws now prohibit courts from asking details about a survivor's sexual past, I would argue that this is not the same as dismantling the assumption that someone who has been victimized is more culpable because of past promiscuity. In other words, legislation does not necessarily change popular opinion.

34 *Nancy Grace Interviews Elizabeth Smart*, 2006, www.youtube.com/watch?v=5x-8ARIxg5lI.

35 Elizabeth Smart on Instagram: "I've noticed a lot of comments about dealing with the shame and embarrassment that I felt after I was rescued and didn't want to tell...," Instagram, November 30, 2020, www.instagram.com/p/CIPRwh8sWes/.

36 Chanel Miller, *Know My Name* (New York: Viking), 47.

37 In my book, *Conceiving Family*, I have written about the parallel complexities between reproductive surrogates and prostitutes regarding their ability to consent. I maintain that consent is difficult to assess when societies impose structural barriers that limit individual and community discernment and make it difficult for people to make decisions out of a true sense of call. See Danielle Tumminio Hansen, *Conceiving Family: A Practical Theology of Surrogacy and Self* (Waco, TX: Baylor University Press), ch. 2. For a more expansive analysis of the parallel ethical concerns that emerge when one considers surrogacy and prostitution in tandem, see Amrita Pande, *Wombs in Labor: Transnational Commercial Surrogacy in India* (New York: Columbia University Press, 2014).

38 M. Farley and H. Barkan, "Prostitution, violence, and posttraumatic stress disorder," *Women & Health* 27, no. 3 (1998): 37–49, https://doi.org/10.1300/J013v27n03_03.

39 Rates of sexual violations remain high among lesbians, with one large survey conducted by the Centers for Disease Control finding that approximately 30% had been violated by another woman. Mikel L. Walters, Jieru Chen, and Matthew J. Breiding, "The National Intimate Partner and Sexual Violence Survey: 2010 findings on victimization by sexual orientation" (American Psychological Association, 2013), https://doi.org/10.1037/e541272013-001.

40 By way of example, many members of the trans community suffer ostracization from their families, with the result that they may become impoverished, homeless, or feel forced to turn to prostitution in order to survive, all of which increases their vulnerability to both sexual and non-sexual forms of harm and exploitation.

41 For an intriguing discussion of sexual violations in the gay community from an international perspective, see Currier and Manuel's study of sexual violations in Malawian gay men, which found that activist socialization impacts how men who have had same-sex experiences of sexual violations label those events. Ashley Currier and Rashida A. Manuel, "When rape goes unnamed: gay Malawian men's responses

to unwanted and non-consensual sex," *Australian Feminist Studies* 29, no. 81 (July 3, 2014): 289–305, https://doi.org/10.1080/08164649.2014.959242.
42 Angela Y. Davis, *Women, Race, & Class*, 175–76.
43 Davis goes on to suggest that this stereotype harmed not only Black women but also white women, creating a kind of trickledown effect that rendered the rape of non-Black women permissible because the rape of Black women was permissible. In this way, she explains, "racism nourishes sexism." Davis, *Women, Race, & Class*, 176.
44 For a rich and detailed exploration of the sexual lives of Black women, including their experiences of sexual violations, see Tricia Rose, *Longing to Tell: Black Women Talk About Sexuality and Intimacy* (New York: Picador, 2004).
45 The forced trafficking and prostitution of Black girls and women in the United States and their subsequent indictment and incarceration—as opposed to therapeutic support and rehabilitation—is but one example of how societal constructs in the United States about race only further enable harmful constructions about the unrapeability of Black women.
46 Linda Adeniji, "The Unrapeable Black Woman: How the Lack of Legal Protection Through the Centuries Promoted the Tradition of Unreported Sexual Assaults," SSRN (Rochester, NY: Social Science Research Network, December 12, 2015), https://doi.org/10.2139/ssrn.2702861.
47 For an analysis of sexual violations inflicted upon male inmates within the prison system, see James Gilligan, *Violence: Reflections on a National Epidemic* (New York: Vintage, 1997). For an important overview of the history and current reality of how racism affects the prison system in the United States and functions as a form of state-sanctioned abuse and control of Black bodies, see Michelle Alexander, *The New Jim Crow: Mass Incarceration in the Age of Colorblindness* (New York: The New Press, 2012).
48 For an important analysis of the way in which dominant culture dehumanizes and takes unwarranted punitive measures against Black men and how pastoral caregivers can respond, see Gregory C. Ellison, *Cut Dead but Still Alive: Caring for African American Young Men* (Nashville, TN: Abingdon Press, 2013).
49 For a groundbreaking analysis of the myth of the Black male rapist, see Davis, *Women, Race, & Class*, 172–202.
50 The gender of those arrested was not identified; however, given other statistics about sexual violations, it is safe to assume a majority of those arrested identified as men. The term "rape" was not defined in the report, but likely adheres to the current FBI definition mentioned earlier in this chapter. See "FBI: arrests by race and ethnicity, 2019," https://ucr.fbi.gov/crime-in-the-u.s/2019/crime-in-the-u.s.-2019/topic-pages/tables/table-43.
51 FBI: arrests by race and ethnicity, 2019.
52 Charlotte Pierce-Baker, *Surviving the Silence: Black Women's Stories of Rape*, (W.W. Norton & Company, 2000), 64. See also pages 75–6 and 84.
53 See Catharine A. Mackinnon, *Towards a Feminist Theory of the State* (Cambridge, MA: Harvard University Press, 1989) and Catharine A. MacKinnon, *Only Words*

(Cambridge, MA: Harvard University Press, 1989). For an article that succinctly explains how hard core pornography negatively impacts women as a class, see Susan J. Brison, "'The price we pay?' Pornography and harm," in *Contemporary Debates in Applied Ethics* edited by Andrew I. Cohen and Christopher Heath Wellman (Malden, MA: Wiley-Blackwell, 2013), 236–350.

54 Debby Herbenick, Tsung-Chieh Fu, Keisuke Kawata, Heather Eastman-Mueller, Lucia Guerra-Reyes, Molly Rosenberg, and Dubravka Svetina Valdivia, "Non-fatal strangulation/choking during sex and its associations with mental health: findings from an undergraduate probability survey," *Journal of Sex & Marital Therapy* 48, no. 3 (2022): 238–50, https://doi.org/10.1080/0092623X.2021.1985025.

55 The term "violence" in and of itself lacks a clear definition, raising questions about whether it is individual, systemic, or both, and whether it is limited to physical forms of harm or whether it includes other forms, such as verbal or state-sanctioned systemic oppression. For a parsing of the term, as well as an analysis of how it has been invoked to promote various political ends, see the introduction to Judith Butler, *The Force of Nonviolence: An Ethico-Political Bind* (London: Verso Books, 2020).

56 "Definition of exotic," accessed November 4, 2019, www.merriam-webster.com/dictionary/exotic.

57 Heather L. Littleton and Danny Axsom, "Rape and seduction scripts of university students: implications for rape attributions and unacknowledged rape," *Sex Roles* 49, no. 9 (November 1, 2003): 473.

58 Littleton and Axsom, "Rape and seduction scripts," 470.

59 Littleton and Axsom, "Rape and seduction scripts," 470.

60 Littleton and Axsom, "Rape and seduction scripts," 466.

61 Catharine MacKinnon, "Sex and violence: a perspective," in *Rape and Society: Readings on the Problem of Sexual Assault*, edited by Patricia Searles and Ronald J. Berger (Boulder, CO: Westview Press, 1995). 30. The lack of self-awareness that she describes points to how misogynistic structures enable those who raped to believe that they have done no wrong. It also tacitly points to the limitations of the criminal justice system to address the kinds of transformation that offending parties need. Punishment, after all, attempts to teach someone not to do the wrong thing by penalizing them for it, but is not primarily interested in helping them to transform in order to want to do the right thing. To that end, restorative justice processes may possess more productive ways to engage offending parties in order to bring about the kind of rehabilitation they need. For more on how restorative justice can benefit both victimized and offending parties in contexts of sexual violations, see Alissa Ackerman and Jill Levenson, *Healing from Sexual Violence* (Brandon, VT: Safer Society Press, 2009); David Karp, *Little Book of Restorative Justice for Colleges and Universities: Repairing Harm and Rebuilding Trust in Response to Sexual Misconduct* (New York: Good Books, 2013); and Judah Oudshoorn, Michelle Jackett, and Lorraine Stutsman Amstutz, *The Little Book of Restorative Justice for Sexual Abuse* (New York: Good Books, 2015).

62 The embeddedness of rape myths in these two words may be one reason why the public in the United States was able to accept allegations made against Harvey Weinstein by multiple women but was divided on those presented by Christine Blasey Ford against Brett Kavanaugh. Though Weinstein was known to the women he victimized, I would assert that the stories his victims collectively provided more closely aligned with rape stereotypes than the one Ford presented. The women who made accusations against Weinstein were by and large not intoxicated, knew him as a work—and not a social—colleague, and their collective testimonies presented a pattern of predatory behavior that was both physically and verbally aggressive. In contrast, Blasey Ford's description deviated more from rape myths, veering more toward the kind of sexual aggression that is normative—which is not the same as acceptable—in a college fraternity. This is not to say that Blasey Ford would have been less traumatized or victimized. Indeed, studies suggest she would have been more traumatized because of the deviations from cognitive schemas that are the accepted basis of rape myths. But it may partially explain why the nation had a more difficult time with her testimony. For a more extensive discussion of both the Weinstein and Kavanaugh accusations, see Kantor and Twohey, *She Said*.

63 See Kristen Leslie, "Pastoral care and acquaintance rape," *Journal of Religion and Abuse* 3, no. 3/4 (2001): 116, fn. 17. See also Audre Lorde, *Sister Outsider* (Trumansburg, NY: Crossing Press, 1984), 120.

64 Susan Brownmiller, *Against Our Will: Men, Women, and Rape* (New York: Fawcett Books, 1975).

65 Ann Cahill summarizes Catharine MacKinnon well on this topic when she states that,

> Rape is here understood as part of an interlocking set of practices, demands, and behaviors that serve to perpetuate the social and political domination of men over women. From this perspective, rape is constituted not as a horrific aberration from normal, healthy sexual encounters, but rather as a necessary element of a particular political structure. (Cahill, *Rethinking Rape*, 184)

66 For a helpful primer on the specifics of clergy sexual abuse, see Marie M. Fortune and James N. Poling, *Sexual Abuse by Clergy: A Crisis for the Church* (Eugene, OR: Wipf and Stock, 2008).

67 Pamela Cooper-White elaborates on the significance of power in sexual harm through the employment of three categories: 1. "Rape is about power, *and* sex;" 2. "Rape is about power, *using* sex;" 3. "Rape is about power, gender, and race." Cooper-White proposes that the first category recognizes that the arousal of the person who enacts the harm is essential to separating rape from other unhealthy forms of aggression—such as physical abuse. However, it is important to recognize that sex and violence ought not to be fused, thereby normalizing rape. This leads her to the second way of understanding the significance of power in rape.

Here, Cooper-White suggests that sex may be used as the tool that inflicts power. However, this definition—along with the first—fails to acknowledge that rape is both an individual crime and a collective one that results from what a theologian might characterize as social sins in which the person who manifests the violation participates. This leads to her third understanding of the role of power in rape. Cooper-White closes by suggesting that these three categories are complementary and all need to be mutually acknowledged in order to truly understand the role power plays in rape. Pamela Cooper-White, *Gender, Violence, and Justice: Collected Essays on Violence against Women* (Eugene, OR: Cascade Books, 2019), 265–75.

68 Cooper-White, *Gender, Violence, and Justice*, 265.
69 Cook, Cortina, and Koss argue that sexual abuse only involves harm done to those in a vulnerable class and not harm done to others as a result of a power imbalance due to the position of the person who inflicted the sexual violation. This more limited definition does not align with state laws or denominational understandings of sexual abuse that pastoral caregivers might employ. I, therefore, do not employ the more limited definition here. See Sarah L. Cook, Lilia M. Cortina, and Mary P. Koss, "What's the difference between sexual abuse, sexual assault, sexual harassment and rape?," *The Conversation*, September 20, 2018, https://theconversation.com/whats-the-difference-between-sexual-abuse-sexual-assault-sexual-harassment-and-rape-88218.
70 By way of definition, "power-over" is the act of exerting power over another person and "power-to-do" is the act of being able to enact one's own agency. In cases of sexual harm, the use of power falls into the former category. For further discussion of these two categories, see Tumminio Hansen, *Conceiving Family*, 134–35. See also Robert A. Dahl, "The concept of power," *Behavioral Science* 2, no. 3 (2007): 1–15; and Hanna F. Pitkin, *Wittgenstein and Justice: On the Significance of Ludwig Wittgenstein for Social and Political Thought* (Berkeley: University of California Press, 1993), 276.
71 For a subset of the extensive research on clergy sexual abuse, see research by Diana Garland, James Poling, David Pooler, and Susan Reynolds.
72 Unlike the terms "rape" and "sexual assault," which have become diffuse and conglomerated together in ways that lead to confusion, "sexual abuse" and "incest" seem more clear about what they are seeking to describe. Having said that, Artime et al., found that researchers had unstable and inconsistent definitions of "child sexual abuse" employed across research conducted with male survivors. See Artime et al., "Men's acknowledgment of their sexual victimization experiences," 313–14.
73 United Nations, *Declaration on the Elimination of Violence Against Women: Proclaimed by the General Assembly*. Resolution 48/104 of 20 December, 1993, 2.
74 United Nations, *Declaration on the Elimination of Violence Against Women*.
75 Brison, *Aftermath*, 89.

Notes   235

76 Brison acknowledges that the fear of rape also impacts women collectively. She writes,

> Sexual violence victimizes not only those women who are directly affected but all women. The fear of rape has long functioned to keep women in their place. Whether or not one agrees with the claims of those, like Susan Brownmiller (1975), who argue that rape is a means by which all men keep all women subordinate, the fact that women's lives are restricted by sexual violence is indisputable.... In the seminar I taught at Dartmouth on violence against women, the men in the class were stunned by the extent to which the women in the class took precautions against assault every day—locking doors and windows, checking the back seat of the car, not walking alone at night, looking in closets on returning home. And this is at a "safe," rural New England campus. (Brison, *Aftermath*, 18)

77 For an extensive analysis of the "gray" area between sex and rape, see Gavey, *Just Sex?*, 97–128.
78 Linda Martín Alcoff, *Rape and Resistance* (Cambridge, UK: Polity, 2018), 9.
79 For a broader discussion of gaslighting's role in misogyny, see Kate Manne, *Down Girl: The Logic of Misogyny* (Oxford, New York: Oxford University Press, 2017), 13–15.
80 Herman, *Trauma and Recovery*, 178–80. Herman also notes that the way that others receive the speech of those who lived through a traumatic event may impact her willingness to speak in the first place. As she observes, "In the absence of a socially meaningful form of testimony, many traumatized people choose to keep their symptoms," 183.
81 Susan J. Brison, "Why I spoke out about one rape but stayed silent about another," *TIME*, December 1, 2014, accessed July 8, 2019, https://time.com/3612283/why-i-spoke-out-about-one-rape-but-stayed-silent-about-another/. Elsewhere in her work, Brison writes that the French lawyer who represented her following her attack in France said that "a certain amount was typically awarded for '*un viol gentil*' ('a gentle rape') and a somewhat larger amount...for '*un viol méchant*' ('a nasty rape')." There is, of course, something ironic about saying that any rape is gentle—synonyms for this French word also include nice and agreeable—though the distinction proves useful for driving home the point that there exists colloquially, collectively, a belief that some forms of sexual harm deserve more sympathy than others do, namely, those that align with rape myths. See Brison, *Aftermath*, 91.
82 Brison, *Aftermath*, 7.
83 Herman, *Trauma and Recovery*, 158.
84 Caruth suggests that the essence of trauma is that the event is not "fully known," and that the survivor's experience of missing the full actuality of the trauma leads to reliving the event in the form of intrusive symptoms. However, an alternative

interpretation is that these intrusive symptoms—symptoms like flashbacks, intrusive memories, and nightmares—are actually signs that the event is known too intensely, too fully, and that it is recalled in somatic forms that are so realistic that they go beyond what could be rightly categorized as a memory and instead become a form of reliving. Cathy Caruth, *Unclaimed Experience: Trauma, Narrative, and History* (Baltimore, MD: Johns Hopkins University Press, 1996). For a more succinct critique of Caruth, see Brison, *Aftermath*, 32.

85 Singing in this context is highly liturgical, and scholars have proposed that liturgy can be transformative in responding to individual and intergenerational trauma. For an important contribution to this body of literature, see Shannon Craigo-Snell, "Generational joy: affections, epigenetics, and trauma," *Liturgy* 35, no. 4 (October 1, 2020): 58–66, https://doi.org/10.1080/0458063X.2020.1832852.

86 Anita Hill, *Believing: Our Thirty-Year Journey to End Gender Violence* (New York: Viking, 2021), 149. Hill notes that LGBTQ+ individuals are statistically more likely to experience sexual violations, making their absence in public discourse even more troublesome. She suggests that their stories are being shared more openly after 2018 and suggests the following book as a resource: Richard Blanco, Caridad Moro, Nikki Moustaki, and Elisa Albo, eds., *Grabbed: Poets & Writers on Sexual Assault, Empowerment & Healing* (Boston: Beacon Press, 2020).

87 For a book-length discussion of consent in the sexual culture of college campuses, see Donna Freitas, *Consent on Campus: A Manifesto* (New York: Oxford University Press, 2018). For a more general discussion of consent, see Marie M. Fortune, *Sexual Violence: The Sin Revisited* (Cleveland, OH: Pilgrim Press, 2005), 42–44, 55–57, 79–84.

88 MacKinnon, *Only Words*.

89 For examples from academic literature, see the work of Charlotte Pierce-Baker and Susan Brison, both survivors of physically violent attacks that threatened their lives, who do not name or describe the people who violated them in their books, though presumably these are a matter of public record, since their cases went to trial and received convictions. Pierce-Baker does mention that the men who attacked her were Black, in order to query the role that race played both in the violation and in the way she processed it. Her husband—who contributes a chapter under a pseudonym in the book—likewise doesn't offer identifying information beyond the race of the men. The same can be said of how Roxane Gay writes about the people who raped her in her memoir written for a popular audience. One notable exception to this trend is Chanel Miller's memoir, though in Miller's case, Brock Turner was a household name for years while she was known to the public under the pseudonym of "Emily Doe," and so she explains that one of the reasons she wrote the book was because everyone in the case had been named except her. Miller explains her choice to name Brock Turner but not the defense attorney or judge in the introduction, explaining that she chose to leave the latter two individuals nameless in order "to demonstrate the roles they played." About Brock Turner, she writes, "I will use

Brock's name, but the truth is he could be Brad or Brody or Benson, and it doesn't matter." Chanel Miller, *Know My Name* (New York: Viking), vii. See also Susan J. Brison, *Aftermath* (Princeton, NJ: Princeton University Press, 2003); Charlotte Pierce-Baker, *Surviving the Silence: Black Women's Stories of Rape* (New York: W. W. Norton & Company, 2000); Roxane Gay, *Hunger: A Memoir of (My) Body* (New York: Harper Perennial, 2018).

90 Ann J. Cahill, *Rethinking Rape* (Ithaca, NY: Cornell University Press, 2001), 200.

91 Chanel Miller, "The Full Letter Read by Brock Turner's Father at His Sentencing Hearing," *The Stanford Daily*, June 8, 2016, www.stanforddaily.com/2016/06/08/the-full-letter-read-by-brock-turners-father-at-his-sentencing-hearing/.

92 Theologically, constructing identity like this is problematic because it presses against one of the core principles of Christian thought, namely, that all human beings are created *imago Dei* (in the image of God), and therefore, they are essentially good. This theological assumption separates the kinds of arguments that can be made about human beings between theologians, philosophers, and non-Christian ethicists, as the former two disciplines can make a wider scope of arguments about human nature because they do not need to take essential goodness into account. On the one hand, this opens the possibility for broader conversation about human nature, but on the other, it makes permissible offensive ones as well, such as Peter Singer's utilitarian argument that intellect determines moral value such that it becomes permissible to murder a baby with Down's syndrome and that cognitively disabled individuals have less moral worth than a pig.

93 If a person who experiences sexual victimization cannot name the person who violated them because of the risk of libel and slander, and if they can't call them reductive names like "offender" or "perpetrator," then speaking becomes very cumbersome unless one chooses between two unideal linguistic options or gets creative. In an effort to find alternatives to commonly used terms like "perpetrator," Lacy Crawford explains her reasons for choosing "men" and "boys" to describe the individuals who forced her to engage in oral sex in a dorm room at their elite boarding school, noting that she considered her options to be unideal: "The two males might be called *boys* or *men*, and I use the terms largely interchangeably. They were both eighteen years of age, so legally they were adults. Men. But they were also high school students, and in high school we were not *men* and *women* but *boys* and *girls*." She also gives the boys/men who assaulted her pseudonyms and refers to them by these names throughout the book. Lacy Crawford, *Notes on a Silencing* (New York: Little Brown and Company), 2020, 16.

94 My conception of systemic and epistemic misorientation falls under the overall category of cultural misorientation, which I define as a dominant culture's overall brokenness, a brokenness that individuals must navigate in ways that inevitably cause them to both be victims and perpetuators of harm. For more on cultural misorientation, see chapter 4 of *Conceiving Family*—especially page 81—where I elaborate on the term "cultural misorientation" and its substantial

overlap with corporate sin. Danielle Tumminio Hansen, *Conceiving Family: A Practical Theology of Surrogacy and Self* (Waco: Baylor University Press, 2019).
95 Brett Kavanaugh, "I am an independent, impartial judge," *Wall Street Journal*, October 4, 2018, www.wsj.com/articles/i-am-an-independent-impartial-judge-1538695822.
96 Miller, *Know My Name*, vii–viii.
97 See chapter 6 (176–203) of Alcoff's *Rape and Resistance*, in which she shows the way that media coverage crafts victim stories in ways that eradicate their narrative agency and subjectivity. This chapter was co-authored with Laura Gray-Rosendale. Linda Martín Alcoff, *Rape and Resistance* (Cambridge, UK: Polity Press, 2018).

CHAPTER 2

1 "On #MeToo, Americans more divided by party than gender," NPR.org, accessed June 3, 2020, www.npr.org/2018/10/31/662178315/on-metoo-americans-more-divided-by-party-than-gender.
2 Crawford, 7.
3 Corinne Saunders, *Rape and Ravishment in the Literature of Medieval England* (Cambridge, UK: D.S. Brewer, 2001), 20.
4 Chaucer would have been familiar with the term, as his father was a victim of rape in the platonic sense—he was abducted by his aunt, who intended to marry him to her daughter.
5 For contrasting views, see Cannon and Pearsall, who propose the violation was of a sexual nature, and Kelly, who suggests it was not. Christopher Cannon, "Raptus in the Chaumpaigne release and a newly discovered document concerning the life of Geoffrey Chaucer," *Speculum* 68, no. 1 (1993): 74–94; Derek Pearsall, *The Life of Geoffrey Chaucer: A Critical Biography* (Oxford: Wiley-Blackwell, 1995); Henry Ansgar Kelly, "Meanings and uses of raptus in Chaucer's time," *Studies in the Age of Chaucer* 20 (1998): 101–65.
6 For a brief history of English rape law, see Keith Burgess-Jackson, "A history of rape law," in *A Most Detestable Crime: New Philosophical Essays on Rape*, edited by Keith Burgess-Jackson (New York: Oxford University Press, 1999), 15–31.
7 For but one example, see *The State of Missouri v. Celia, a Slave*. Celia killed and burned the body of Robert Newsom, her slave master, who had repeatedly raped her and forced her to bear children with him. She was convicted by a jury of 12 white men, and when her defense attorneys asked for a new trial, the judge denied it. They then took their claims to the Missouri Supreme Court, stating that the murder was an act of self-defense to prevent further sexual violations. The state Supreme Court denied the request and Celia was hanged on December 21, 1855.
8 Back in 2006, Tom Jones explained to National Public Radio that he had no concerns about the term "rape" being used in the musical when it debuted in 1960.

However, he began to realize the significance of using the term as the topic of sexual harm gained widespread public attention; he then attempted to change the lyrics, but initially encountered obstacles to so doing. He was eventually able to change the lyrics and did so on several occasions. As he stated in the interview, "For years, I didn't think. And then it gradually began to seep into my consciousness—my consciousness was raised. I really began to think, you know, rape isn't funny. It began to become distasteful to me about 10 years into the run." See "Tom Jones, updating 'The Fantasticks' for a new revival," *National Public Radio*, August 23, 2006, www.npr.org/templates/story/story.php?storyId=5697901.

9   United States Department of Justice, "An updated definition of rape," January 6, 2012, www.justice.gov/archives/opa/blog/updated-definition-rape.
10 Chanel Miller, *Know My Name* (New York: Penguin Random House, 2019), 33.
11 Federal Bureau of Investigation, "Rape," https://ucr.fbi.gov/crime-in-the-u.s/2013/crime-in-the-u.s.-2013/violent-crime/rape.
12 Susan Brownmiller, *Against Our Will: Men, Women, and Rape*, reprinted edition (New York: Ballantine Books, 1993), 15.
13 Cooper-White, *Gender, Violence, and Justice*, 266.
14 Cooper-White, *Gender, Violence, and Justice*, 265–66, 271, 274.
15 I take my definition of agency from previously published work. See Danielle Tumminio Hansen, *Conceiving Family: A Practical Theology of Surrogacy and Self* (Waco, TX: Baylor University Press, 2019).
16 For more on the distinction between healthy and unhealthy aggression in sex acts, see Kathleen J. Greider, *Reckoning with Aggression: Theology, Violence, and Vitality*, (Louisville, KY: Westminster John Knox Press, 1997).
17 Tumminio Hansen, *Conceiving Family*, 134–35. See also Robert A. Dahl, "The concept of power," *Behavioral Science* 2, no. 3 (2007): 1–15 and Hanna F. Pitkin, *Wittgenstein and Justice: On the Significance of Ludwig Wittgenstein for Social and Political Thought* (Berkeley, CA: University of Berkeley Press, 1993), 276.
18 "Sexual abuse" is the term Stevens has used to describe her own experience of harm.
19 Name changed to protect privacy.
20 Catharine A. MacKinnon, *Feminism Unmodified: Discourses on Life and Law*, (Cambridge, MA: Harvard University Press, 1987), 164. Here, as Susan Brison acknowledges, there is significant overlap between the understanding of power that MacKinnon postulates and the one that Foucault advocates for in his work. The overlap—in concepts, if not in the words used to describe them—may provide a converging point for Foucauldian feminists and MacKinnonites. See Susan J. Brison, "Can we end the feminist 'sex wars' now? Comments on Linda Martín Alcoff, *Rape and Resistance: Understanding the Complexities of Sexual Violation*," *Philosophical Studies* 177, no. 2 (February 1, 2020): 307.
21 MacKinnon, *Feminism Unmodified*, 164.
22 Susan Ehrlich, *Representing Rape: Language and Sexual Consent* (Abingdon: Routledge, 2003), 14–15.
23 Susan Ehrlich, *Representing Rape*, 43.

24 Susan Ehrlich, *Representing Rape*, 31.
25 Susan J. Brison, *Aftermath: Violence and the Remaking of a Self* (Princeton, NJ: Princeton University Press, 2003), 98; Brison, "Can we end the feminist 'sex wars' now?," 307.
26 See Alcoff, *Rape and Resistance*, 41.
27 Brison, "Can we end the feminist sex wars now?," 307–8.
28 Alcoff, *Rape and Resistance*, 8.
29 Emily Bazelon, "Maryville rape case: the horrifying details of what happened to Daisy Coleman feel all too familiar," October 14, 2013, accessed June 11, 2020, https://slate.com/human-interest/2013/10/maryville-rape-case-the-horrifying-details-of-what-happened-to-daisy-coleman-feel-all-too-familiar.html.
30 Barnett later pled guilty to a lesser charge of misdemeanor child endangerment as part of a plea deal, following public outcry about the initial dismissal of charges and an investigation by a special prosecutor.
31 *Audrie and Daisy*, directed by Bonni Cohen and John Shenk (Netflix, 2016).
32 Brison, "Can we end the feminist sex wars now?," 56.
33 See Jay Asher, *13 Reasons Why* (London: Razorbill, 2017), 225–26.
34 See Toni Morrison, *Beloved*, reprint edition (New York: Vintage, 2004), 81.
35 Studies on sexual arousal and orgasm during acts of sexual harm remain scarce; however, evidence exists that sexual arousal/orgasm can occur during such acts, even if the victim did not consent to the act occurring. For a review of the psychological literature, see Roy J. Levin and Willy van Berlo, "Sexual arousal and orgasm in subjects who experience forced or non-consensual sexual stimulation: a review," *Journal of Clinical Forensic Medicine* 11, no. 2 (April 2004): 82–88, https://doi.org/10.1016/j.jcfm.2003.10.008.
36 Lisa Taddeo, "Opinion: The specific horror of unwanted oral sex," *New York Times*, February 13, 2020, sec. Opinion, www.nytimes.com/2020/02/13/opinion/harvey-weinstein-trial.html.
37 Raniere is currently serving a 120-year sentence for racketeering and sex trafficking. A small number of former NXIVM members continue to insist that their participation in Raniere's sexual demands was consensual. Nicole Hong, "Nxivm's leader is guilty of ugly crimes. these die-hards stand by him," *New York Times*, November 10, 2020, www.nytimes.com/2020/11/10/nyregion/keith-raniere-nxivm.html.
38 *Audrie and Daisy*.
39 Catharine A. MacKinnon, *Women's Lives, Men's Laws* (Cambridge, MA: Belknap Press, 2007), 303.
40 Priscilla Alvarez, "ICE whistleblower alleges high rate of hysterectomies and medical neglect at Georgia facility," CNN, September 16, 2020, www.cnn.com/2020/09/15/politics/immigration-customs-enforcement-medical-care-detainees/index.html.
41 Amy Jean-Jacques and Sam Rowlands, "Legalised non-consensual sterilisation—eugenics put into practice before 1945, and the aftermath. Part 1: USA, Japan,

Canada and Mexico," *European Journal of Contraception & Reproductive Health Care* 23, no. 2 (March 4, 2018), 121–29.
42 Harriet B. Presser, "The role of sterilization in controlling Puerto Rican fertility," *Population Studies* 23, no. 3 (1969): 343–61, https://doi.org/10.2307/2172875.
43 Oliver Wendell Holmes Jr., "Buck v. Bell, 274 U.S. 200 (1927)," May 2, 1927, https://supreme.justia.com/cases/federal/us/274/200/.
44 *Buck v. Bell* was never overturned, though the United States Department of Health and Human Services issued Federal Sterilization Guidelines in 1978 that prohibited many of the practices being used to coerce sterilization. Despite the guidelines, news reports of forced sterilizations continued to appear in the ensuing decades.
45 Charlotte Pierce-Baker, *Surviving the Silence: Black Women's Stories of Rape* (W.W. Norton & Company, 2000), 58.
46 Ann J. Cahill, *Rethinking Rape* (Ithaca, NY: Cornell University Press, 2001), 132.
47 For a more extensive consideration of my understanding of the role of agency in constituting the self, see Tumminio Hansen, *Conceiving Family*, specifically pages 15–16. Additionally, while agency is oftentimes paramount in this process, other scholars question the privilege of agency in the construction of the self instead of innate human dignity or the soul. For a particularly insightful commentary on the ability to do versus the ability to be, see Eva Kittay, *Learning from My Daughter: The Value and Care of Disabled Minds* (Oxford, New York: Oxford University Press, 2019), 53–54.
48 Pierce-Baker, *Surviving the Silence*, 58.
49 The second man who raped Pierce-Baker was never located.
50 For a particularly insightful, detailed example, see Chanel Miller's description of her cross-examination in the trial against Brock Turner. Chanel Miller, *Know My Name* (New York: Penguin Random House, 2019), 180–81.
51 Pierce-Baker, *Surviving the Silence*, 50–60.
52 Put into more formal language, this participant in the Thistle Farms program echoes the view that Susan Brison and other feminist philosophers have of "the self as fundamentally relational—capable of being undone by violence, but also of being remade in connection with others." See Brison, *Aftermath*, xi.
53 Ann J. Cahill, "Recognition, desire, and unjust sex," *Hypatia* 29, no. 2 (2014): 303–19, https://doi.org/10.1111/hypa.12080. While Cahill uses the term "masculine norm" here, she also indicates that she recognizes the problem of gender binaries in such an assertion.
54 Cahill, "Recognition, desire, and unjust sex," 314.
55 Cahill, "Recognition, desire, and unjust sex," 313.
56 "Recognition, desire, and unjust sex," 315.
57 "Recognition, desire, and unjust sex," 315.
58 Desire, explained in this way, is therefore distinct from consenting to a sexual activity because it is possible for a person to give consent to an activity in which one does not desire to participate.

59 See Tumminio Hansen, *Conceiving Family*, 13–15.
60 The root desires that I identify loosely derive from Maslow's hierarchy of needs. Contrary to Maslow, however, they are not enumerated in a particular order or hierarchy, as scholars have critiqued the ordering both for its individualistic orientation and because evidence does not lead to the conclusion that one needs to progress through the needs in the order in which Maslow conceived them. For more on Maslow and critiques against the hierarchy, see Tumminio Hansen, *Conceiving Family*, 148n6 and 149n7.
61 Susan Brison, "Justice and gender-based violence," *Revue Internationale de Philosophie* 67, no. 3 (2013): 273.
62 Brison, "Justice and gender-based violence," 273–74.
63 Alcoff, *Rape and Resistance*, 155. Arguments about consent in sex work closely echo arguments about consent in surrogacy. Scholars, including myself, have made similar arguments concerning the consent a surrogate gives to carry a child to term for intended parents who have offered her money to carry the pregnancy, because if economic deprivation makes surrogacy the only option for survival, then the suggestion that she could freely choose not to participate becomes complicated. See Tumminio Hansen, *Conceiving Family*, 39–61, 79–105.
64 Alcoff, *Rape and Resistance*, 81.
65 Cahill, *Rethinking Rape*, 191.
66 Cahill, "Recognition, desire, and unjust sex," 303–19.
67 This is a distinctly theological claim which asserts that humans do not exist in isolation but rather are essentially connected. This belief is reflected in a number of biblical passages (e.g., 1 Cor. 12:12–27) and doctrinal assertions (i.e., *perichoresis*) as well as in the writings of numerous theologians, including Catherine Keller, Rosemary Radford Ruether, Emilie Townes, and Howard Thurman.
68 For a helpful primer on moral injury and spiritual care, see Nancy Ramsay and Carrie Doehring, eds., *Military Moral Injury and Spiritual Care: A Resource for Religious Leaders and Professional Caregivers* (St. Louis, MO: Chalice Press, 2019).
69 Mary Gaitskill, "On not being a victim: sex, rape, and the trouble with following rules," *Harper's*, March 1994.
70 This professor would not have been obligated to report what I told her to the university, as professors were not mandated reporters at the time.
71 Much evidence exists to support the assertion that myths and stereotypes about rape affect whether victim testimonies are believed. Police, for instance, utilize rape myths as they determine the veracity of sexual assault/rape claims that are brought to their attention. In addition, research suggests that those who hold more firmly entrenched sex role stereotypes are more likely to doubt the veracity of rape claims. Research also suggests that Americans are less likely to believe accusations brought by Black women than white women. Interestingly, researchers have replicated across cultures the finding that victims are more likely to be believed if their accusations are more strongly tied to stereotypes or myths of

rape. For more on the role that race and sex role stereotypes play in how others evaluate the veracity of rape accusations, see Jessica Shaw, Rebecca Campbell, Debi Cain, and Hannah Feeney, "Beyond surveys and scales: how rape myths manifest in sexual assault police records," *Psychology of Violence* 7, no. 4 (2017): 602–14, and Cynthia E. Willis, "The effect of sex role stereotype, victim and defendant race, and prior relationship on rape culpability attributions," *Sex Roles* 26, no. 5–6 (1992). Several cross-cultural studies reinforce domestic ones. Researchers in Denmark, for instance, found that accusations of rape were more likely to be prosecuted if the crime reflected culturally held stereotypes of rape, specifically if the person who caused the sexual violation was a stranger to the victimized party, if the victimized party actively resisted the attack, if the victimized party sustained physical injuries, and if the victimized party was sober. See N.B. Hansen, M. Hansen, R. Campbell, A. Elklit, O.I. Hansen, and R.H. Bramsen, "Are rape cases closed because of rape stereotypes? Results from a Danish police report," *Nordic Psychology* 71, no. 1 (2018): 51–61. Similarly, Australian researchers found that when victimized parties and offending parties did not share a cultural heritage, the victimized person was more likely to be blamed when her cultural background differed from that of the person who sexually violated her. In cases where the rape was more stereotypical, culture did not factor into blame attribution. See Renata Bongiorno, Blake M. McKimmie, and Barbara M. Masser, "The selective use of rape-victim stereotypes to protect culturally similar perpetrators," *Psychology of Women Quarterly* 40, no. 3 (2016).

CHAPTER 3

1 For an extended exploration of the concepts of embedded beliefs, see the introduction and first chapter—particularly pages 18–25—of Carrie Doehring, *The Practice of Pastoral Care: A Postmodern Approach*, revised and expanded edition (Louisville, KY: John Knox Press, 2015).
2 In this way, one wonders whether dependency care extends not just to the physical act of taking care of others but also to the act of narrating the self for others. There are some parallels, then, between speaking on behalf of an infant and speaking on behalf of a dependent adult who cannot speak. For more on the latter, see Eva Kittay's explanation of why it is justifiable for her to speak on behalf of her daughter, who is cognitively disabled and unable to speak. See Eva Kittay, *Learning from My Daughter: The Value and Care of Disabled Minds* (Oxford: Oxford University Press, 2019), 7.
3 For a book-length exploration of the concept of dependency and dependency care, particularly in relation to women's labor and disability, see Eva Feder Kittay, *Love's Labor: Essays on Women, Equality, and Dependency* (New York: Routledge, 1999).
4 Anita Hill, *Believing: Our Thirty-Year Journey to End Gender Violence* (New York: Viking, 2021), 82–83.

5   For an extended analysis of the emergence and construction of the reproductive self as well as how assumptions about the primacy of the biological family limit its expression, see Kittay, *Love's Labor*.
6   For an important resource on how the reproductive self can experience trauma, see Janet Jaffe and Martha O. Diamond, *Reproductive Trauma* (Washington, DC: American Psychological Association, 2010).
7   Here I employ "postfeminism" to mean the end of feminism and not the site of feminist politics, per another use of the word.
8   I have written more expansively on the concept of mutual self-construction and self-defeat in Danielle Tumminio Hansen, *Conceiving Family: A Practical Theology of Surrogacy and Self* (Waco, TX: Baylor University Press), 129–45.
9   For an extensive and insightful philosophical analysis of how time affects the interpretation of sexual violations, see Megan Burke, *When Time Warps: The Lived Experience of Gender, Race, and Sexual Violence* (Minneapolis: University of Minnesota Press, 2019).
10 For a more thorough theological exploration of memory's role in trauma, see Danielle Tumminio Hansen, "Remembering rape in Heaven: a constructive proposal for memory and the eschatological self," *Modern Theology* 37, no. 3 (September 21, 2020): 662–78, accessed October 27, 2020, https://doi.org/10.1111/moth.12651.
11 Chanel Miller, *Know My Name* (New York: Viking), 9.
12 Susan J. Brison, *Aftermath: Violence and the Remaking of a Self* (Princeton, NJ: Princeton University Press, 2003), 56.
13 Bessel van der Kolk, *The Body Keeps the Score: Brain, Mind, and Body in the Healing of Trauma* (New York: Viking, 2014), 43–44.
14 Bessel van der Kolk, *The Body Keeps the Score*, 70.
15 Danielle Tumminio Hansen, "Four ways faith leaders can shift to trauma-informed ministry," *The Christian Century* 137, no. 21 (2020), www.christiancentury.org/article/recommendations/four-ways-faith-leaders-can-shift-trauma-informed-ministry.
16 Judith L. Herman, *Trauma and Recovery: The Aftermath of Violence—From Domestic Abuse to Political Terror* (New York: Basic Books, 2015), 176.
17 Herman, *Trauma and Recovery*, 177–78.
18 For but one of many examples of this kind of linguistic catharsis, see the conversations between Harry Potter and Dumbledore toward the end of each *Harry Potter* book, excepting, of course, book six of the series.
19 For historical background and contemporary analysis of how slavery, the hypersexualization of Black women's bodies, and systemic oppression intersected to construct Black women's bodies as unrapeable, see Kimberlé Crenshaw, "Mapping the margins: intersectionality, identity politics, and violence against women of color," *Stanford Law Review* 43, no. 6 (July 1991): 1241–99; bell hooks, *Ain't I a Woman: Black Women and Feminism* (New York: Routledge, 2015).

20 Crawford, 7.
21 Crawford, 199, 201.
22 Crawford, 265–67.
23 Maya Angelou, *Maya Angelou "Rape" = Her Mute Years*, 2017, www.youtube.com/watch?v=yMNSpN-Gi3g.
24 Crawford, 236–50.
25 Bessel A. van der Kolk et al., "Yoga as an adjunctive treatment for posttraumatic stress disorder: a randomized controlled trial," *Journal of Clinical Psychiatry* 75, no. 6 (June 15, 2014): e559–65, https://doi.org/10.4088/JCP.13m08561.
26 Kate Elizabeth Russell, *My Dark Vanessa* (New York: William Morrow, 2020), 252.
27 Russell, *My Dark Vanessa*, 270.

CHAPTER 4

1 For two accessible introductions to purity culture and its negative effect on those who experience sexual violations, see Emily Joy Allison and Lyz Lenz, *#ChurchToo: How Purity Culture Upholds Abuse and How to Find Healing* (Minneapolis: Broadleaf Books, 2021), and Linda Kay Klein, *Pure: Inside the Evangelical Movement That Shamed a Generation of Young Women and How I Broke Free* (New York; London: Atria Books, 2019).
2 Elizabeth Smart, quoted in Molly Oswaks, "Elizabeth Smart is standing up for rape victims—and tearing down purity culture," *Vice*, September 1, 2016, www.vice.com/en/article/mbqjka/elizabeth-smart-is-standing-up-for-rape-victimsand-tearing-down-purity-culture.
3 Oswaks, "Elizabeth Smart is standing up for rape victims."
4 It is worth noting that Mormon leaders removed a controversial verse of scripture that appeared to endorse purity culture (Moroni 9:9) from a study book (called a Personal Progress book) that Mormon girls routinely keep as part of their education. Meanwhile, the website on abuse run by the Church of Jesus Christ of Latter-Day Saints specifically states:

> If you have been a victim of rape or other sexual abuse, whether you have been abused by an acquaintance, a stranger, or even a family member, you are not guilty of sexual sin. Know that you are innocent and that your Heavenly Father loves you. (Church of Jesus Christ of Latter-Day Saints, "Abuse")

See also Peggy Fletcher Stack, "LDS feminists applaud as church removes troublesome Book of Mormon verse on rape from Youth Book," *The Salt Lake Tribune*, September 29, 2016, https://sltrib.com/religion/2016/09/29/lds-feminists-applaud-as-church-removes-troublesome-book-of-mormon-verse-on-rape-from-youth-book.

5   For an example of how this can potentially manifest, again in relation to the LDS community, though not in relation to Elizabeth Smart, see the case of Madi Barney. Barney was a sophomore at Brigham Young University (BYU) when she experienced a sexual violation in her off-campus apartment. When she reported the harm, the university responded by bringing an honor code violation against her, presumably because a person not of the same sex was in her bedroom. See Annie Knox, "Protest of BYU planned in wake of honor code criticisms," *The Salt Lake Tribune*, May 3, 2016, https://archive.sltrib.com/article.php?id=3794990&itype=CMSID.

6   Scholars have observed that this kind of logic may have motivated the spa shootings in the Atlanta area in 2021, which were undertaken by a Southern Baptist who adhered to the kinds of beliefs embedded in purity culture. "Purity culture and the subjugation of women: Southern Baptist beliefs on sex and gender provide context to Spa suspect's 'motive,'" *The Conversation*, accessed April 25, 2021, http://theconversation.com/purity-culture-and-the-subjugation-of-women-southern-baptist-beliefs-on-sex-and-gender-provide-context-to-spa-suspects-motive-157496.

7   This kind of ideology is precisely what motivated the prominent Southern Baptist Beth Moore to leave the denomination in 2021 in what became a well-publicized instance of an evangelical woman calling out the role of misogyny within evangelical Christianity.

8   Kenneth Pargament, Margaret Feuille, and Donna Burdzy, "The brief RCOPE: current psychometric status of a short measure of religious coping," *Religions* 2, no. 1 (March 2011): 51–76, https://doi.org/10.3390/rel2010051.

9   Mary Claire Jalonick and Elana Schor, "No 'dogma': Democrats walk tightrope on Barrett's faith," AP NEWS, April 20, 2021, https://apnews.com/article/donald-trump-ruth-bader-ginsburg-amy-coney-barrett-dianne-feinstein-judiciary-2aaf6821079ac0c5c6fe50699ad745ba.

10 A notable exception, historically, comes from Julian of Norwich, who uses female pronouns—including "Mother"—to describe God. Julian, who lived in England during the Middle Ages, was making a bold theological claim with these pronouns, defiantly bucking tradition, though she does so with just enough care as to avoid charges of heresy. For a helpful primer on Julian's theology, see Amy Laura Hall, *Laughing at the Devil: Seeing the World with Julian of Norwich* (Durham, NC: Duke University Press Books, 2018). For the original text in a modern English translation, see Julian of Norwich, *Revelations of Divine Love*, trans. Elizabeth Spearing (London; New York: Penguin Books, 1999).

11 In the early Church, many scholars agree that women undertook leadership roles in Christianity; however, as the faith codified and gained more power culturally, women's leadership roles declined and women were not allowed to participate in the priesthood.

12 For one important authoritative source laying out an argument for how the priest acts in the image of Christ (*in persona Christi*) when consecrating the bread and

wine during a Mass, see Thomas Aquinas, *Summa Theologica* (Claremont, CA: Coyote Canyon Press, 2010), III, 83, 1, 3.

13 For the groundbreaking article documenting the sexual abuse scandal in the Roman Catholic Church and documenting the opposition faced by victimized individuals who brought forward claims, see "Church allowed abuse by priest for years," *The Boston Globe*, accessed April 25, 2021, www.bostonglobe.com/news/special-reports/2002/01/06/church-allowed-abuse-priest-for-years/cSHfGkTIrAT25qKGvBuDNM/story.html.

14 For popularized examples of such instances, see *The Keepers* (Netflix, 2017); *Spotlight* (Open Road Films, 2015).

15 For a historical overview of research in posttraumatic stress, beginning with Charcot's research, see chapter 1 of Judith Herman, *Trauma and Recovery: The Aftermath of Violence—from Domestic Abuse to Political Terror* (New York: Basic Books, 1997).

16 Oppenheim's proposal met with significant opposition from other psychological experts as well as politicians, who saw in it the possibility that false victims could make illegitimate claims to government compensation based on their condition, which would affect German's economy and workforce. See Roger K. Pitman, "A brief nosological history of PTSD," *Journal of Traumatic Stress Disorders & Treatment* 2, no. 1 (2013), https://doi.org/10.4172/2324-8947.1000101.

17 The Committee on Nomenclature and Statistics of the American Psychiatric Association, *Diagnostic and Statistical Manual: Mental Disorders* (Washington, DC: American Psychiatric Association Mental Hospital Services, 1952), 40.

18 The current *DSM-5* includes posttraumatic stress in a category known as "Trauma- and Stressor-Induced Disorders." Other disorders included here include Reactive Attachment Disorder, Disinhibited Social Engagement Disorder, Acute Stress Disorder, and Adjustment Disorders. The category of Trauma and Stressor-Related Disorders is new to the *DSM-5*. See American Psychiatric Association, *Diagnostic and Statistical Manual of Mental Disorders, Fifth Edition* (Washington, DC: American Psychiatric Publishing, 2013), 265–90.

19 The prominence of "shell shock" within the news following the world wars no doubt raised the mental health community's awareness of combat-based trauma. However, again, it is worth reiterating that clinicians believed that if symptoms of distress persisted indefinitely, then a soldier likely was not negatively impacted by combat but rather suffered from an underlying form of neurosis that was independent from it.

20 Jennifer A. Bennice and Patricia A. Resick, "Marital rape: history, research, and practice," *Trauma, Violence & Abuse* 4, no. 3 (2003): 228–46.

21 Harkening to the work of Miranda Fricker, one might say that the early *DSM*'s exclusion of rape mirrors the law's exclusion of sexual harassment prior to Catharine MacKinnon's popularizing of the term in the late 1970s. In both cases, epistemic injustice occurred when a lack of acknowledgment by systems of power resulted in paltry frameworks to speak about and address the harm. Catharine A. MacKinnon,

Sexual Harassment of Working Women (New Haven, CT: Yale University Press, 1979); Miranda Fricker, *Epistemic Injustice: Power and the Ethics of Knowing* (Oxford: Oxford University Press, USA, 2009).

22 Unlike the original *DSM*, the *DSM-II* does not attempt to classify what might constitute an environmental stressor, though it does give examples of them based on the age of the patient. The Committee on Nomenclature and Statistics of the American Psychiatric Association, *DSMII: Diagnostic and Statistical Manual of Mental Disorders*, second edition (Washington, DC: American Psychiatric Association, 1968), 48–49.

23 See American Psychiatric Association, *DSMIII: Diagnostic and Statistical Manual of Mental Disorders*, 3rd ed (Washington, DC: American Psychiatric Association, 1980), 309.89. See also Lori A. Zoellner, Michele A. Bedard-Gilligan, Janie J. Jun, Libby H. Marks, and Natalia M. Garcia, "The evolving construct of Posttraumatic Stress Disorder (PTSD): *DSM-5* criteria changes and legal implications," *Psychological Injury and Law* 6, no. 4 (2013): 277–89.

24 Herman goes on to suggest that what traumatic events have in common is that they "generally involve threats to life or bodily integrity, or a close personal encounter with violence and death. They confront human beings with the extremities of helplessness and terror, and evoke the responses of catastrophe" (Herman, *Trauma and Recovery*, 33). Such a description conjures in the mind the extremes of violence.

25 Herman, *Trauma and Recovery*, 33. In addition, it may be that the parameters of what constitutes trauma still remain overly narrow. Gold, Marx, Soler-Baillo, and Sloan interviewed 454 undergraduates at Temple University and determined that students were more likely to develop symptoms of PTSD when they experienced a stressor not defined as traumatic by the *DSM* than those who had experienced a stressor that met the criterion for a traumatic stressor. Incidents not included in the *DSM* included, but were not limited to, the imprisonment of a loved one or divorce of parents. This finding calls into question the validity of what defines a traumatic stressor in the *DSM*. In relation to this particular project, one also wonders whether symptoms of posttraumatic stress may be exacerbated because the events in question are not named as being traumas. See Sari D. Gold, Brian P. Marx, Jose M. Soler-Baillo, and Denise M. Sloan, "Is life stress more traumatic than traumatic stress?" *Journal of Anxiety Disorders* 19, no. 6 (2005): 687–98.

26 Once every nine minutes, the victimized person is a minor. See Emily R. Dworkin, Anna E. Jaffe, Michele Bedard-Gilligan, and Skye Fitzpatrick, "PTSD in the year following sexual assault: a meta-analysis of prospective studies," *Trauma, Violence, & Abuse*, July 19, 2021, https://doi.org/10.1177/15248380211032213.

27 Data show that rape is more likely to result in PTSD than other potentially traumatic events, and that PTSD may persist longer. The authors recognize that the scope of the study is limited by those who identified the harm as rape. It is not clear

how many of the meta-analysis participants engaged in therapy in the aftermath of the harm. Dworkin et al., "PTSD in the year following sexual assault."
28. American Psychiatric Association, *Diagnostic and Statistical Manual of Mental Disorders, Fourth Edition (DSM-IV)* (Washington, DC: American Psychiatric Association, 1994), 426–27.
29. Dworkin, Jaffe, Bedard-Gilligan, and Fitzpatrick, "PTSD in the year following sexual assault: a meta-analysis of prospective studies," *Trauma Violence Abuse 2*, (April 2023): 497–514. See also Gerald Rosen and Scott O. Lillenfeld, "Posttraumatic stress disorder: an empirical evaluation of core assumptions," *Clinical Psychology Review*, 28, no. 5 (June 2008): 837–68.
30. A 2021 meta-analysis indicated that roughly 75% of those who reported a sexual violation met the criteria for PTSD in the month after the event; at one year, 41% met the criteria. It is unclear from the meta-analysis how many individuals sought therapy within the year. These data do not include those who did not report or recognize that harm occurred. Dworkin et al., "PTSD in the year following sexual assault."
31. George A. Bonanno, Sandro Galea, Angela Bucciarelli, and David Vlahov, "Psychological resilience after disaster: New York City in the aftermath of the September 11th terrorist attack," *Psychological Science* 17, no. 3 (March 2006): 181–86, https://doi.org/10.1111/j.1467-9280.2006.01682.x; Isaac R. Galatzer-Levy, Sandy H. Huang, and George A. Bonanno, "Trajectories of resilience and dysfunction following potential trauma: a review and statistical evaluation," *Clinical Psychology Review* 63 (July 2018): 41–55, https://doi.org/10.1016/j.cpr.2018.05.008; Katharina Schultebraucks, Karmel W. Choi, Isaac T. Galatzer-Levy, and George A. Bonanno, "Discriminating heterogeneous trajectories of resilience and depression after major life stressors using polygenic scores," *JAMA Psychiatry*, March 31, 2021, https://doi.org/10.1001/jamapsychiatry.2021.0228.
32. Sarah Woodhouse, Susan Ayers, and Andy P. Field, "The relationship between adult attachment style and posttraumatic stress symptoms: a meta-analysis," *Journal of Anxiety Disorders* 35 (October 2015): 103–17, https://doi.org/10.1016/j.janxdis.2015.07.002; Emma M. Marshall and Patricia A. Frazier, "Understanding posttrauma reactions within an attachment theory framework," *Current Opinion in Psychology* 25 (February 2019): 167–71, https://doi.org/10.1016/j.copsyc.2018.08.001.
33. For an extensive and incisive womanist critique of suffering's value, see Delores S. Williams, *Sisters in the Wilderness: The Challenge of Womanist God-Talk*, anniversary edition (Maryknoll, NY: Orbis, 2013).
34. For more of Amy's story and an insightful analysis of it, see Donna Freitas, *Consent on Campus: A Manifesto* (New York: Oxford University Press, 2018), 3.
35. Freitas, *Consent on Campus*, 4.
36. *Lethelogica* derives from the Greek words "*Lethe*" (the river in Hades that caused travelers to forget their past) and "*logica*," which here means "word" instead of

"logic" or "reason." To describe the phenomenon in question, I am substituting the Greek word for body, "*soma*" to create the word "*lethesoma*," or the phenomenon of forgetting one's body.

37 Mary Koss has conducted studies that suggest large numbers of women with experiences of sexual violations fail to identify their experiences as such, and while we can only postulate why, perhaps one reason among others is that women who do not show PSTD symptoms think no harm has been done if they are not psychologically traumatized by it.

38 I remain particularly concerned about the ways that certain thought leaders believe that knowledge is both static and certain. This is a particular tendency among legal originalists and biblical literalists, both of whom assume that the writers of the documents which they interpret have absolute truth as of the time of writing, that a literal interpretation is the only and correct interpretation, and that their contemporary ability to interpret is infallible. Their hubris is as alarming as it is dangerous.

39 Herman, *Trauma and Recovery*, 133–54, 175–95.

40 This same hermeneutic of humility is important not only for those who practice therapy but also for others who offer care to those who have experienced a sexual violation, including doctors, nurses, chaplains, and priests.

41 It may be the case that individuals who are already vulnerable to PTSD can also develop symptoms following exposure to traumatic images broadcast by the media, though the *DSM-5* explicitly states that "criterion A4 does not apply to exposure through electronic media, television, movies, or pictures unless it is work-related" (*DSM-5*, 231). Limited research has found that PTSD symptoms may emerge following media exposure outside of the workplace. In a study done following the Boston Marathon bombings, researchers found that adolescents were more likely to experience symptoms of PTSD if they had been exposed to violence prior to the attacks, had a previous history of psychopathology, as well as exposure to media reporting and images of the attacks. The same study found that adolescents with hyporeactive sympathetic nervous systems only developed symptoms if they had high media exposure following the attacks. See Daniel S. Busso, Katie A. McLaughlin, and Margaret A. Sheridan, "Media exposure and sympathetic nervous system reactivity predict PTSD symptoms after the Boston Marathon bombings," *Depression and Anxiety* 31, no. 7 (July 31, 2014): 551–58.

42 For more on the psychology of those who believe in alien abduction, see the research of Richard McNally. For an article on posttraumatic stress in those who believe they were abducted by aliens specifically from his corpus, see Richard J. McNally, "Explaining 'memories' of space alien abduction and past lives: an experimental psychopathology approach," *Journal of Experimental Psychopathology* 3 (2012): 2–16. See also Jatinder Takhar and Sandra Fisman, "Alien abduction in PTSD," *Journal of the American Academy of Child & Adolescent Psychiatry* 34, no. 8 (August 1, 1995): 974–75, https://doi.org/10.1097/00004583-199508000-00005.

43 Matthew C. Fadus et al., "Unconscious bias and the diagnosis of disruptive behavior disorders and ADHD in African American and Hispanic youth," *Academic Psychiatry* 44, no. 1 (February 1, 2020): 95–102, https://doi.org/10.1007/s40596-019-01127-6.
44 I use the term "sexual assault" in relation to this incident as this is the term utilized by the accuser—who goes by the pseudonym Grace—in her description of the events. In contrast, media coverage of Ansari's denial of the claims referred to the allegations as ones of "sexual misconduct." Katie Way, "I went on a date with Aziz Ansari. It turned into the worst night of my life," babe.net, January 13, 2018, https://babe.net/2018/01/13/aziz-ansari-28355.
45 Way, "I went on a date with Aziz Ansari."
46 Way, "I went on a date with Aziz Ansari."
47 Way, "I went on a date with Aziz Ansari."
48 Inez Stepman, "Inez Stepman on Twitter," Twitter, January 14, 2018, https://twitter.com/InezFeltscher/status/952673765359538176.
49 Please note that Banfield insists that Grace ought to have gone to the police if she indeed experienced a form of sexual violation, including sexual harassment. However, Banfield also goes on to identify herself as someone who experienced workplace sexual harassment, though there appears to be no record of her filing any police report about the incident. "Banfield slams Ansari accuser in open letter," January 15, 2018, CNN, www.youtube.com/watch?v=y4bAULTwAJU.
50 "Bari Weiss on Twitter," Twitter, January 14, 2018, https://twitter.com/bariweiss/status/952647595880525826.
51 Caitlin Flanagan, "'Babe' turned a movement into a racket," *The Atlantic*, January 19, 2018.
52 Jodi Kantor and Megan Twohey, *She Said: Breaking the Sexual Harassment Story That Helped Ignite a Movement* (New York: Random House, 2019), 185. Here, Kantor and Twohey seem to imply that wrongdoing is made worse by intent on the part of the accused. It is, however, worth asking whether impact differs based on intent, given that a victimized party can be traumatized by a sexual act that the perpetrating party believed was within his rights to undertake. Indeed, the fact that the perpetrating party did not take the victimized party's perspective into account or did not question his own actions or the collective patriarchal assumptions that may have enabled them can add to the victimized party's trauma.
53 Letter from personal files.
54 For more on gender construction in rape, including whether women can rape, see Gavey, 193–213.
55 Peter Martinez, "Aziz Ansari responds to woman's claim of sexual misconduct," accessed January 14, 2021, www.cbsnews.com/news/aziz-ansari-woman-claims-sexual-misconduct-report/.
56 Hanna Stotland, a college admissions consultant explains that perhaps we can believe both perspectives. As she wrote in a piece for the *New York Times*:

> When someone is accused of sexual assault, we often think one person is telling the truth and the other is lying, but from what I've seen, both students are sincerely reporting their biased, externally influenced, and often drunken memories. . . . We shouldn't frame every disagreement as a disagreement between a truthteller and a liar. There are a lot of other possibilities. (Stotland, "Opinion: I advise students accused of sexual assault. Expelling them isn't the answer.")

57 Grace, quoted in Way, "I went on a date with Aziz Ansari."
58 Catharine A. MacKinnon, *Toward a Feminist Theory of the State*, reprint edition (Cambridge, MA: Harvard University Press, 1991), 130.
59 Ann J. Cahill, *Rethinking Rape* (Ithaca, NY: Cornell University Press, 2001), 200.
60 For an expansive exploration of the concept of *habitus*, see Edward Farley, *Theologia: The Fragmentation and Unity of Theological Education*, reprint edition (Eugene, OR: Wipf and Stock, 2001).
61 Given the instability of the foster system and the forms of abuse that can occur within it, this may not be an unreasonable explanation for a child to make. For an explanation of why one child who was sexually violated by her father did not report what happened, see various interviews with lawyer, restorative justice advocate, and MacArthur Fellow Sujatha Baliga, including "Sujatha Baliga," accessed November 23, 2020, www.macfound.org/fellows/1029/. For a comprehensive overview of the struggles faced by foster children in the United States, see Cris Beam, *To the End of June: The Intimate Life of American Foster Care* (Boston: Mariner Books, 2013). See also Danielle Tumminio Hansen, "Even more tenuous connections: a pastoral theological analysis of foster care during COVID-19," *Journal of Pastoral Theology* 31, nos. 2–3 (September 2, 2021): 207–23, https://doi.org/10.1080/10649867.2021.1921403.
62 Angela Y. Davis, *Women, Race, & Class* (New York: Vintage, 1983), 172. For a more extensive analysis of this topic, see pages 173–201.
63 Charlotte Pierce-Baker, *Surviving the Silence: Black Women's Stories of Rape* (New York: W. W. Norton & Company, 2000), 64.

CHAPTER 5

1 Gavey, 159.
2 Alcoff, *Rape and Resistance*, 73. Linda Martín Alcoff makes a convincing argument for the value of "know-how" or the embodied knowledge that arises in the aftermath of a sexual violation. Alcoff rightly recognizes that experience need not diminish epistemic credibility but rather can enhance it; however, here her focus is on establishing the value of the victimized party's credibility rather than the value

of the interpretative process that takes place over time or the evolving perspective a person might have of the event.
3   For a defense of epistemic liberation in theology, particularly in relation to memory, see Danielle Tumminio Hansen, "Remembering rape in Heaven: a constructive proposal for memory and the eschatological self," *Modern Theology* 37, no. 3 (September 21, 2020): 662–78.
4   Alcoff, *Rape and Resistance*, 6.
5   Gendered pronouns have been changed to gender neutral ones.
6   Gendered pronouns have been changed to gender neutral ones.
7   Brison, *Aftermath*, xi.
8   Tricia Rose, *Longing to Tell: Black Women Talk About Sexuality and Intimacy* (New York: Farrar, Straus and Giroux, 2004), 6.
9   In general, I refrain from using the Foucauldian term "dominant discourses" because I find Foucault to be a problematic partner to engage constructively on this issue, given his own writings about sexuality, which at times appear to endorse abusive practices. I therefore care to give him no airtime in this work, especially when there are other terms from my own discipline—specifically Carrie Doehring's term "embedded beliefs"—that represent a similar concept. For more extensive analysis of embedded and deliberative beliefs, especially in relation to the practice of listening and offering support and care to those who have survived harm, see Carrie Doehring, *The Practice of Pastoral Care, Revised and Expanded Edition: A Postmodern Approach* (Louisville, KY: Westminster John Knox Press, 2015).
10 While Italian Americans are often treated as a monolith when it comes to discussing their immigration to the United States, they themselves did not identify this way, and neither did the American public respond to them as a monolith. Northern Italians—who were more likely to be light skinned and wealthy—were less likely to be stigmatized than were their Southern counterparts, who had darker skin, eyes, and hair and were more likely to be financially destitute. The racial privileges granted to white Americans did not extend to these immigrants from Southern Italy, raising important questions about the social construction of race in the United States. Upon their arrival in the United States, the Italian immigrants themselves tended to identify themselves not by their country of origin but by the region they came from (i.e., Sicily or Naples or Milan). See Stefano Luconi, "Becoming Italian in the US: through the lens of life narratives," *MELUS* 29, no. 3/4 (2004): 151–64, https://doi.org/10.2307/4141848.
11 The anti-Italian rhetoric that was common during the early twentieth century in the United States arguably emerged from a combination of anti-immigrant bias, anti-Catholic bias, and systemic racism. As Linda Martín Alcoff explains, the dark complexion—especially of Southern Italian immigrants—led them to be seen not as white but as Black, a sentiment that changed over time, though, as Alcoff reflects,

"Arguably, southern Europeans and Jews are even today only borderline whites, culturally marked as distinct and problematic, with less evidence of the mythical values of honesty, cool-headedness, and hard work associated with Protestants." The extent to which Italian Americans continue to be stereotyped as ill-educated Brooklynites with strong accents, Mafia ties, and minimal education can be seen in media representations. Linguistically, the extent to which their last names continue to be heard as "strange" or "difficult to spell" harkens to the way they continue to be othered—if not overtly discriminated against—in the dominant culture of the United States. Linda Martín Alcoff, *The Future of Whiteness* (Cambridge, UK: Polity, 2015), 13.

12 For more on racial covering, see Kenji Yoshino, *Covering: The Hidden Assault on Our Civil Rights* (New York: Random House Trade Paperbacks, 2007), 111–42.

13 The marginalization and pressure to assimilate that many Italian Americans experienced in the early part of the twentieth century mirrors the experience of many other groups that have immigrated to the United States. For a helpful overview of issues commonly faced by immigrant groups, see Rita J. Simon, "Immigration and public opinion," *In Defense of the Alien* 18 (1995): 58–68.

14 Salisbury Cathedral established the first English cathedral girls' choir decades later, in 1991. In 2019, the number of girls in English cathedral choirs exceeded the number of boys for the first time in history, there being 739 girl choristers and 737 boy choristers. The study did not ask about either trans or gender nonconforming children, who would need to identify with one gender binary or another in order to participate. Katherine Dienes-Williams, the first woman appointed as a choir director in an English cathedral stated that "It is imperative that we continue to work passionately and energetically in our respective cathedrals to endeavor to allow children identifying as any gender to access and enhance this musical heritage and culture." Other cathedral choir directors, such as Paul McCreesh, worried that the data were yet another sign of the power of gendered constructions that make it appropriate for girls but not boys to participate in the arts. The English choral tradition had, up until 2016, at least, been an exception to that norm. As he stated, "Without a doubt, it's great to increase opportunities for girl choristers, but at the same time it's boys who are underrepresented in most youth choirs." McCreesh also seems to imply that the presence of girls is a threat to boys in the choral tradition, once again pitting the genders against one another. He continued the aforementioned quotation by saying, "Boys need safe spaces to sing, and not to feel intimidated by (older) girls." Kyle Macdonald, "Girl choristers now outnumber boys in English cathedrals for the first time in history," *Classic fM Digital Radio*. December 20, 2019, www.classicfm.com/music-news/girl-choristers-outnumber-boys-english-cathedrals/

15 It is widely assumed that the dispassionate, ethereal style of the English choral tradition emerged in the Middle Ages and perpetuates through the present day. However, Timothy Day asserts that this style only emerged in most English church settings

in the 1930s and that, prior, the tradition was highly emotive, even bombastic at times. Day also reminds the reader that the use of the musical voice does not emerge in isolation but rather emerges in reaction to other cultural beliefs and norms such that the musical voice itself can best be understood as a social construction derived from other social constructions. See Timothy Day, *I Saw Eternity the Other Night: King's College Cambridge, and an English Singing Style* (New York: Penguin, 2020).

16 Judith Butler, known for her theory of gender performativity, first presented the term in *Gender Trouble: Feminism and the Subversion of Identity* (New York: Routledge, 2006).

17 The cathedral where I sang established a woman's choir shortly after I graduated, around the year 2001.

18 Men also sing with vibratos and are equally as able to suppress their vibratos as women are if they are trained to do so. There are also choirs that operate in the English choral tradition composed entirely of men and women. In England, some of the most notable are the choirs of Trinity College and Clare College at Cambridge University. In the United States, Anglo-Catholic churches like the ones at Christ Church (New Haven, CT) and the Church of the Advent (Boston, MA) also represent this tradition.

19 Purity culture plays a far lesser role for Episcopalians than it does for some other Christians, such as Mormons and some evangelical Christian groups who place a premium on women's piety and chastity.

20 Our physical appearance also encouraged us to see the body as somehow lesser or worthy of ignoring. In church services, we wore robes that covered up our bodies so that we would be uniform and so the visual focus wouldn't be on any of us physically. The robes visually disembodied us, exposing us only from the neck up, covering up any curves, any bodily specificity.

21 For a selection of key pastoral theology books on active listening, see Emma J. Justes, *Hearing Beyond the Words: How to Become a Listening Pastor* (Nashville, TN: Abingdon Press, 2002); Emma J. Justes, *Please Don't Tell: What to Do with the Secrets People Share* (Nashville, TN: Abingdon Press, 2014). For a helpful resource on active listening with survivors of sexual violations, see Kristen J. Leslie, *When Violence Is No Stranger: Pastoral Counseling with Survivors of Acquaintance Rape* (Minneapolis: Fortress Press, 2003).

22 For a primer to posttraumatic growth and its dimensions, see R.G. Tedeschi and L.G. Calhoun, "The posttraumatic growth inventory: measuring the positive legacy of trauma," *Journal of Traumatic Stress* 9, no. 3 (July 1996): 455–71, https://doi.org/10.1007/BF02103658. For further reading, including in relation to posttraumatic growth and rape, see Tanja Zoellner and Andreas Maercker, "Posttraumatic growth in clinical psychology: a critical review and introduction of a two component model," *Clinical Psychology Review* 26, no. 5 (September 2006): 626–53, https://doi.org/10.1016/j.cpr.2006.01.008; Kanako Taku, Arnie Cann, Lawrence G. Calhoun,

and Richard G. Tedeschi, "The factor structure of the posttraumatic growth inventory: a comparison of five models using confirmatory factor analysis," *Journal of Traumatic Stress* 21, no. 2 (April 2008): 158–64, https://doi.org/10.1002/jts.20305; Laura Sinko, Robert Ploutz-Snyder, Michelle Munro Kramer, Terri Conley, and Denise Saint Arnault, "Trauma history as a significant predictor of posttraumatic growth beyond mental health symptoms in women-identifying survivors of undergraduate non-consensual sexual experiences," *Violence and Victims* 37, no. 3 (June 1, 2022): 396–421, https://doi.org/10.1891/VV-D-20-00082; Christopher Peterson, Nansook Park, Nnamdi Pole, Wendy D'Andrea, and Martin E.P. Seligman, "Strengths of character and posttraumatic growth," *Journal of Traumatic Stress* 21, no. 2 (April 2008): 214–17, https://doi.org/10.1002/jts.20332.
23 Alcoff, *Rape and Resistance*, 73.
24 Susan J. Brison, *Aftermath* (Princeton, NJ: Princeton University Press, 2003), 20.

CHAPTER 6

1 Lacy Crawford describes this phenomenon when she writes:

   I know I'm stacking the deck in my own defense. Which I should not have to do, because I was a minor and the boys were eighteen and there were *two of them*—one of whom was on that night almost a foot taller and a hundred pounds heavier than me. I was a virgin. They pushed me down and—I'm doing it again. (Crawford, 11)

2 Angela D. Sims, *Lynched: The Power of Memory in a Culture of Terror* (Waco, TX: Baylor University Press, 2016), 79.
3 Sims, *Lynched*, 80–82.
4 Nottingham Sr., Junius, quoted in Sims, *Lynched*, 102.
5 For more on misfires in performatives, see lecture three in J.L. Austin, *How to Do Things with Words* (Eastford, CT: Martino Fine Books, 2018).
6 Austin differentiates between failed performatives—what he calls "infelicities" and what I term statements that "fail to perform"—as either "abuses" or "misfires." Misfires occur when what seeks to be performed is not allowed or goes wrong; an abuse involves a hollow act. I use the terminology of "fail to perform" rather than "infelicities" for the sake of simplification and clarity. See Austin, *How to Do Things with Words*, 167.
7 Here I am assuming a context in which the necessary felicity conditions obtain.
8 Chanel Miller, *Know My Name* (New York: Viking), 47.
9 Note that Trump is not consistent in asserting that one is innocent until proven guilty—see the repeated rallies in which he encouraged crowds to chant "Lock her up" in regard to unsubstantiated claims of crimes committed by Hillary Clinton

for but one instance of Trump's willingness to violate his own assertion that a person in the United States deserves to be seen as innocent until proven guilty. It is particularly ironic that Trump judged Hillary Clinton this way, given his assertion, quoted above, that it was really a dangerous time to be a man in the United States and not to be a woman.

10 For one example of why those who were raped may minimize harm and defend the person who raped them, see Judith L. Herman, *Trauma and Recovery: The Aftermath of Violence—From Domestic Abuse to Political Terror* (New York: Basic Books, 2015), 82–83. Herman uses a hypothetical example of a woman being battered by her partner to explain that a victimized person may minimize the harm or defend the person inflicting it for complex reasons, ranging from fear and denial to the love and empathy she may have for the person who raped her to emotional dependence and her partner's persuasive attempts to get her to stay in the relationship. Herman goes on to explain that the woman who is experiencing this kind of intimate partner violence will need to instead discover a new way of naming and reacting to the relationship if she is going to leave the abuse and process the trauma.

11 One reason victimized individuals may not report an incidence of rape to police is because they believe the criminal justice system is ill-equipped to provide the kind of response they are looking for, which might involve an apology or forms of accountability that they personally find meaningful. Many feel restorative justice is better equipped to accomplish these goals than the criminal justice system is because it gives the harmed party agency to identify the contours of meaningful accountability, rather than relying exclusively on punishment mechanisms, including the prison system and sex offender registries. For a summary and statistics concerning what victims do see as effective accountability and the role that restorative justice can play, see Jo-Anne Wemmers, "Judging victims: restorative choices for victims of sexual violence," *Victims of Crime Research Digest* no. 10, June 2, 2017, www.justice.gc.ca/eng/rp-pr/cj-jp/victim/rd10-rr10/p3.html.

12 "De facto" being the key term here, because the speech of those who were raped can do this, especially when they appear to be an ideal victim, but such instances are rare in comparison to instances where their credibility is attacked and those who inflicted the harm are defended against the accusation, emerging, ultimately, unscathed in the eyes of many and especially in the eyes of the powerful, including in the eyes of judges, juries, police officers, and those who have the ability to terminate jobs or contracts.

13 Kyubo Kim has proposed that vulnerability can be an important addition to care practices and one that is theologically grounded by the way that Jesus practiced vulnerability in his life. See Kyubo Kim, "The power of being vulnerable in Christian soul care: common humanity and humility," *Journal of Religion and Health* 56, no. 1 (February 2017): 355–69, https://doi.org/10.1007/s10943-016-0294-8.

14 I'm working here from Brené Brown's definition of vulnerability, which reads that vulnerability is "uncertainty, risk, and emotional exposure. But vulnerability is not weakness; it's our most accurate measure of courage." For more on vulnerability, see Brené Brown, *Braving the Wilderness: The Quest for True Belonging and the Courage to Stand Alone* (New York: Random House, 2017), 154.

15 Disclosure is even more complicated for those individuals who are also vulnerable for other reasons, perhaps due to economics, physical or intellectual ability, race, gender, sexual orientation, or age. Marie Fortune writes in particular about the latter issue, explaining that disclosure may be especially complicated for children because of the vulnerabilities wrought by age, because they are afraid of the offender's power, or because they do not have the language to describe the wrongdoing. See Marie M. Fortune, *Sexual Violence: The Sin Revisited* (Cleveland, OH: Pilgrim Press, 2005), 178–80.

16 Pastoral and practical theologians have invoked the topic of vulnerability in nuanced and creative ways to explain why vulnerability is so valuable as a caregiving resource. For a sampling of the literature from the field on the many dimensions of vulnerability—including economic vulnerability—see James Newton Poling, *Render Unto God: Economic Vulnerability, Family Violence, and Pastoral Theology* (Eugene, OR: Wipf and Stock, 2012).

17 For a helpful overview of how to navigate complex boundaries related to power and vulnerability in caregiving relationships, see Jan Berry, "A safe space for healing: boundaries, power and vulnerability in pastoral care," *Theology & Sexuality* 20, no. 3 (September 1, 2014): 203–13, https://doi.org/10.1179/1355835815Z.00000000050.

18 Susan Brison offers an example from one listener following her own experience of a rape and attempted murder who exhibited this kind of reaction and what the effect on her was.

> An aunt, with whom I had been close since childhood, did not write or call at all until three months after the attack, and then sent a belated birthday card with a note saying that she was sorry to hear about my "horrible experience" but pleased to think that as a result I "will become stronger and will be able to help so many people. A real blessing from above for sure." Such attempts at a theodicy discounted the horror I had to endure. (Brison, *Aftermath*, 11)

As Brison intimates, the problem with this kind of reaction is that it shuts down vulnerability and robs the survivor of narrative agency, dictating what their reaction should be instead of creating space for the survivor to name and process it in their own words.

19 The tendency to deny is both collective as well as individual. Judith Herman historically charts the dialectic between society's ability to name and engage with trauma and subsequently disengage and attempt to forget or deny it. See Herman, *Trauma and Recovery*, 7–33.

20 Shame may emerge not only from feelings about the event but also from feelings about subsequent reactions to it, including reactions emerging from posttraumatic stress. Shame may also lead to behaviors that make it difficult to connect with others, as Bessel van der Kolk remarks when he notes that his chronically traumatized patients often have difficulty making eye contact because of their intense feelings of shame. Van der Kolk goes on to explain that the neurological response in patients who struggle with eye contact also makes it difficult for them to emotionally connect with others. See *The Body Keeps the Score: Brain, Mind, and Body in the Healing of Trauma* (New York: Viking, 2014), 67, 102.

21 I addressed the need for social belonging as a primary need for human flourishing and the successful embodiment of theological anthropology in chapter 1 of *Conceiving Family*. Willie James Jennings also extensively discusses the significance of social belonging within theological education at large and the way in which white, masculine, individualist epistemologies have all too often thwarted the manifestation of social belonging within the lives of individuals and communities. See Willie James Jennings, *After Whiteness: An Education in Belonging* (Grand Rapids, MI: Eerdmans, 2020).

22 For more on humility in listening, see Emma J. Justes, *Hearing Beyond the Words: How to Become a Listening Pastor* (Nashville, TN: Abingdon Press, 2002), 21–42.

23 Pastoral theology at large privileges placing the needs of the most vulnerable first in a pastoral encounter. Emmanuel Lartey discusses human vulnerability in relation to God's identity in complex and nuanced ways, identifying that God is at times simultaneously inscrutable, invulnerable, and inviolable while also recognizing that the biblical accounts of Jesus's life and embodied vulnerability create the possibility of solidarity for humans who are seeking a point of contact and commonality with the divine. See Emmanuel Y. Lartey, *Pastoral Theology in an Intercultural World* (Eugene, OR: Wipf and Stock, 2013), 106–11.

24 To that end, Kristen Leslie rightly observes that the process of interpretation and meaning-making ultimately belongs to the person who experienced the violation and not the listener, again reinforcing the listener's role as primarily non-directive. See Kristen J. Leslie, *When Violence Is No Stranger: Pastoral Counseling with Survivors of Acquaintance Rape* (Minneapolis: Fortress Press, 2003), 54.

25 This way of listening also demonstrates humility on the part of the listener instead of dominance. See Justes, *Hearing Beyond the Words*, 21–42.

26 Put differently, while Susan Brison is right that "*Saying* something about the memory *does* something to it," I would add that "The way a listener *responds* to the memory *does* something to it." Brison, *Aftermath*, xi.

27 Doehring, *The Practice of Pastoral Care*, 56–63.

28 Doehring, *The Practice of Pastoral Care*, 64–65.

29 I have also discussed this particular aspect of listening in Danielle Tumminio Hansen, "Absent a word: how the language of sexual trauma keeps survivors silent,"

Journal of Pastoral Theology 30, no. 2 (May 2020): 136–49, https://doi.org/10.108 0/10649867.2020.1748920.
30 Justes, *Hearing Beyond the Words*, 45.
31 For a helpful primer on empathy, see Doehring, *The Practice of Pastoral Care*, 37–43.
32 For a rich resource on pastoral imagination, see Eileen R. Campbell-Reed, *Pastoral Imagination: Bringing the Practice of Ministry to Life* (Minneapolis: Fortress Press, 2021).
33 For more on fusion and disengagement, see Doehring, *The Practice of Pastoral Care*, 39–43.
34 Doehring, *The Practice of Pastoral Care*, 39–43.
35 Emma Justes offers an important resource for caregivers to better understand best practices of confidentiality and boundary keeping in *Please Don't Tell*, 41–55. For an exploration of boundaries, specifically boundary violations, in pastoral sexual misconduct, see "Sexual exploitation and other boundary violations in pastoral ministries," in Pamela Cooper-White, *Gender, Violence, and Justice: Collected Essays on Violence against Women* (Eugene, OR: Cascade Books, 2019), 96–118. See also chapter 10 of Marie Fortune, *Sexual Violence*, 185–218.
36 For a helpful analysis of the role that culture plays in naming and contextualizing rape, see chapter 5, "Decolonizing terms," in Linda Martín Alcoff's *Rape and Resistance* (Cambridge, UK: Polity, 2018), 148–75.
37 For a set of profiles and analyses of how Black women name, interpret, and integrate sexual violations into their lives, with attention given to how these violations affect their spirituality, see Stephanie M. Crumpton, *A Womanist Pastoral Theology Against Intimate and Cultural Violence* (Palgrave Macmillan, 2014), 25–65.
38 Phillis Isabella Sheppard, *Self, Culture, and Others in Womanist Practical Theology* (New York: Palgrave Macmillan, 2011), 121–22.
39 Phillis Isabella Sheppard remarks that race and gender often impact our ways of seeing the world such that care seekers may feel that there are limitations to what can be discussed with someone who does not share their background. She explains that Black women often experience barriers wrought by imposed norms that exclude their experiences and voices. This, in turn, also affects the resources available to them for spiritual support. Citing the research of Marjorie Lewis, she proposes that Black women may feel they cannot bring concerns to white male pastors because they are unable to empathize with their experiences. See Phillis Isabella Sheppard, "Womanist pastoral theology and black women's experience of gender, religion, and sexuality," in *Pastoral Theology and Care: Critical Trajectories in Theory and Practice*, edited by Nancy J. Ramsay (Hoboken, NJ: Wiley-Blackwell, 2018), 129–30. See also Marjorie Lewis, "Diaspora dialogue: womanist theology in engagement with aspects of the Black British and Jamaican experience," *Black Theology* 2, no. 1 (January 1, 2004): 85–109, https://doi.org/10.1558/blth.2004.2.1.85.
40 It may be helpful for listeners to familiarize themselves with the literature on epistemic injustice, beginning with the work of Miranda Fricker, who coined the term. Fricker proposes two kinds of epistemic injustice. Testimonial injustice occurs when

someone's story is not trusted or believed. Hermeneutical injustice occurs when someone lacks frameworks to interpret or contextualize their lives. Both may be evident in the ways that victims speak and are listened to by others. For more on these forms of epistemic injustice, see Miranda Fricker, *Epistemic Injustice: Power and the Ethics of Knowing* (Oxford: Oxford University Press, USA, 2009), 9–17, 149–69. For a helpful analysis of how epistemic justice plays out specifically in sexual violations, see Debra L. Jackson, "'Me too': epistemic injustice and the struggle for recognition," *Feminist Philosophy Quarterly* 4, no. 4 (December 17, 2018), https://doi.org/10.5206/fpq/2018.4.6231.

41 Kristen Leslie recognizes that many survivors will encounter a lack of support from their communities and loved ones. She offers a number of guidelines and recommendations for how pastoral care providers can listen in ways that start with belief in the survivor's narrative. See Leslie, *When Violence Is No Stranger*, 133–55.

42 Both Carrie Doehring and Jeanne Stevenson-Moessner have eloquently written about the role that music can play in trauma recovery. See Carrie Doehring, "Searching for wholeness amidst traumatic grief: the role of spiritual practices that reveal compassion in embodied, relational, and transcendent ways," *Pastoral Psychology*, 68 (December, 2018): 241–59; Jeanne Stevenson-Moessner, *Overture to Practical Theology: The Music of Religious Inquiry* (Eugene, OR: Cascade Books, 2016).

43 For a vision of how faith communities might respond in the aftermath of a sexual violation within the community, see Fortune, *Sexual Violence*, 219–25. See also Margaret Kennedy, "Sexual abuse of women by priests and ministers to whom they go for pastoral care and support," *Feminist Theology* 11, no. 2 (January 1, 2003): 226–35, https://doi.org/10.1177/096673500301100213; John D. Vogelsang, "From denial to hope: a systemic response to clergy sexual abuse," *Journal of Religion and Health* 32, no. 3 (September 1, 1993): 197–208, https://doi.org/10.1007/BF00995653. For a church-based resource, see Evangelical Lutheran Church in America, "Healing in congregations after clergy sexual abuse: a resource to assist synodical leaders and local congregations" (ELCA, 2005), 116.

44 For a sampling of well-publicized examples of this kind of coverup in educational institutions, see reports about allegations of sexual misconduct at Penn State University, Michigan State University, University of Southern California, and St. Paul's School, an elite boarding school in New Hampshire. For an incisive book-length analysis how Title IX procedures foster an environment that does not encourage institutional accountability, see Donna Freitas, *Consent on Campus: A Manifesto* (New York: Oxford University Press, 2018).

CHAPTER 7

1 Allison Manning, "St. Paul's graduate and convicted felon Owen Labrie could go to jail for alleged curfew violations," *The Boston Globe*, March 15, 2016, accessed

April 19, 2021, www.boston.com/news/local-news/2016/03/15/st-pauls-graduate-and-convicted-felon-owen-labrie-could-go-to-jail-for-alleged-curfew-violations.

2 Chessy Prout and Jenn Abelson, *I Have the Right To: A High School Survivor's Story of Sexual Assault, Justice, and Hope* (New York: Margaret K. McElderry Books, 2018).

3 For a book-length exploration of the journey of one survivor who experienced a rape at St. Paul's School, see Lacy Crawford's *Notes on a Silencing*.

4 Chessy Prout's book offers a poignant example of how that dominant epistemology—which included doubt of survivor speech—seeped into the student body. She writes about how she tried to return to St. Paul's after she reported the harm that Labrie inflicted, but many of the girls who she previously thought of as close friends turned her into a pariah because they believed that their own social status would decline on-campus if they maintained a friendship with her. Their alienation became one of the factors that eventually caused her to withdraw from the school. See chapter 10 of Prout and Abelson, *I Have the Right To*.

5 The examples cited all illustrate how human beings need proxies to support them because they cannot meet all of their needs on their own. I propose elsewhere in my scholarship that reproductive surrogacy relationships can teach us something about how to construct non-reproductive relationships where one individual serves as a proxy (or non-reproductive surrogate) for others. Such relationships function best when they mutually value subjectivity and a person's sense of identity or calling. See the final chapter of Danielle Tumminio Hansen, *Conceiving Family: A Practical Theology of Surrogacy and Self* (Waco, TX: Baylor University Press, 2019) as well as "Even more tenuous connections: a pastoral theological analysis of foster care during COVID-19," *Journal of Pastoral Theology*, 31, nos. 2–3 (2021): 207–23. Reprinted in *Justice Matters: Spiritual Care and Pastoral Theological Imaginations in Times of the COVID-19 Pandemic*, eds. Kyungsig Samuel Lee and Danjuma Gibson (New York: Routledge, 2022), 137–54.

6 For an analysis of how neoliberalism inflicts trauma on Black Americans and practices of care that can help dismantle its effects, see Cedric C. Johnson, *Race, Religion, and Resilience in the Neoliberal Age* (New York: Palgrave Macmillan, 2015).

7 For more on my development of the term "cultural misorientation," see chapter 4 of Tumminio Hansen, *Conceiving Family*.

8 Danielle Sered, *Until We Reckon: Violence, Mass Incarceration, and a Road to Repair* (New York: The New Press, 2019), 3.

9 For a helpful feminist theological analysis about the self that ultimately advocates for greater awareness of the relational self, see Catherine Keller, *From a Broken Web: Separation, Sexism and Self* (Boston, MA: Beacon Press, 1988).

10 For detailed information about the case and appeals, see New Hampshire Judicial Branch, "Information on Cases for the Public and Media: State of NH v. Owen Labrie," www.courts.state.nh.us/caseinfo/pdf/labrie/index.htm.

11 For a helpful primer on the problems that Title IX policies broadly pose, see Donna Freitas, *Consent on Campus: A Manifesto* (New York, NY: Oxford University Press, 2018), especially chapter 1.
12 For an overview of the limitations to the legalistic approach of Title IX committees and a practical vision for restorative justice as an alternative, see Mary P. Koss, Jay K. Wilgus, and Kaaren M. Williamsen, "Campus sexual misconduct: restorative justice approaches to enhance compliance with Title IX guidance," *Trauma, Violence, and Abuse* 15, no. 3 (July 2014): 242–57, https://doi.org/10.1177/1524838014521500.
13 Susan Ehrlich, *Representing Rape: Language and Sexual Consent* (New York: Routledge, 2003), 38, 40. See also Marianne LaFrance and Eugene Hahn, "The disappearing agent: gender stereotypes, interpersonal verbs, and implicit causality," in *The Women and Language Debate: A Sourcebook*, edited by Camille Roman, Suzanne Juhasz, and Christine Miller (New Brunswick, NJ: Rutgers University Press, 1993).
14 Ehrlich, *Representing Rape*, 47.
15 Ehrlich, *Representing Rape*, 54–55.
16 Ehrlich, *Representing Rape*, 76.
17 Ehrlich, *Representing Rape*, 77; emphasis Ehrlich.
18 Ehrlich, *Representing Rape*, 78; emphasis Ehrlich.
19 Ehrlich, *Representing Rape*, 78.
20 This deprivation of narrative agency also occurs in the courtroom for those accused of harm. See Sered, *Until We Reckon*, 92–93.
21 Nancy Scheper-Hughes, "James X: a reflection on rape, race, and redemption," *Anthropology Today* 32, no. 5 (2016): 21–25, https://doi.org/10.1111/1467-8322.12299.
22 For a groundbreaking book-length treatment of the history of Jim Crow laws and their impact on mass incarceration policies, see Michelle Alexander, *The New Jim Crow: Mass Incarceration in the Age of Colorblindness* (New York: The New Press, 2012). For an important treatment of the pastoral theological consequences of a racist carceral system, see Gregory Ellison, *Cut Dead but Still Alive: Caring for African American Young Men* (Nashville, TN: Abingdon Press, 2013).
23 Sered, *Until We Reckon*, 8.
24 For more on the barriers that incarcerated individuals and their communities face, see Sered, *Until We Reckon*, 7–10.
25 Sered, *Until We Reckon*, 11–12.
26 Sered, *Until We Reckon*, 7.
27 United States Sentencing Commission. "Recidivism Among Federal Violent Offenders," January 23, 2019, www.ussc.gov/research/research-reports/recidivism-among-federal-violent-offenders.
28 United States Sentencing Commission. "Recidivism Among Federal Violent Offenders."

29 The punitive structure of the criminal justice system ironically inflicts further concrete harm upon those that it incarcerates, as demonstrated through practices like solitary confinement that can harm the mental health of inmates, in essence functioning as a form of torture. The United Nations has drawn attention to and expressed concern at the way that the United States treats prisoners, particularly in relation to its use of solitary confinement as a form of torture, and has singled out the United States for violating the Mandela Rules, which provides minimum standards for the human treatment of prisoners. For more details, see Nils Melzer, "Torture and other cruel, inhuman or degrading treatment or punishment: report of the Special Rapporteur on torture and other cruel, inhuman or degrading treatment or punishment," January 22, 2021, https://undocs.org/A/HRC/46/26.
30 Sered, *Until We Reckon*, 68–69.
31 In his analysis of violence in the prison system, James Gilligan explains that prison inmates may use rape as a tool to maintain their power, and that prison guards often "play dumb" in order to maintain order in the prison system, as well as to maintain their own power. In this way, the guards become complicit in the enactment of sexual harm. See James Gilligan, *Violence: Reflections on a National Epidemic* (New York: Vintage, 1997), 170.
32 For more on how shame is integrally entwined in the enactment of violence and in the practices of the prison system, see Gilligan, *Violence*, 103–38, 163–90.
33 In 2019, researchers found that 37% of parents spanked their children, with the rate rising to 49% in children 0–9. They documented that rates of spanking were higher for boys than girls, higher in the southern portion of the United States than the northeastern portion, and that Black families were more likely to spank their children than white families were. Rates were also higher in families where parents did not have a graduate degree and where there were more than three children. See David Finkelhor, Heather Turner, Brittany Kaye Wormuth, Jennifer Vanderminden, and Sherry Hamby, "Corporal punishment: current rates from a national survey," *Journal of Child and Family Studies* 28, no. 7 (July 1, 2019): 1991–97, https://doi.org/10.1007/s10826-019-01426-4.
34 For but one example of the handcuffing of a child under the age of ten by law enforcement, see Michael George, "'We want you to beat him': Maryland police seen in body camera footage handcuffing 5-year-old boy," CBS Evening News, March 28, 2021, www.cbsnews.com/news/maryland-police-5-year-old-boy-handcuffed-berated/.
35 Punishment can be best understood as a form of operant conditioning designed to eradicate behavior by making it unappealing. Warrants for its use draw on behavior modification studies, such as those done by B.F. Skinner. Critics argue that punishment only deters behavior but does not teach alternatives or encourage better choices or accountability.
36 Thordis Elva and Tom Stranger, *South of Forgiveness: A True Story of Rape and Responsibility* (New York: Skyhorse Publishing, 2017), 8–9.

37 Elva and Stranger, *South of Forgiveness*, 13.
38 Elva and Stranger, *South of Forgiveness*, 14.
39 For more on restorative justice in indigenous contexts in North America, see Howard Zehr, Allan McRae, Kay Pranis, and Lorraine Stutzman Amstutz, *The Big Book of Restorative Justice: Four Classic Justice & Peacebuilding Books in One Volume* (Good Books, 2015), 20–21, 56. Zehr explains, in the introduction to the book, that he has often been credited as being the founder of restorative justice practices and recognizes that the credit given to him falsely covers the contributions of centuries of indigenous people for whom restorative justice was normative.
40 The murder of Ann Grosmaire by her boyfriend Connor McBride and the subsequent use of restorative justice by Ann's parents is perhaps the most well-publicized example of restorative justice being used in the aftermath of a murder. Andy and Kate Grosmaire were motivated by their Roman Catholic faith commitments to see a supplement to the criminal justice system and engaged in the process with the support of the prosecutor in the case. The conversations between the Grosmaires and McBride allowed the parents to ask questions of McBride that felt important to their healing and created space for him to take accountability and ask what needed to be done to make things right. The Grosmaires felt a prison sentence was a necessary form of accountability for McBride, who agreed and is now serving a sentence. The Grosmaires continue to visit him in prison.
41 For a groundbreaking study showing that restorative justice processes where victimized and offending individuals meet can yield positive outcomes, see Mary Koss's 2014 study. The size of the study—which qualitatively analyzes twenty-two cases of sexual harm which utilized restorative processes—limits the ability to generalize outcomes. Nonetheless, the findings offer cautious optimism that restorative processes provide a positive alternative to the criminal justice system in cases of sexual harm. Mary P. Koss, "The RESTORE Program of Restorative Justice for Sex Crimes: vision, process, and outcomes," *Journal of Interpersonal Violence* 29, no. 9 (June 1, 2014): 1623–60, https://doi.org/10.1177/0886260513511537.
42 The organization Circles of Support and Accountability (CoSA) has created an intensive support system for sex offenders that suggests that, with the right level of social accountability and support, sex offenders are capable of rehabilitation and reintegration. Additionally, Alissa Ackerman and Jill Levenson note that it is something of a vicious circle when it comes to the public believing that someone who has been labeled by the government as a "sex offender" is beyond rehabilitation because the public has inherited the embedded belief that the proper response to such individuals is to isolate them. Without support, however, offenders have no chance at rehabilitation. See Alissa Ackerman and Jill Levenson, *Healing from Sexual Violence* (Brandon, VT: Safer Society Press, 2009).
43 For more details on the petition created by Elwakil and the logic behind it, see Amira Elwakil, "Petition: rapist should not be given platform at Southbank Centre's

2017 WoW Festival," Change.Org, accessed April 22, 2021, www.change.org/p/rapist-should-not-be-given-platform-at-southbank-centre-s-2017-wow-festival.

44 For a defense of restorative justice in matters of sexual harm from a feminist perspective, see Leigh Goodmark, "Restorative justice as feminist practice," *International Journal of Restorative Justice* 1 (November 1, 2018): 372–84, https://doi.org/10.5553/IJRJ/258908912018001003003.

45 For an accessible introduction to how restorative justice creates space for accountability and speech, see chapters 3 and 4 of Judah Oudshoorn, Lorraine Stutzman Amstutz, and Michelle Jackett, *The Little Book of Restorative Justice for Sexual Abuse: Hope through Trauma* (New York: Good Books, 2015).

46 See Ackerman and Levenson, *Healing from Sexual Violence*, specifically chapters two and six.

47 For an overview and vision of how victim voice can be privileged in response processes, especially in underserved or diverse settings, via the use of listening practices, see Mary Koss, J.W. White, and E.C. Lopez, "Victim voice in reenvisioning responses to sexual and physical violence nationally and internationally," *American Psychologist* 72, no. 9 (2017): 1019–30.

48 For an example of what this looks like outside of the sphere of sexual violations, see the Derek Chauvin trial, in which Genevieve Hansen, an EMT worker, gave what the judge perceived to be an angry response to questions about George Floyd's size that Chauvin's defense attorney posed. "I'm advising you," said Judge Peter A. Cahill, "Do not argue with counsel and specifically, do not argue with the court. They have the right to ask questions, your job is to answer them." It is worth noting here that Hansen did answer the question—even correcting a prior statement she made. The judge's issue, therefore, was with the assertive tone of her voice rather than the contents of her speech. For more on Hansen's testimony, see Koss et al., "Victim voice."

49 The importance of removing punitive measures and dismantling the power the prison system holds as the sole locus of accountability for wrongdoing also affects the power that system has to inflict racial injustice and perpetuate the wrongful imprisonment of Black bodies. Restorative justice, therefore, also offers an important opportunity to address racial injustice in the United States. For a sustained and accessible consideration of what restorative justice can contribute to the eradication of racial injustice and systemic oppression, see Fania E. Davis, *The Little Book of Race and Restorative Justice: Black Lives, Healing, and US Social Transformation* (New York: Good Books, 2019).

50 In an important study concerning sexual violations on college campuses, researchers found that recidivism rates are also lower for those who sexually offend when restorative justice is employed. See David Karp and Casey Sacks, "Student conduct, restorative justice, and student development: findings from the STARR Project: a student accountability and restorative research project,"

Contemporary Justice Review 17 (June 23, 2014), https://doi.org/10.1080/1028 2580.2014.915140.

51 Danielle Sered writes that it is important to remember that violent behavior does not emerge in a vacuum but rather often emerges out of previous suffering. As she explains it, "Nearly everyone who commits violence has also survived it, and few have gotten formal support to heal. Although people's history of victimization never excuses the harm they cause, it does implicate our society for not having addressed their pain earlier." Sered, *Until We Reckon*, 4.

52 In the spring of 2016, *The Boston Globe*'s Spotlight team published a detailed report on cases of sexual misconduct over a period of decades not just at St. Paul's School but at numerous other boarding schools. See Jonathan Saltzman, Jenn Abelson, Bella English, and Todd Wallack, "Private schools, painful secrets," *Boston Globe*, May 6, 2016, www.bostonglobe.com/metro/2016/05/06/private-schools-painful-secrets/OaRI9PFpRnCTJxCzko5hkN/story.html.

53 Eileen O'Grady, "St. Paul's School compliance officer abruptly quits post," *Concord Monitor*, October 19, 2020, www.concordmonitor.com/St-Pauls-School-Overseer-Resigns-36866420.

54 For a comprehensive workbook that includes sample formats for restorative justice circles related to gender and power, see Mariame Kaba and Shira Hassan, *Fumbling Towards Repair: A Workbook for Community Accountability Facilitators*, Workbook edition (Chicago: Project NIA, 2019).

55 Ann J. Cahill, *Rethinking Rape* (Ithaca, NY: Cornell University Press, 2001), 200.

CONCLUSION

1 Susan J. Brison, *Aftermath: Violence and the Remaking of a Self* (Princeton, NJ: Princeton University Press, 2003), 21.

2 Anita Hill, *Believing: Our Thirty-Year Journey to End Gender Violence* (New York: Viking, 2021), 149.

3 Miranda Pilipchuk, "Good survivor, bad survivor: #MeToo and the moralization of survivorship," *Feminism and Philosophy* 19, no. 1 (Fall 2019): 5–10.

4 Andrea Johnson, Ramya Sekaran, and Sasha Gombar, "2020 Progress Update: MeToo Workplace Reforms in the States," *National Women's Law Center*, September 2020, 25.

5 For a transcript of Donald Trump's statements, see "Transcript: Donald Trump's taped comments about women," *The New York Times*, October 8, 2016, sec. U.S., www.nytimes.com/2016/10/08/us/donald-trump-tape-transcript.html.

6 Hill, *Believing*, 296.

7 In the case of Anita Hill, who stated that Clarence Thomas sexually harassed her, two other women—Angela Wright and Lillian McEwen—made similar allegations. Neither was allowed to testify during the Thomas nomination. In the case of Christine

Blasey Ford, who alleged that Brett Kavanaugh attempted to rape her, two other women—Deborah Ramirez and Julie Swetnick—made allegations of misconduct. Neither Ramirez nor Swetnick were allowed to testify before the Senate Judiciary Committee.

8   Judith Jarvis Thomson, "A defense of abortion," *Philosophy & Public Affairs* 1, no. 1 (1971): 47–66.
9   Danielle Elizabeth Tumminio Hansen, "The body of God, sexually violated: a trauma-informed reading of the climate crisis," *Religions* 13, no. 3 (March 2022): 249–61, https://doi.org/10.3390/rel13030249.
10 Tumminio Hansen, "The body of God," 257.
11 Senator Dianne Feinstein told Amy Coney Barrett that the "The dogma lives loudly within you" in her confirmation hearing to be a judge on the United States Court of Appeals in 2017, three years prior to her nomination to the United States Supreme Court. "Feinstein: 'The dogma lives loudly within you, and that's a concern,'" accessed August 15, 2022, www.washingtonpost.com/video/politics/feinstein-the-dogma-lives-loudly-within-you-and-thats-a-concern/2017/09/07/04303fda-93cb-11e7-8482-8dc9a7af29f9_video.html.

BIBLIOGRAPHY

Ackerman, Alissa, and Jill Levenson. *Healing from Sexual Violence*. Brandon, Vermont: Safer Society Press, 2009.
Adeniji, Linda. "The Unrapeable Black Woman: How the Lack of Legal Protection Through the Centuries Promoted the Tradition of Unreported Sexual Assaults." SSRN. Rochester, NY: Social Science Research Network, December 12, 2015. https://doi.org/10.2139/ssrn.2702861.
Alcoff, Linda Martín. *The Future of Whiteness*. Cambridge, UK: Polity, 2015.
———. *Rape and Resistance*. Cambridge, UK: Polity, 2018.
Alexander, Michelle. *The New Jim Crow: Mass Incarceration in the Age of Colorblindness*. New York: The New Press, 2012.
Allison, Emily Joy, and Lyz Lenz. *#ChurchToo: How Purity Culture Upholds Abuse and How to Find Healing*. Minneapolis: Broadleaf Books, 2021.
Alvarez, Priscilla. "ICE Whistleblower Alleges High Rate of Hysterectomies and Medical Neglect at Georgia Facility." CNN, September 16, 2020. www.cnn.com/2020/09/15/politics/immigration-customs-enforcement-medical-care-detainees/index.html.
American Psychiatric Association. *DSMIII: Diagnostic and Statistical Manual of Mental Disorders*, third edition. Washington, DC: American Psychiatric Association, 1980.
———. *Diagnostic and Statistical Manual of Mental Disorders, Fourth Edition (DSM-IV)*. Washington, DC: American Psychiatric Association, 1994.
———. *Diagnostic and Statistical Manual of Mental Disorders, Fifth Edition*. Washington, DC: American Psychiatric Publishing, 2013.
Anderson, RaeAnn E., Lesley A. Tarasoff, Nicole VanKim, and Corey Flanders. "Differences in Rape Acknowledgment and Mental Health Outcomes Across Transgender, Nonbinary, and Cisgender Bisexual Youth." *Journal of Interpersonal Violence* 36, no. 13–14 (July 2021): NP7717–39. https://doi.org/10.1177/0886260519829763.
Aquinas, Thomas. *Summa Theologica*. Claremont, CA: Coyote Canyon Press, 2010.
Asher, Jay. *13 Reasons Why*. Reissue edition. London: Razorbill, 2017.
Audrie & Daisy | Netflix Official Site, 2016. www.netflix.com/title/80097321.
Austin, J.L. *How to Do Things with Words*. Edited by J. O. Urmson. Eastford, CT: Martino Fine Books, 2018.

Banfield Slams Ansari Accuser in Open Letter, 2018. www.youtube.com/watch?v=y4bAULTwAJU.

"Bari Weiss on Twitter." Twitter. Accessed December 31, 2020. https://twitter.com/bariweiss/status/952647595880525826.

Beam, Cris. *To the End of June: The Intimate Life of American Foster Care*. New York: Houghton Mifflin Harcourt, 2013.

Bennice, Jennifer A., and Patricia A. Resick. "Marital Rape: History, Research, and Practice." *Trauma, Violence & Abuse* 4, no. 3 (2003): 228–46.

Berry, Jan. "A Safe Space for Healing: Boundaries, Power and Vulnerability in Pastoral Care." *Theology & Sexuality* 20, no. 3 (September 1, 2014): 203–13. https://doi.org/10.1179/1355835815Z.00000000050.

Blanco, Richard, Caridad Moro, Nikki Moustaki, and Elisa Albo, eds. *Grabbed: Poets & Writers on Sexual Assault, Empowerment & Healing*. Boston: Beacon Press, 2020.

Bogel-Burroughs, Nicholas. "An Outspoken Off-Duty Firefighter Testified: 'There Was a Man Being Killed.'" *The New York Times*, March 30, 2021, sec. U.S. www.nytimes.com/2021/03/30/us/genevieve-hansen-testimoy.html.

Bonanno, George A., Sandro Galea, Angela Bucciarelli, and David Vlahov. "Psychological Resilience after Disaster: New York City in the Aftermath of the September 11th Terrorist Attack." *Psychological Science* 17, no. 3 (March 2006): 181–6. https://doi.org/10.1111/j.1467-9280.2006.01682.x.

Brison, Susan. "Justice and Gender-Based Violence." *Revue Internationale de Philosophie* 67, no. 3 (2013): 259–77.

———. *Aftermath: Violence and the Remaking of a Self*. Princeton, NJ: Princeton University Press, 2003.

———. "Can We End the Feminist 'Sex Wars' Now? Comments on Linda Martín Alcoff, *Rape and Resistance: Understanding the Complexities of Sexual Violation*." *Philosophical Studies* 177, no. 2 (February 1, 2020): 303–09. https://doi.org/10.1007/s11098-019-01392-z.

Brown, Brené. *Braving the Wilderness: The Quest for True Belonging and the Courage to Stand Alone*. New York: Random House, 2017.

Brownmiller, Susan. *Against Our Will: Men, Women, and Rape*. New York: Ballantine Books, 1993.

Burgess-Jackson, Keith. "A History of Rape Law." In *A Most Detestable Crime: New Philosophical Essays on Rape*, edited by Keith Burgess-Jackson, 15–31. New York: Oxford University Press, 1999.

Burke, Megan. *When Time Warps: The Lived Experience of Gender, Race, and Sexual Violence*. Minneapolis: University of Minnesota Press, 2019.

Butler, Judith. *Gender Trouble: Feminism and the Subversion of Identity*. New York: Routledge, 2006.

———. *The Force of Nonviolence: An Ethico-Political Bind*. London: Verso Books, 2020.

Cahill, Ann J. *Rethinking Rape*. Ithaca: Cornell University Press, 2001.

———. "Recognition, Desire, and Unjust Sex." *Hypatia* 29, no. 2 (2014): 303–19. https://doi.org/10.1111/hypa.12080

Campbell-Reed, Eileen R. *Pastoral Imagination: Bringing the Practice of Ministry to Life*. Minneapolis: Fortress Press, 2021.

Cannon, Christopher. "Raptus in the Chaumpaigne Release and a Newly Discovered Document Concerning the Life of Geoffrey Chaucer." *Speculum* 68, no. 1 (1993): 74–94.

"Church Allowed Abuse by Priest for Years." *The Boston Globe*. Accessed April 25, 2021. www.bostonglobe.com/news/special-reports/2002/01/06/church-allowed-abuse-priest-for-years/cSHfGkTIrAT25qKGvBuDNM/story.html.

Church of Jesus Christ of Latter-Day Saints. "Abuse." Accessed April 25, 2021. www.churchofjesuschrist.org/study/manual/true-to-the-faith/abuse?lang=eng.

Coleman, Monica A. *Bipolar Faith: A Black Woman's Journey with Depression and Faith*. Minneapolis: Fortress Press, 2016.

Cooper-White, Pamela. *Gender, Violence, and Justice: Collected Essays on Violence against Women*. Eugene, OR: Cascade Books, 2019.

Craigo-Snell, Shannon. "Generational Joy: Affections, Epigenetics, and Trauma." *Liturgy* 35, no. 4 (October 1, 2020): 58–66. https://doi.org/10.1080/0458063X.2020.1832852.

Crawford, Lacy. *Notes on a Silencing*. New York: Little Brown, 2020.

Crenshaw, Kimberlé. "Mapping the Margins: Intersectionality, Identity Politics, and Violence against Women of Color." *Stanford Law Review* 43, no. 6 (July 1991): 1241–99.

Crumpton, Stephanie M. *A Womanist Pastoral Theology Against Intimate and Cultural Violence*. New York: Palgrave Macmillan, 2014.

Currier, Ashley, and Rashida A. Manuel. "When Rape Goes Unnamed: Gay Malawian Men's Responses to Unwanted and Non-Consensual Sex." *Australian Feminist Studies* 29, no. 81 (July 3, 2014): 289–305. https://doi.org/10.1080/08164649.2014.959242.

Davis, Angela Y. *Women, Race, & Class*. New York: Vintage, 1983.

Davis, Fania E. *The Little Book of Race and Restorative Justice: Black Lives, Healing, and US Social Transformation*. New York: Good Books, 2019.

"Definition of EXOTIC." Accessed November 4, 2019. www.merriam-webster.com/dictionary/exotic.

Day, Timothy. *I Saw Eternity the Other Night: King's College Cambridge, and an English Singing Style*. New York: Penguin, 2020.

Doehring, Carrie. *The Practice of Pastoral Care: A Postmodern Approach*. Revised and expanded edition. Louisville, KY: Westminster John Knox Press, 2015.

———. "Searching for Wholeness Amidst Traumatic Grief: The Role of Spiritual Practices That Reveal Compassion in Embodied, Relational, and Transcendent Ways." *Pastoral Psychology* 68 (December, 2018): 241–59.

Doehring, Carrie, and Allison Kestenbaum. "Interpersonal Competencies for Cultivating Spiritual Trust." In *Chaplaincy and Spiritual Care in the Twenty-First Century: An Introduction*, edited by Wendy Cadge and Shelly Rambo, 134–55. Chapel Hill, NC: University of North Carolina Press, 2022. https://uncpress.org/book/9781469667607/chaplaincy-and-spiritual-care-in-the-twenty-first-century/.

Dworkin, Emily R., Anna E. Jaffe, Michele Bedard-Gilligan, and Skye Fitzpatrick. "PTSD in the Year Following Sexual Assault: A Meta-Analysis of Prospective Studies." *Trauma, Violence, & Abuse* 24, no. 2 (2023): 497–514. https://doi.org/10.1177/15248380211032213.

Ehrlich, Susan. *Representing Rape: Language and Sexual Consent*. Abingdon: Routledge, 2003.

"Elizabeth Smart on Instagram: 'I've Noticed a Lot of Comments about Dealing with the Shame and Embarrassment That I Felt after I Was Rescued and Didn't Want to Tell . . . .'" Instagram. Accessed January 9, 2021. www.instagram.com/p/CIPRwh8sWes/.

Ellison, Gregory C. *Cut Dead But Still Alive: Caring for African American Young Men*. Nashville, TN: Abingdon Press, 2013.

Elva, Thordis, and Tom Stranger. *South of Forgiveness: A True Story of Rape and Responsibility*. New York: Skyhorse Publishing, 2017.

Elwakil, Amira. "Petition: Rapist Should Not Be Given Platform at Southbank Centre's 2017 WoW Festival." Change.org, accessed April 22, 2021. www.change.org/p/rapist-should-not-be-given-platform-at-southbank-centre-s-2017-wow-festival.

Evangelical Lutheran Church in America. "Healing in Congregations After Clergy Sexual Abuse: A Resource to Assist Synodical Leaders and Local Congregations," 2005, 116.

Fadus, Matthew C., Kenneth R. Ginsburg, Kunmi Sobowale, Colleen A. Halliday-Boykins, Brittany E. Bryant, Kevin M. Gray, and Lindsay M. Squeglia. "Unconscious Bias and the Diagnosis of Disruptive Behavior Disorders and ADHD in African American and Hispanic Youth." *Academic Psychiatry* 44, no. 1 (February 1, 2020): 95–102. https://doi.org/10.1007/s40596-019-01127-6.

Farley, Edward. *Theologia: The Fragmentation and Unity of Theological Education*. Eugene, OR: Wipf and Stock, 2001.

Farley, M., and H. Barkan. "Prostitution, Violence, and Posttraumatic Stress Disorder." *Women & Health* 27, no. 3 (1998): 37–49. https://doi.org/10.1300/J013v27n03_03.

"Feinstein: 'The Dogma Lives Loudly within You, and That's a Concern.'" *Washington Post*. Accessed August 15, 2022. www.washingtonpost.com/video/politics/feinstein-the-dogma-lives-loudly-within-you-and-thats-a-concern/2017/09/07/04303fda-93cb-11e7-8482-8dc9a7af29f9_video.html.

Finkelhor, David, Heather Turner, Brittany Kaye Wormuth, Jennifer Vanderminden, and Sherry Hamby. "Corporal Punishment: Current Rates from a National

Survey." *Journal of Child and Family Studies* 28, no. 7 (July 1, 2019): 1991–97. https://doi.org/10.1007/s10826-019-01426-4.
Flanagan, Caitlin. "'Babe' Turned a Movement Into a Racket." *The Atlantic*, January 19, 2018.
Fletcher Stack, Peggy. "LDS Feminists Applaud as Church Removes Troublesome Book of Mormon Verse on Rape from Youth Book." *The Salt Lake Tribune*, September 29, 2016. https://sltrib.com/religion/2016/09/29/lds-feminists-applaud-as-church-removes-troublesome-book-of-mormon-verse-on-rape-from-youth-book.
Fortune, Marie M. *Sexual Violence: The Sin Revisited*. Cleveland, OH: Pilgrim Press, 2005.
Fortune, Marie M., and James N. Poling. *Sexual Abuse by Clergy: A Crisis for the Church*. Reissue edition. Eugene, OR: Wipf and Stock, 2008.
Franco, Zeno E., Kathy Blau, and Philip G. Zimbardo. "Heroism: A Conceptual Analysis and Differentiation between Heroic Action and Altruism." *Review of General Psychology* 15, no. 2 (2011): 99–113.
Freitas, Donna. *Consent on Campus: A Manifesto*. New York: Oxford University Press, 2018.
Fricker, Miranda. *Epistemic Injustice: Power and the Ethics of Knowing*. New York: Oxford University Press, 2009.
Gafney, Wilda C. *Womanist Midrash: A Reintroduction to the Women of the Torah and the Throne*. Louisville, KY: Westminster John Knox Press, 2017.
Gaitskill, Mary. "On Not Being a Victim: Sex, Rape, and the Trouble with Following Rules." *Harper's*, March 1994.
Galatzer-Levy, Isaac R., Sandy H. Huang, and George A. Bonanno. "Trajectories of Resilience and Dysfunction Following Potential Trauma: A Review and Statistical Evaluation." *Clinical Psychology Review* 63 (July 2018): 41–55. https://doi.org/10.1016/j.cpr.2018.05.008.
Gavey, Nicola. *Just Sex? The Cultural Scaffolding of Rape*. New York: Routledge, 2004.
Gay, Roxane. *Hunger: A Memoir of (My) Body*. New York: HarperCollins, 2018.
George, Michael. "'We Want You to Beat Him': Maryland Police Seen in Body Camera Footage Handcuffing 5-Year-Old Boy." CBS Evening News, March 28, 2021. www.cbsnews.com/news/maryland-police-5-year-old-boy-handcuffed-berated/.
Gilligan, James. *Violence: Reflections on a National Epidemic*. New York: Vintage, 1997.
Goodmark, Leigh. "Restorative Justice as Feminist Practice." *The International Journal of Restorative Justice* 1 (November 1, 2018): 372–84. https://doi.org/10.5553/IJRJ/258908912018001003003.
Greider, Kathleen J. *Reckoning with Aggression: Theology, Violence, and Vitality*. Louisville, KY: Westminster John Knox Press, 1997.
Herbenick, Debby, Tsung-Chieh Fu, Keisuke Kawata, Heather Eastman-Mueller, Lucia Guerra-Reyes, Molly Rosenberg, and Dubravka Svetina Valdivia.

"Non-Fatal Strangulation/Choking During Sex and Its Associations with Mental Health: Findings from an Undergraduate Probability Survey." *Journal of Sex & Marital Therapy* 48, no. 3 (2022): 238–50. https://doi.org/10.1080/0092 623X.2021.1985025.

Herman, Judith. *Trauma and Recovery: The Aftermath of Violence—from Domestic Abuse to Political Terror.* New York: Basic Books, 1997.

Hill, Anita. *Believing: Our Thirty-Year Journey to End Gender Violence.* New York: Viking, 2021.

Hong, Nicole. "Nxivm's Leader Is Guilty of Ugly Crimes. These Die-Hards Stand by Him." *The New York Times*, November 10, 2020, www.nytimes.com/2020/11/10/nyregion/keith-raniere-nxivm.html.

hooks, bell. *Ain't I a Woman: Black Women and Feminism.* New York: Routledge, 2015.

"Insane Nancy Grace Gets Owned by Elizabeth Smart." YouTube, 2006. www.youtube.com/watch?v=5x8ARIxg5lI.

Jackson, Debra L. "'Me Too': Epistemic Injustice and the Struggle for Recognition." *Feminist Philosophy Quarterly* 4, no. 4 (December 17, 2018). https://doi.org/10.5206/fpq/2018.4.6231.

Jaffe, Janet, and Martha O. Diamond. *Reproductive Trauma.* Washington, DC: American Psychological Association, 2010.

Jalonick, Mary Claire, and Elana Schor. "No 'Dogma': Democrats Walk Tightrope on Barrett's Faith." AP NEWS, April 20, 2021. https://apnews.com/article/donald-trump-ruth-bader-ginsburg-amy-coney-barrett-dianne-feinstein-judiciary-2aaf6821079ac0c5c6fe50699ad745ba.

Jean-Jacques, Amy, and Sam Rowlands. "Legalised Non-Consensual Sterilisation – Eugenics Put into Practice before 1945, and the Aftermath. Part 1: USA, Japan, Canada and Mexico." *The European Journal of Contraception & Reproductive Health Care* 23, no. 2 (March 4, 2018): 121–29. https://doi.org/10.1080/136251 87.2018.1450973.

Jennings, Willie James. *After Whiteness: An Education in Belonging.* Grand Rapids, MI: Eerdmans, 2020.

Johnson, Andrea, Ramya Sekaran, and Sasha Gombar. "2020 Progress Update: MeToo Workplace Reforms in the States." *National Women's Law Center*, September 2020.

Johnson, Cedric C. *Race, Religion, and Resilience in the Neoliberal Age.* New York: Palgrave Macmillan, 2015.

Jones, Tom. "Updating 'The Fantasticks' for a New Revival." National Public Radio, August 23, 2006. www.npr.org/templates/story/story.php?storyId=5697901.

Julian of Norwich. *Revelations of Divine Love.* Trans. Elizabeth Spearing. London; New York: Penguin Books, 1999.

Justes, Emma J. *Hearing Beyond the Words: How to Become a Listening Pastor.* Nashville, TN: Abingdon Press, 2002.

———. *Please Don't Tell: What to Do with the Secrets People Share.* Nashville, TN: Abingdon Press, 2014.

Kaba, Mariame, and Shira Hassan. *Fumbling Towards Repair: A Workbook for Community Accountability Facilitators.* Chicago, IL: Project NIA, 2019.

Karp, David, and Casey Sacks. "Student Conduct, Restorative Justice, and Student Development: Findings from the STARR Project: A Student Accountability and Restorative Research Project." *Contemporary Justice Review* 17 (June 23, 2014). https://doi.org/10.1080/10282580.2014.915140.

Kavanaugh, Brett. "I Am an Independent, Impartial Judge." *Wall Street Journal*, October 4, 2018. www.wsj.com/articles/i-am-an-independent-impartial-judge-1538695822.

Keller, Catherine. *From a Broken Web: Separation, Sexism and Self.* Boston, MA: Beacon Press, 1988.

Kelly, Henry Ansgar. "Meanings and Uses of Raptus in Chaucer's Time." *Studies in the Age of Chaucer* 20 (1998): 101–65.

Kelly, Liz, Sheila Burton, and Linda Regan. "Beyond Victim or Survivor: Sexual Violence, Identity and Feminist Theory and Practice." In *Sexualizing the Social*, edited by Lisa Adkins and Vicki Merchant, 77–101. New York: Palgrave Macmillan, 1996.

Kennedy, Margaret. "Sexual Abuse of Women by Priests and Ministers to Whom They Go for Pastoral Care and Support." *Feminist Theology* 11, no. 2 (January 1, 2003): 226–35. https://doi.org/10.1177/096673500301100213.

Kim, Kyubo. "The Power of Being Vulnerable in Christian Soul Care: Common Humanity and Humility." *Journal of Religion and Health* 56, no. 1 (February 2017): 355–69. https://doi.org/10.1007/s10943-016-0294-8.

Kittay, Eva. *Learning from My Daughter: The Value and Care of Disabled Minds.* Oxford; New York: Oxford University Press, 2019.

Kittay, Eva Feder. *Love's Labor: Essays on Women, Equality, and Dependency.* New York: Routledge, 1999.

Klein, Linda Kay. *Pure: Inside the Evangelical Movement That Shamed a Generation of Young Women and How I Broke Free.* New York; London: Atria Books, 2019.

Knox, Annie. "Protest of BYU Planned in Wake of Honor Code Criticisms." *The Salt Lake Tribune*, May 3, 2016. https://archive.sltrib.com/article.php?id=3794990&itype=CMSID.

Koss, Mary P. "The RESTORE Program of Restorative Justice for Sex Crimes: Vision, Process, and Outcomes." *Journal of Interpersonal Violence* 29, no. 9 (June 1, 2014): 1623–60. https://doi.org/10.1177/0886260513511537.

Koss, Mary P., Jay K. Wilgus, and Kaaren M. Williamsen. "Campus Sexual Misconduct: Restorative Justice Approaches to Enhance Compliance with Title IX Guidance." *Trauma, Violence, and Abuse* 15, no. 3 (July 2014): 242–57. https://doi.org/10.1177/1524838014521500.

Koss, Mary, J.W. White, and E.C. Lopez. "Victim Voice in Reenvisioning Responses to Sexual and Physical Violence Nationally and Internationally." *American Psychologist* 72, no. 9 (2017): 1019–30.

LaFrance, Marianne, and Eugene Hahn. "The Disappearing Agent: Gender Stereotypes, Interpersonal Verbs, and Implicit Causality." In *The Women and Language Debate: A Sourcebook*, edited by Camille Roman, Suzanne Juhasz, and Christine Miller. New Brunswick, NJ: Rutgers University Press, 1993.

Lartey, Emmanuel Y. *Pastoral Theology in an Intercultural World*. Eugene, OR: Wipf and Stock, 2013.

Leslie, Kristen J. *When Violence Is No Stranger: Pastoral Counseling with Survivors of Acquaintance Rape*. Minneapolis, MN: Fortress Press, 2002.

Levin, Roy J., and Willy van Berlo. "Sexual Arousal and Orgasm in Subjects Who Experience Forced or Non-Consensual Sexual Stimulation—a Review." *Journal of Clinical Forensic Medicine* 11, no. 2 (April 2004): 82–88. https://doi.org/10.1016/j.jcfm.2003.10.008.

Lewis, Marjorie. "Diaspora Dialogue: Womanist Theology in Engagement with Aspects of the Black British and Jamaican Experience." *Black Theology* 2, no. 1 (January 1, 2004): 85–109. https://doi.org/10.1558/blth.2004.2.1.85.

Luconi, Stefano. "Becoming Italian in the US: Through the Lens of Life Narratives." *MELUS* 29, no. 3/4 (2004): 151–64. https://doi.org/10.2307/4141848.

MacKinnon, Catharine A. *Sexual Harassment of Working Women*. New Haven, CT: Yale University Press, 1979.

———. *Feminism Unmodified: Discourses on Life and Law*. Cambridge, MA: Harvard University Press, 1987.

———. *Women's Lives, Men's Laws*. Cambridge, MA: Belknap Press, 2007.

Manne, Kate. *Down Girl: The Logic of Misogyny*. New York: Oxford University Press, 2017.

Manning, Allison. "St. Paul's Graduate and Convicted Felon Owen Labrie Could Go to Jail for Alleged Curfew Violations." Boston.Com. Accessed April 19, 2021. www.boston.com/news/local-news/2016/03/15/st-pauls-graduate-and-convicted-felon-owen-labrie-could-go-to-jail-for-alleged-curfew-violations.

Marshall, Emma M., and Patricia A. Frazier. "Understanding Posttrauma Reactions within an Attachment Theory Framework." *Current Opinion in Psychology* 25 (February 2019): 167–71. https://doi.org/10.1016/j.copsyc.2018.08.001.

Martinez, Peter. "Aziz Ansari Responds to Woman's Claim of Sexual Misconduct." CBS News. Accessed January 14, 2021. www.cbsnews.com/news/aziz-ansari-woman-claims-sexual-misconduct-report/.

"Maryville Rape Case: The Horrifying Details of What Happened to Daisy Coleman Feel All Too Familiar." *Slate*. Accessed June 11, 2020. https://slate.com/human-interest/2013/10/maryville-rape-case-the-horrifying-details-of-what-happened-to-daisy-coleman-feel-all-too-familiar.html.

"Maya Angelou 'Rape' = Her Mute Years. . . ." YouTube, 2017. www.youtube.com/watch?v=yMNSpN-Gi3g.

McFague, Sallie. *Metaphorical Theology: Models of God in Religious Language*. Philadelphia: Fortress Press, 1982.

McNally, Richard J. "Explaining 'Memories' of Space Alien Abduction and Past Lives: An Experimental Psychopathology Approach." *Journal of Experimental Psychopathology* 3 (2012): 2–16.

Melzer, Nils. "Torture and Other Cruel, Inhuman or Degrading Treatment or Punishment: Report of the Special Rapporteur on Torture and Other Cruel, Inhuman or Degrading Treatment or Punishment." January 22, 2021. https://undocs.org/A/HRC/46/26.

Miller, Chanel. *Know My Name*. New York: Viking, 2019.

Morrison, Toni. *Beloved*. Reprint edition. New York: Vintage, 2004.

New Hampshire Judicial Branch. "Information on Cases for the Public and Media: State of NH v. Owen Labrie." Accessed April 21, 2021. www.courts.state.nh.us/caseinfo/pdf/labrie/index.htm.

NPR.org. "On #MeToo, Americans More Divided By Party Than Gender." Accessed June 3, 2020. www.npr.org/2018/10/31/662178315/on-metoo-americans-more-divided-by-party-than-gender.

O'Grady, Eileen. "St. Paul's School Compliance Officer Abruptly Quits Post." *Concord Monitor*, October 19, 2020. www.concordmonitor.com/St-Pauls-School-Overseer-Resigns-36866420.

Oswaks, Molly. "Elizabeth Smart Is Standing Up for Rape Victims—And Tearing Down Purity Culture." *Vice*, September 1, 2016. www.vice.com/en/article/mbqjka/elizabeth-smart-is-standing-up-for-rape-victimsand-tearing-down-purity-culture.

Oudshoorn, Judah, Lorraine Stutzman Amstutz, and Michelle Jackett. *The Little Book of Restorative Justice for Sexual Abuse: Hope through Trauma*. New York: Good Books, 2015.

Pande, Amrita. *Wombs in Labor: Transnational Commercial Surrogacy in India*. New York: Columbia University Press, 2014.

Pargament, Kenneth, Margaret Feuille, and Donna Burdzy. "The Brief RCOPE: Current Psychometric Status of a Short Measure of Religious Coping." *Religions* 2, no. 1 (March 2011): 51–76. https://doi.org/10.3390/rel2010051.

Pargament, Kenneth. *The Psychology of Religion and Coping: Theory, Research, Practice*. Revised edition. New York: The Guilford Press, 2001.

Pargament, Kenneth I., ed. *APA Handbook of Psychology, Religion, and Spirituality*. Washington, DC: American Psychological Association, 2013.

Pearsall, Derek. *The Life of Geoffrey Chaucer: A Critical Biography*. Oxford: Wiley-Blackwell, 1995.

Peterson, Christopher, Nansook Park, Nnamdi Pole, Wendy D'Andrea, and Martin E. P. Seligman. "Strengths of Character and Posttraumatic Growth." *Journal of Traumatic Stress* 21, no. 2 (April 2008): 214–17. https://doi.org/10.1002/jts.20332.

Peterson, Zoë D., Emily K. Voller, Melissa A. Polusney, and Maureen Murdoch. "Prevalence and consequences of adult sexual assault in men: review of empirical

findings and state of the literature." *Clinical Psychology Review* 31, no. 1 (February 2011): 1–24.
Pew Research Center. "Religion in America: U.S. Religious Data, Demographics and Statistics." *Pew Research Center's Religion & Public Life Project*. Accessed October 21, 2020. www.pewforum.org/religious-landscape-study/.
Pierce-Baker, Charlotte. *Surviving the Silence: Black Women's Stories of Rape*. W. W. Norton & Company, 2000.
Pilipchuk, Miranda. "Good Survivor, Bad Survivor: #MeToo and the Moralization of Survivorship." *Feminism and Philosophy* 19, no. 1 (Fall 2019): 5–10.
Pitman, Roger K. "A Brief Nosological History of PTSD." *Journal of Traumatic Stress Disorders & Treatment* 2, no. 1 (2013). https://doi.org/10.4172/2324-8947.1000101.
Platow, Michael J., and John A. Hunter. "Intergroup Relations and Conflict: Revisiting Sherif's Boys' Camp Studies." In *Social Psychology: Revisiting the Classic Studies*, edited by Joanne R. Smith and S. Alexander Haslam, 146–63. London: SAGE Publications Ltd, 2017.
Poling, James Newton. *Render Unto God: Economic Vulnerability, Family Violence, and Pastoral Theology*. Eugene, OR: Wipf and Stock, 2012.
Presser, Harriet B. "The Role of Sterilization in Controlling Puerto Rican Fertility." *Population Studies* 23, no. 3 (1969): 343–61. https://doi.org/10.2307/2172875.
Prout, Chessy, and Jenn Abelson. *I Have the Right To: A High School Survivor's Story of Sexual Assault, Justice, and Hope*. New York: Margaret K. McElderry Books, 2018.
"Purity Culture and the Subjugation of Women: Southern Baptist Beliefs on Sex and Gender Provide Context to Spa Suspect's 'Motive.'" *The Conversation*. Accessed April 25, 2021. http://theconversation.com/purity-culture-and-the-subjugation-of-women-southern-baptist-beliefs-on-sex-and-gender-provide-context-to-spa-suspects-motive-157496.
Ramsay, Nancy. "Compassionate Resistance: An Ethic for Pastoral Care and Counseling." *The Journal of Pastoral Care* 52, no. 3 (Fall 1998): 217–26.
———. "Intersectionality: A Model for Addressing the Complexity of Oppression and Privilege." *Pastoral Psychology* 63 (2014): 453–69. Accessed February 13, 2020. http://dx.doi.org/10.1007/s11089-013-0570-4.
Ramsay, Nancy J., ed. *Pastoral Theology and Care: Critical Trajectories in Theory and Practice*. Chichester, UK; Hoboken, NJ: Wiley-Blackwell, 2018.
Ramsay, Nancy, and Carrie Doehring, eds. *Military Moral Injury and Spiritual Care: A Resource for Religious Leaders and Professional Caregivers*. St. Louis, MO: Chalice Press, 2019.
Rose, Tricia. *Longing to Tell: Black Women Talk About Sexuality and Intimacy*. New York: Picador, 2004.
Russell, Kate Elizabeth. *My Dark Vanessa*. New York: William Morrow, 2020.
Saltzman, Jonathan, Jenn Abelson, Bella English, and Todd Wallack. "Private Schools, Painful Secrets." *Boston Globe*, May 6, 2016. www.

bostonglobe.com/metro/2016/05/06/private-schools-painful-secrets/
OaRI9PFpRnCTJxCzko5hkN/story.html.
Saunders, Corinne. *Rape and Ravishment in the Literature of Medieval England*. Cambridge, UK: D.S. Brewer, 2001.
Schaberg, Jane. *The Illegitimacy of Jesus: A Feminist Theological Interpretation of the Infancy Narratives*. Expanded twentieth anniversary edition. London: Sheffield Phoenix Press Ltd, 2005.
Scheper-Hughes, Nancy. "James X: A Reflection on Rape, Race, and Redemption." *Anthropology Today* 32, no. 5 (2016): 21–25. https://doi.org/10.1111/1467-8322.12299.
Schneider, Elizabeth M. "Feminism and the False Dichotomy of Victimization and Agency." *New York Law School Law Review* 38 (1993): 387–99.
Scholz, Susanne. *Sacred Witness: Rape in the Hebrew Bible*. Minneapolis, MN: Fortress Press, 2010.
Schultebraucks, Katharina, Karmel W. Choi, Isaac R. Galatzer-Levy, and George A. Bonanno. "Discriminating Heterogeneous Trajectories of Resilience and Depression After Major Life Stressors Using Polygenic Scores." *JAMA Psychiatry*, March 31, 2021. https://doi.org/10.1001/jamapsychiatry.2021.0228.
Searles, Patricia, and Ronald J. Berger eds. *Rape and Society: Readings on the Problem of Sexual Assault*. Boulder, CO: Westview Press, 1995.
Sebold, Alice. *Lucky*. Reprint edition. New York: Scribner, 2017.
Sered, Danielle. *Until We Reckon: Violence, Mass Incarceration, and a Road to Repair*. New York: The New Press, 2019.
Sheppard, Phillis Isabella. *Self, Culture, and Others in Womanist Practical Theology*. New York: Palgrave Macmillan, 2011.
Simon, Rita J. "Immigration and Public Opinion." *In Defense of the Alien* 18 (1995) 58–68.
Sims, Angela D. *Lynched: The Power of Memory in a Culture of Terror*. Waco, TX: Baylor University Press, 2016.
Sinko, Laura, Robert Ploutz-Snyder, Michelle Munro Kramer, Terri Conley, and Denise Saint Arnault. "Trauma History as a Significant Predictor of Posttraumatic Growth Beyond Mental Health Symptoms in Women-Identifying Survivors of Undergraduate Non-Consensual Sexual Experiences." *Violence and Victims* 37, no. 3 (June 1, 2022): 396–421. https://doi.org/10.1891/VV-D-20-00082.
Spotlight. Open Road Films, 2015.
"Statistics | RAINN." Accessed December 29, 2020. www.rainn.org/statistics.
Stepman, Inez. "Inez Stepman on Twitter." Twitter. Accessed December 31, 2020. https://twitter.com/InezFeltscher/status/952673765359538176.
Stevenson-Moessner, Jeanne. *Overture to Practical Theology: The Music of Religious Inquiry*. Eugene, OR: Cascade Books, 2016.

Stotland, Hanna. "Opinion: I Advise Students Accused of Sexual Assault. Expelling Them Isn't the Answer." *The New York Times*, sec. Opinion. Accessed April 10, 2020. www.nytimes.com/video/opinion/100000006326199/sexual-assault-students-campus.html.

"Sujatha Baliga." Accessed November 23, 2020. www.macfound.org/fellows/1029/.

Taddeo, Lisa. "Opinion: The Specific Horror of Unwanted Oral Sex." *The New York Times*, February 13, 2020, sec. Opinion. www.nytimes.com/2020/02/13/opinion/harvey-weinstein-trial.html.

Takhar, Jatinder, and Sandra Fisman. "Alien Abduction in PTSD." *Journal of the American Academy of Child & Adolescent Psychiatry* 34, no. 8 (August 1, 1995): 974–75. https://doi.org/10.1097/00004583-199508000-00005.

Taku, Kanako, Arnie Cann, Lawrence G. Calhoun, and Richard G. Tedeschi. "The Factor Structure of the Posttraumatic Growth Inventory: A Comparison of Five Models Using Confirmatory Factor Analysis." *Journal of Traumatic Stress* 21, no. 2 (April 2008): 158–64. https://doi.org/10.1002/jts.20305.

Tedeschi, R.G., and L.G. Calhoun. "The Posttraumatic Growth Inventory: Measuring the Positive Legacy of Trauma." *Journal of Traumatic Stress* 9, no. 3 (July 1996): 455–71. https://doi.org/10.1007/BF02103658.

The Committee on Nomenclature and Statistics of the American Psychiatric Association. *Diagnostic and Statistical Manual: Mental Disorders*. Washington, DC: American Psychiatric Association Mental Hospital Services, 1952.

———. *DSMII: Diagnostic and Statistical Manual of Mental Disorders*. Second edition. Washington, DC: American Psychiatric Association, 1968.

The Stanford Daily. "The Full Letter Read by Brock Turner's Father at His Sentencing Hearing," June 8, 2016. www.stanforddaily.com/2016/06/08/the-full-letter-read-by-brock-turners-father-at-his-sentencing-hearing/.

The Keepers. Netflix, 2017.

Thomson, Judith Jarvis. "A Defense of Abortion." *Philosophy & Public Affairs* 1, no. 1 (1971): 47–66.

The New York Times. "Transcript: Donald Trump's Taped Comments About Women," October 8, 2016, sec. U.S. www.nytimes.com/2016/10/08/us/donald-trump-tape-transcript.html.

Trible, Phyllis. *Texts of Terror: Literary-Feminist Readings of Biblical Narratives*. Philadelphia: Fortress Press, 1984.

Tumminio Hansen, Danielle. "Absent a Word: How the Language of Sexual Trauma Keeps Survivors Silent." *Journal of Pastoral Theology*, n.d. https://doi.org/10.1080/10649867.2020.1748920.

———. *Conceiving Family: A Practical Theology of Surrogacy and Self*. Waco, TX: Baylor University Press, 2019.

———. "Four Ways Faith Leaders Can Shift to Trauma-Informed Ministry." *The Christian Century*. Accessed December 21, 2020. www.christiancentury.org/article/recommendations/four-ways-faith-leaders-can-shift-trauma-informed-ministry.

———. "Remembering Rape in Heaven: A Constructive Proposal for Memory and the Eschatological Self." *Modern Theology* (September 21, 2020). Accessed October 27, 2020. https://doi.org/10.1111/moth.12651.

———. "Even More Tenuous Connections: A Pastoral Theological Analysis of Foster Care During COVID-19." *Journal of Pastoral Theology* 31, no. 2–3 (September 2, 2021): 207–23. https://doi.org/10.1080/10649867.2021.1921403.

———. "The Body of God, Sexually Violated: A Trauma-Informed Reading of the Climate Crisis." *Religions* 13, no. 3 (March 2022): 249–61. https://doi.org/10.3390/rel13030249.

United States Department of Justice. "An Updated Definition of Rape." January 6, 2012. www.justice.gov/archives/opa/blog/updated-definition-rape.

United States Sentencing Commission. "Recidivism Among Federal Violent Offenders." January 23, 2019. www.ussc.gov/research/research-reports/recidivism-among-federal-violent-offenders.

van der Kolk, Bessel A., Laura Stone, Jennifer West, Alison Rhodes, David Emerson, Michael Suvak, and Joseph Spinazzola. "Yoga as an Adjunctive Treatment for Posttraumatic Stress Disorder: A Randomized Controlled Trial." *The Journal of Clinical Psychiatry* 75, no. 6 (June 15, 2014): e559–65. https://doi.org/10.4088/JCP.13m08561.

van der Kolk, Bessel. *The Body Keeps the Score: Brain, Mind, and Body in the Healing of Trauma*. New York: Viking, 2014.

Vogelsang, John D. "From Denial to Hope: A Systemic Response to Clergy Sexual Abuse." *Journal of Religion and Health* 32, no. 3 (September 1, 1993): 197–208. https://doi.org/10.1007/BF00995653.

Walters, Mikel L., Jieru Chen, and Matthew J. Breiding. "The National Intimate Partner and Sexual Violence Survey: 2010 Findings on Victimization by Sexual Orientation." American Psychological Association, 2013. https://doi.org/10.1037/e541272013-001.

Way, Katie. "I Went on a Date with Aziz Ansari. It Turned into the Worst Night of My Life." babe.net, January 13, 2018. https://babe.net/2018/01/13/aziz-ansari-28355.

Weems, Renita. *Battered Love (Overtures to Biblical Theology)*. Minneapolis: Augsburg Fortress Press, 1995.

Welch, Graham F., and David M. Howard. "Gendered Voice in the Cathedral Choir." *Psychology of Music* 30, no. 1 (April 1, 2002): 102–20.

Wemmers, Jo-Anne. "Judging Victims: Restorative Choices for Victims of Sexual Violence." *Victims of Crime Research Digest* No. 10, June 2, 2017. www.justice.gc.ca/eng/rp-pr/cj-jp/victim/rd10-rr10/p3.html.

Wendell Holmes, Jr., Oliver. "Buck v. Bell, 274 U.S. 200 (1927)." May 2, 1927. https://supreme.justia.com/cases/federal/us/274/200/.

Williams, Delores S. *Sisters in the Wilderness: The Challenge of Womanist God-Talk*. Anniversary edition. Maryknoll, NY: Orbis, 2013.

Wittgenstein, Ludwig. *Tractatus Logico-Philosophicus*. London: Kegan Paul, Trench, Trubner, & Co., Ltd, 1922.
Woodhouse, Sarah, Susan Ayers, and Andy P. Field. "The Relationship between Adult Attachment Style and Post-Traumatic Stress Symptoms: A Meta-Analysis." *Journal of Anxiety Disorders* 35 (October 2015): 103–17. https://doi.org/10.1016/j.janxdis.2015.07.002.
Yoshino, Kenji. *Covering: The Hidden Assault on Our Civil Rights*. New York: Random House Trade Paperbacks, 2007.
Zehr, Howard, Allan MacRae, Kay Pranis, and Lorraine Stutzman Amstutz. *The Big Book of Restorative Justice: Four Classic Justice & Peacebuilding Books in One Volume*. New York: Good Books, 2015.
Zoellner, Tanja, and Andreas Maercker. "Posttraumatic Growth in Clinical Psychology: A Critical Review and Introduction of a Two Component Model." *Clinical Psychology Review* 26, no. 5 (September 2006): 626–53. https://doi.org/10.1016/j.cpr.2006.01.008.

INDEX

active listening, 155, 173–176, 255n21
Amanda, 52–54, 67. *See also* Thistle Farms
Ansari, Aziz, 123, 125, 126, 128, 132, 251n55, 252n57, 276, 281
Audrie & Daisy, 56, 57, 61, 240n31, n38, 269
Austin, J.L., 163, 164, 222n7, 256n5, 269. *See* performativity

Blasey Ford, Christine, 40, 233, 267–268n7
Book of Job, xvii
Brison, Susan, xx, xxiv, 7, 31, 55, 58, 70, 89, 138, 154, 157, 209, 220, 221n1, 223n17–18, 225n2, 225–226n3, 232n53, 235n76, n81, 236–237n89, 239n20, 241n52, 258n18, 259n26, 270
Buck, Carrie, 64. *See also Buck v. Bell*
Buck v. Bell, 64, 241n44, 281

Cahill, Ann, 38, 65, 68, 69, 72, 130, 208, 233n65, 241n53, 270, 271
Catholic sex abuse scandal, 73, 107, 108, 176, 247n13
Central Park jogger case, 15

Charcot, Jean-Martin, 109–111
Clinton, Bill, 7, 92, 212
Coleman, Daisy, 57, 58, 240n29, 276
conduct disorder (CD), 122, 123
conversational work, xix, 26, 27, 78
coverture, 110
Crawford, Lacy, 46, 92, 93, 205, 219, 237n93, 256n1, 262n3, 271
criminal sexual misconduct, 27. *See also* sexual misconduct
cyberbullying, 56, 58, 66, 70

Davis, Lanny, 9–10
Declaration on the Elimination of Violence Against Women, 24, 234n73
desire
  desire to do, 69
  desire within, 69
  projected desire, 70
  root desire, 69, 70, 242n60
Diagnostic and Statistical Manual of Mental Disorders (DSM), 109–115, 117, 120, 121, 218, 247n17, n18, 248n22, n23, 269, 280
dominant stories, vii, 101–103

embedded belief, xvi, xxi, xxvii, 6, 27, 39–42, 61, 70, 72, 73, 83, 84, 90, 91, 98, 102–106, 108, 112, 117, 121–123, 135–137, 139, 140, 143, 150, 152–157, 159, 160, 171, 173, 177–179, 185–188, 190, 192, 204, 206, 207, 208, 222n10, 243n1, 246n6, 253n9, 265n42
Episcopal Church, xxiii, 52, 148, 152, 255n19
epistemic clash, xviii
etiological event, 109–110, 117, 121, 122. *See also* originating event

foundational setting, 140, 141, 142

Gavey, Nicola, 69, 135, 136, 235n77, 251n54, 273
gender-based violence, 24–26, 34, 84
Genesis 19, 7
Genesis 39, 7
God as "Father," 8, 106
Grace, Nancy, 11, 230n34, 274
gray rape, 2, 27, 28, 235n77
gross sexual imposition, 5, 26, 27
gross stress reaction, 109, 111
Gulf War, 56

habitus, 130, 252n60
Haleyi, Mimi, 60
hermeneutic of belief, 91, 92
hermeneutic of disbelief, 91
Hill, Anita, 33, 34, 84, 210, 211, 212, 236n86, 274
hysterectomies, 63, 65, 269

ideal perpetrator, 11, 15, 26
ideal victim, 11–14, 26, 28, 33, 91, 92, 196, 211, 237n93, 257n12
Immigration and Customs Enforcement (ICE), 63, 64, 269
incest, 2, 22–23, 234n72

Janet, Pierre, 109
Jim Crow Laws, 56, 263n22
Judges 19, 7

Kantor, Jodi, 9, 126, 127, 233n62, 251

Labrie, Owen, 181, 182, 187, 262n4, 276, 277
layered listening, 172, 175, 176, 177, 179
Lewinsky, Monica, 7
lethelogica, 249n36
lethesoma, 116, 250n36
linguistic gaslighting, 28, 189
linguistic rape, 29, 58, 59

MacKinnon, Catharine, 17, 19, 54, 62, 63, 112, 128, 129, 130, 154, 223n13, 231n53, 232n61, 233n65, 239n20, 240n39, 247n21, 252, 276
male model for God, 8
manslaughter, 35
McFague, Sallie, xxv, 8, 9, 15, 20, 23, 106–108, 154, 276
McGowan, Rose, 9, 10
#MeToo, xxviii, 1, 33, 34, 45, 123, 177, 210, 211, 229n27, 277, 278
Meili, Trisha, 14, 15
Miller, Chanel, 12, 42, 48, 88, 93, 165, 236n89, 241n50, 277

Index

Ministry of Presence, 93
Mississippi appendectomies, 64
Mitchell, Brian, 12
moral injury, 73, 242n68, 278
myth of our own immunity, 7

narrative trust, 172, 177, 178, 179
NXIVM, 61, 240n37, 274

Oppenheim, Hermann, 109, 247
oppositional defiant disorder (ODD), 122, 123
originating event, 109, 110, 111, 112, 114, 115, 120, 122, 123
Oxenberg, India, 61

Panamanian Defense Forces, 56
performativity, 8, 101, 163, 171, 219, 222n7, 255
Pierce-Baker, Charlotte, 15, 65–67, 131, 236n89, 278
postfeminism, 85, 244n7
post-rape script, 109, 115, 116, 132
Pott, Audrie, 56, 57, 61, 62, 269
Pott, Larry, 61, 62
power-over, 23, 51, 53, 54, 234n70
power-to-do, 23, 51, 234n70
pre-accomplice, 208
pre-victim, 38, 43, 98, 99, 130, 208
problems of idolatry and irrelevance, 9
Prout, Chessy, 181–183, 187, 203, 262n4, 278
purity culture, 103–106, 245n1, n4, 246n6, 255n19, 269, 277, 278

Raniere, Keith, 61, 240n37, 274
rape shield laws, 12, 230n33
Roman Catholic Church, 73, 107, 108, 229n34, 247n13
Rose, Tricia, 139, 140, 142, 231, 231n44, 253, 278
Rosie the Riveter, 84, 85

Scheper-Hughes, Nancy, 191, 279
Sciorra, Annabella, 60
second rape, 66
secondary trauma, 73
self
 aspirational self, 85, 86
 autonomous self, 83, 86
 narrative self, vii, 81, 84, 94, 198, 200
 relational self, xxiv, 138, 241n52, 262n9
self-destruction, 87
self-reflexivity, 6, 228n14
sexual abuse, xxv, 2, 5, 22–24, 52, 71, 81, 131, 132, 174, 221n4, 226n7, 233n66, 234n69, n71, n72, 239n18, 245n4, 247n13, 261n43, 272, 273, 275, 277, 281
sexual misconduct, 27, 73, 251n44, 260n35, 261n44, 263, 267n52, 268, 275, 276
shame, 32, 34, 41, 66, 77, 81, 96, 100, 105, 107, 136, 151, 155, 169, 186, 190, 192–194, 211, 225n1, 230n35, 259n20, 264n32, 272, 275
Sims, J. Marion, 63
slut-shaming, 56, 58, 66
Smart, Elizabeth, 11, 12, 104, 105, 230n35, 245n2, 246n5, 272, 274, 277

social belonging, 70, 83, 169–171, 175, 185, 206, 259n21
St. Paul's School, 92, 181–182, 187, 203–204, 205, 261n44, 262n3, n4, 267n52
Stanford University, 12
Starr, Kenneth, 7
Stevens, Becca, 52, 218. *See also* Thistle Farms

Taylor, Recy, 15
Thistle Farms, 51–53, 67, 218, 241n52
Till, Emmett, 167
tip-of-the-tongue syndrome, 116. *See lethelogica*
tip-of-the-body syndrome, 116. *See lethesoma*
Title IX, 118, 170, 188, 212, 261n44, 263n11, n12, 275

Turner, Brock, 12, 39, 48, 88, 93, 165, 236n89, 237n91, 241n50, 280
Twohey, Megan, 9, 126, 127, 229n28, 233n62, 251n52

unideal victims, 12, 13, 237n93

violence against women, 24–26, 63, 235n76, 244n19, 260, 271
Virgin Mary, 8
vulnerability, 12, 13, 19, 22, 33, 51, 76, 83, 96, 129, 156, 167–169, 171, 172, 176, 194, 217, 230n40, 257n13, 258n14, n16, n17, n18, 259n23

Way, Katie, 123, 125–127, 251n44, 281
Weinstein, Harvey, 9, 10, 60, 61, 126, 127, 233n62, 280
Wooten, Dawn, 63

www.ingramcontent.com/pod-product-compliance
Ingram Content Group UK Ltd.
Pitfield, Milton Keynes, MK11 3LW, UK
UKHW010428300625
460100UK00010B/46/J